How Video Games Made the Metaverse

This book offers an unflinching look at the creative and structural challenges of storytelling in interactive media. Drawing on over 30 years of industry experience, Kelly Vero explores the rich interplay between narrative, design and technology, making the case for why story, far from being a cosmetic layer, is foundational to player engagement, emotional investment and lasting value in games and virtual worlds.

The book unpacks how narrative design works across different genres and platforms: from AAA games and sandbox titles to immersive metaverses, offering a toolkit of questions and techniques to help creators build experiences that resonate. Vero brings the reader inside the design process, examining iterative workflows, empathy versus hypothesis testing, and the importance of building for diverse, evolving user bases. She draws from case studies including *The Legend of Zelda*, *BTS Universe Story*, *Final Fantasy XIV* and even *RuneScape*'s infamous party hat, showing how stories are told not just through dialogue, but also through User Interface (UI), environment, mechanics and player choice.

Crucially, *How Video Games Made the Metaverse: From Pixels to Portals* is about building worlds that people want to live in. Whether you're a product lead, a writer or a designer, this book explores how to integrate content, interaction and community into a unified whole. It challenges creators to abandon ego-led development and instead embrace deep user understanding as the compass for creative direction.

By the end, readers will understand how to apply storytelling techniques not only to games and metaverses, but also to digital products more broadly, from loyalty programmes and education platforms to virtual retail and Artificial Intelligence (AI) companions. Vero's reflections on narrative, purpose and legacy offer a roadmap for creating digital experiences that matter, not just ones that entertain.

Kelly Vero is a game developer, futurist and technology pioneer with 30 years of experience in the interactive entertainment industry. She has worked with leading studios and brands worldwide, and is a frequent keynote speaker on the metaverse, narrative design and AI. Her previous book *Breaking Through Bytes* was published in 2025.

How Video Games Made the Metaverse

From Pixels to Portals

Kelly Vero

CRC Press
Taylor & Francis Group
Boca Raton London New York

CRC Press is an imprint of the
Taylor & Francis Group, an **informa** business

Designed cover image: Kelly Vero

First edition published 2026
by CRC Press
2385 NW Executive Center Drive, Suite 320, Boca Raton FL 33431

and by CRC Press
4 Park Square, Milton Park, Abingdon, Oxon, OX14 4RN

CRC Press is an imprint of Taylor & Francis Group, LLC

© 2026 Kelly Vero

ISBN: 9781041015345 (hbk)
ISBN: 9781041015321 (pbk)
ISBN: 9781003615248 (ebk)

DOI: 10.1201/9781003615248

Typeset in Minion
by Deanta Global Publishing Services, Chennai, India

Contents

Acknowledgements

I am really privileged to have a great support network around me who, like me, continually challenge the status quo. It's not an echo chamber, no way, these people are pretty vocal when my opinions, research or presentations are way off. Although this book is short, I don't think I would have been able to write a word without the encouragement and occasional criticism from the following people:

Chris Newson and Marc Mikulich – thanks so much for supporting me.

Shawn Crocker – sorry that I ditched our holidays, but I've got more bad news… I'm gonna keep writing.

Debra Stewardson, Georgina Wellman, Ben Hanson, Dave Bradley and Pengfei Clyde Zhang – I really respect every single thing you do. If you keep doing it, I will keep writing about it.

Christian Wittmer – you have been the best co-founder.

Nelle Stahl – my hubris knows no bounds, thank you for putting me back in my cage.

Claire Blackshaw – your arguments are sound, now, buy me a cocktail!

Dave, Ivy and Goku – thank you for letting me pet you when I didn't know what to write. RIP Vivvy and Seon-hye.

Thank you to Gabriel Fidalgo, Jak Marshall and Tommy Thompson for providing just the facts over the years.

Hugs to you good people who believe in the future.

Foreword

By Some People Whose Opinions I Value and Whose Beliefs I Really Admire

IN THE BEGINNING THERE WAS... SOMETHING

We've been sharing visions of the metaverse in literature for decades. Every science fiction aficionado knows about the potential of shared online spaces, from the books of Neal Stephenson and William Gibson to *The Matrix* and *Ready Player One*. Gaming platforms have provided crucial and reliable perspectives (and statistics). However, the metaverse has developed organically through the wider evolution of innovative technologies, and the growing need for more meaningful interactive and immersive experiences that transcend traditional gaming and/or social platforms. People want to congregate and share experiences. It is human nature to socialise in any format.

It says a lot that, in the earliest days of computing, engineers gravitated towards finding ways to create fun, shared experiences. People (and corporate entities) like creating and sharing worlds, and right now they have unprecedented power to do that.

Technological advances like high-speed internet and cheap graphics processors have made this something we can realistically and comfortably use today. Virtual reality (VR) has had some stops and starts, but it's becoming something people are ready to use, as the development of usable headsets in the last couple of decades enabled more immersive 3D digital spaces. Meanwhile, the explosion of blockchain tech over the last 15 years means that digital items can be tracked and traded reliably.

Massively Multiplayer Online games (MMOs) are nothing new, but it's easier to use MMOs to explain the metaverse as a concept. Massively multiplayer games are one manifestation of an idea that has even deeper roots in the original multi-user dungeons (MUDs). These evolve from pen and paper role-playing. Whatever the medium, people demonstrably want to find ways to create new worlds from fresh clay, and then to share them with others. Real-time rendering engines, good coding practice and instancing are the most powerful mediums we've had to bring that universal need to life on a global scale. Whether you call that "the metaverse" or just a logical through-line from small-scale *D&D* campaigns to *Battlebit Remastered* doesn't really matter.

There wasn't a metaverse, per se, nor the infrastructure to make it a thing until Internet of Things (IoT) and blockchain began to mature. Adoption (of those technologies) has enabled the metaverse to become something more tangible as what we have today. But the role of games in making this happen cannot be overstated. Massively Multiplayer Online games helped popularise the idea of shared digital worlds. Gamers were playing in shared spaces like text-only dungeons and early fantasy games like *Ultima* back in the 1990s, so the concept of a metaverse – whether or not it took that name – was not only understood by gamers but purposefully and regularly entered. *Second Life* was hugely instrumental, but *Eve Online* and fantasy games like *World of Warcraft* brought gamers together like never before.

However, not everything we have right now can be called an actual *metaverse*. People and companies are working/experimenting hard to shape what the future metaverse could be. The metaverse has emerged as these precursors converged to make whole virtual worlds increasingly popular. Today, experiences like *Roblox* and *Fortnite* have turned every young person with a joypad into a metaverse inhabitant.

THE NEW STYLE

Some of us are naturally inclined to be a technophile and autodidact, especially if we work in tech or games. We're always looking for new ways to work. We love to find that one new tool which will improve our lives (and productivity). While the metaverse and blockchain are still emerging concepts, we experiment with them to better understand the sector.

At conferences such as Game Developers Conference (GDC) and Pocket Gamer Connects or Gamescom, it has become more apparent that the blockchain gaming sector is moving towards truly AAA experiences using Web3.

Developments in the metaverse, Web3 and Non-Fungible Token (NFT) technologies continually present new opportunities and ways of working; strategically, there is no one-size-fits-all approach in most daily tech practice: it's about adapting to different needs and utilising different parts of these technologies to drive unique ideas, experiences and/or interactions that can "speak to" or connect with diverse audiences.

If we take a definition of "the metaverse" that represents it as just an extension of multi-player video games and the communities around them, then that's something that can be used by everyone as a primary means of staying in touch with both real-world friends and massive Discord communities. Living and breathing the metaverse, or 3D virtual worlds, as some might prefer to call it/them, allows us to dip in and out of every day, even if it is just to change our avatar's look *du jour*. From transacting in virtual currencies (crypto) to trading NFTs as investments – much like interacting with stocks on traditional exchanges – everything has changed. We can do all that and meet/hang out with colleagues, friends and communities in the metaverse using holograms instead of Zoom if we want to, simultaneously. There is no escape from Web3.

GOOD INTENTIONS

Metaverse and spatial technologies will continually evolve. The development of these technologies will prove to be continually beneficial to game developers, and gamers alike, particularly as we see more technological convergence in the future, the potential is huge.

It's an open secret that office workers are using campfires in *Red Dead Redemption* to hold meetings rather than holding their corporate stand-ups in Zoom. What an innovative way to make the office huddle a more enjoyable experience? This kind of thing will become more and more common with or without a pandemic locking us at home.

It's rare these days for a game to be released without some social or shared online features, and these all contribute to the growth of the metaverse, especially now younger gamers expect these as standard.

Concerts inside *Roblox* and *Fortnite* were formative experiences for many kids. That generation will be raised with a mobile phone in one hand and a joypad in the other – it will be second nature for them to play games, share music and work together in the metaverse. But there's a lot of friction between where we are now (online worlds that are ring-fenced by publisher ownership and demarcated by the engines they run on) and the vision of a universal, shared digital platform. That friction is commercial, creative, architectural and cultural. Perhaps it's too much friction to overcome for some? The future of real-time multi-user experiences is going to be made up of a bunch of different walled gardens and ecosystems, with the responsibility for interoperability and universality of content and identity being devolved to third parties.

The road ahead is challenging – here's why: *choice*. Choice is imperative where we choose what we share, with whom and how we entertain ourselves and others. I think one shared metaverse to rule them all is unlikely. People having real, meaningful social experiences inside shared multiplayer gaming experiences isn't just possible – it's already happening.

We can still read books (like this one) if we want to; however, gaming currently offers one of the best forms of immersive storytelling. For some, it is way better medium than books/movies/TV or any other format. The metaverse, using gaming as a tool in its development, offers something less passive, allowing us to "live" through the story and experiences. And those of who don't just stream, we still go to the cinema.

By the natural order of things, there are "non-believers" who will tell us that the metaverse and everything in it is a game, a fad. Ironically, these conversations could have happened on a phone call rather than as a video call! It took the pandemic to show us how much we rely on shared digital spaces, but the instruments of this convergence were already there.

As exciting as the idea of interoperability is, owning a single outfit that transcends different worlds perhaps faces a much more prosaic reality: a future of forum posts complaining about how the deprecation of a feature in one-walled garden's API has broken an integration that used to work. Look at what's happened with Reddit this year, now extrapolate that to a 3D, real-time experience – not a very rosy future, but probably a realistic one. But with virtual identity, economy, UGC, socialisation and interconnectivity comes parity. It sure does sound like the actual world we are living in. More challenges will come from our creativity, privacy being a big one. With more activity moving online, data privacy will only become an even bigger issue. It's already obvious that your virtual self duplicated across avatars and platforms, but the sentience of this poses challenges for regulation and safety.

How do we balance the reality and virtuality of ourselves as living, breathing humans who have a facsimile in a digital world? When almost everything can be done virtually, what will be the eventual point of reality? Will we be able to separate the virtual from the physical? And will reality even matter in the end?

NOOBS, NERFS AND NETWORKS ARE LEVELLING US UP!

When it comes to efficiency, it's almost hard to imagine a world without game-based technologies. It is the subtle things; from streamlining a process and gamifying it, it empowers the end user to find creative solutions and gives us the data/outcome we need. The journey to what you want to achieve is more enjoyable in technology. Almost everything that we create and experience nowadays has been touched by game technologies. Sure, we can use online gaming spaces to goof off. Not everyone is using or understands the metaverse and gaming together in a way that directly impacts their efficiency.

Interactive or immersive elements we take for granted, from chat applets to learning new skills, have game technology at their heart. Interaction within the metaverse has the potential to enhance efficiency through immersive simulations. They offer training platforms where users can develop skills, solve problems and work as teams, and these offer solutions applicable beyond gaming. Metaverse technologies enable seamless collaboration and communication, streamlining remote work and meetings. Users can enjoy engaging, productive interactions by combining games and the metaverse, fostering creativity and productivity. These innovations make work enjoyable and empower individuals to learn and perform more efficiently in an ever-evolving digital landscape.

Even the language of gaming has made its way into the metaverse just as it has infiltrated the physical world. N00bs, networking and nerfs: all terms from gaming that find their way into the modern workplace. Even the UK government had a minister for Levelling Up, but that hasn't aged well in the current zeitgeist.

This is a great time to be alive and creating. We can really make a place we want to exist, in 3D or physically, so the don't-be-a-dick mantra will help everyone. Of course, there will be rocky roads, but the journey is how we grow. Mmm, Rocky Road ice cream! Let's choose that instead.

Debra Stewardson
Dave Bradley
Georgina Wellman
Ben Hanson
Pengfei Clyde Z

CHAPTER 1

Introduction to Technology

MANCHESTER–CAMBRIDGE–PENNSYLVANIA–NEW JERSEY– EVERYBODY TALK ABOUT: POST-WAR COMPUTERS

Of course, I prefer New York–London–Paris–Munich (bonus points if you sang that). Can you imagine a world without computers? I can't. When it comes to computing history, there were gods and titans: Manchester, Cambridge, Pennsylvania and New Jersey were the gods. These institutions were already driving innovation in stored-program architecture as early as 1947 (Copeland, 2006; Campbell-Kelly and Aspray, 2004). The WWII-era COLOSSUS and Electronic Numerical Integrator and Computer (ENIAC) were remarkable achievements in cryptography and calculation (Randell, 1976; Ceruzzi, 2003), but they weren't designed to be reprogrammable in the modern sense. That leap came shortly after, with teams at the University of Manchester, the University of Cambridge, Princeton's Institute for Advanced Study and Bell Labs: the big four. These titans of teamwork whose efforts introduced the concept of reprogrammable stacks: a precursor to that well-known catch-all. *Software.*

In simple terms: reprogrammable meant we could finally write code, test it (QA) and iterate. Today that sounds ordinary, but at the time, it was revolutionary. Unless you're deep in the trenches, coding has always been more about outcome than obsession. Code, though definitely not new, needed a new proving ground.

Video games in the earliest days of computing arguably fell into three emerging categories, even if no one at the time would have labelled them that way. First, we had instructional or training programmes, often used in military, aerospace or educational settings – what we now recognise as serious games (Michael and Chen, 2006). Second, R&D-driven software emerged to simulate Artificial Intelligence (AI), logic trees and basic environment modelling. These laid the groundwork for what we might now call digital twins (virtual replicas of real-world systems), simulations or system emulators. And third, there were demonstration models, designed less for player enjoyment and more to showcase hardware capability, but nonetheless laying the groundwork for entertainment.

DOI: 10.1201/9781003615248-1

These early games weren't made in garages, they were born in labs. Often, the hardware filled an entire room (Ceruzzi, 2003). In my early years of working in the games industry, our dev kits were stacked across full-length racks the size of a small office. Today, they've shrunk down to handheld consoles, SDK sticks and, in some cases, cloud-enabled testbeds. But the DNA is the same: build, test, iterate-repeat.

Back in the 1940s and 1950s, porting software: that is, moving it between systems, was almost impossible. Code may have been "reprogrammable," but only in relation to the specific institution and hardware it was written for. Each machine was bespoke, often running on thermionic valves (vacuum tubes), and could take hours to warm up (Ceruzzi, 2003; Edwards, 1996).

There's a romantic rumour I heard when I was working at a games studio nearby that the first engineers working on these systems at Cambridge's Mathematical Laboratory had time for a pint (or two) at The Eagle while waiting for the machine to boot because it really took that long. That might be apocryphal, but it captures how much patience early computing required.

Game distribution, as we know it today, whether through sharing Steam codes or slotting in a console cartridge, was unimaginable. Playing a "game" meant undergoing lab security protocols, possibly waiting on code to compile for hours, and navigating the scepticism of white-coated researchers who didn't always see the value in "play." Moore's Law? *Hardly.* Processing capacity was measured in patience, not power.

From those lab-grown rounds of *tic-tac-toe* to entire worlds built using AI tools, video games have been instrumental in pushing the limits of computation, creativity and interactivity (Bogost, 2007). You won't find the first computer game designer credited at the end of a YouTube speedrun or walking the stage at the Game Developers Conference (GDC). That's because, during the decade in which video games were born, many of these so-called "games" were never commercially released. They weren't made to entertain; they were created to test hardware, evaluate software stability or simulate logic problems in research environments (Lowood, 2009). The people behind these breakthroughs weren't indie devs or AAA studios; they were university researchers and lab teams.

This invisible legacy mirrors the challenges we face in tracing the origins of the metaverse. We know when the term was coined: 1992 and where: in *Snow Crash* (Stephenson, 1992), and we can trace early 3D social platforms like *Active Worlds, Habbo Hotel* (2000) or *Second Life.* But identifying the first creator of a genuine metaverse product is more complicated. Like early games, many formative metaverse experiments were collaborative, unpublished or never fully realised. Metaverses, multiverses (parallel narrative universes) and transmedia properties (Intellectual Property (IP) spread across multiple platforms) have existed long before they were named as such. They emerge at the edges of tech, where experimentation outpaces classification. That makes origin stories murky, but it also makes them more interesting.

In 1948, just after the patent filing for the world's first cathode ray tube amusement device, widely considered the earliest interactive electronic game (Wolf, 2008); Alan Turing and David Champernowne wrote what is now recognised as the first computerised chess simulation, a program they dubbed *Turochamp* (Hodges, 2012). Get it? *Turing* + *Champ*ernowne.

The program was, conceptually, a marvel – capable of simulating strategy, prioritising moves and even mimicking beginner and expert styles. But there was one problem: it was impossible to run on the machines of the time. The code was simply too complex for the early processors to handle. GitHub didn't exist, and computational chess couldn't yet go live.

In 1952, Turing did test the algorithm manually by acting as the processor working through each instruction line by line and noting the program's decisions. Turochamp was never run on an actual computer during his lifetime. But its logic, and its ambitions, anticipated a future where software could not only process rules but think.

Bertie the Brain: a towering, room-sized machine that played *tic-tac-toe* was arguably the first publicly demonstrated video game. Built in 1950 by Josef Kates for the Canadian National Exhibition, Bertie wasn't designed for fun (though it was fun); it was a functional tech demo to showcase Kates's innovation: the Additron tube, a compact alternative to bulky vacuum tubes (Malloy, 2014).

Whenever I talk about the real origins of game design, *Bertie* is my go-to game, more than chess. We already know about Garry Kasparov's battle with *Deep Blue* (1996), and if we don't, we all remember Matthew Broderick's tic-tac-dystoe showdown with Joshua in *WarGames* (1983). But before AI took centre stage in Cold War cinema, it was *Bertie* who taught the public that a machine could "play."

From the Mount Othrys of Manchester, Cambridge, Princeton and Bell Labs, we shifted rapidly to the plēthos: *Bertie the Brain* at the Canadian National Exhibition (1950), to Nimrod at the Festival of Britain (1951) and finally to the Berlin Industrial Show. These public showcases not only demonstrated computational power but also seeded the idea of interactive machines in the public imagination (Edwards, 2018). Like *Bertie*, *Nimrod* was a demonstration of computational power, not a consumer product. These events were the GDCs or E3s of their time, public showcases where game mechanics were used to market something else: the hardware.

The seeds planted in these exhibitions would take root decades later, fuelling the rise of arcades, home consoles and ultimately the video game industry as we know it. It's easy to draw a neat line from *Bertie* to *Pong* to PlayStation, but the story is wider and far more global (Kent, 2001) (Table 1.1).

It would be shortsighted to assume that only the West deserves credit for the evolution of video games, or indeed the metaverse. As we'll see throughout this book, milestones

TABLE 1.1   Timeline – from Vacuum Tubes to Virtual Worlds

Year	Milestone	Significance
1947	Stored-program concept	Basis for reprogrammability
1950	*Bertie the Brain*	Public demo of computation via games
1952	Turing tests Turochamp	First simulation of game AI
1992	Snow Crash published	Term "metaverse" coined
2003	Launch of *Second Life*	Emergence of persistent social worlds

in both fields have emerged in every region of the world, from Nakamura's arcade break-throughs in Japan to Pocket Gamer Connects in Aqaba, Jordan. Through early simulation networks in the Soviet Union and virtual social experiments in Korea and China, the digital future is, and always has been, globally co-authored.

These past 50 years of modern technology often feel, to me, like a fever dream – a blur of silicon, sprites, startups and sudden disruption. I've gone from hanging out in arcades, pockets heavy with coins, to working alongside legends of the games industry, all within the blink of an evolutionary eye. If this book achieves anything, I hope it shows that game technology hasn't just shaped entertainment, it has shaped how we think, build and interact (Bogost, 2007). These pages won't drown you in glossaries or treat you like a circuit diagram. I believe that, today more than ever, we're kinaesthetic learners. We learn by doing: by poking, pressing, dragging and remixing (Prensky, 2001).

Growing up, the only way I could spend proper time with my dad was if I had a screwdriver in my hand. I prefer Cosmopolitans these days (priorities evolve), but that early tactile bond with technology taught me that if you want to understand it, you have to get close to it.

The emergence of the young luddite might not really be about fear, perhaps it's about fatigue or frustration or distrust. But emergent tech isn't going away. Whether it's generative AI, digital twins, the metaverse, spatial, edge or modular computing, the next generation will live surrounded by technology, just as we did. And they'll need to figure out which screwdriver or cloud platform is right for the job. As for Moore's law? Let's just say I'm not convinced anymore (Moore, 1965). Have you seen the size of your new smartphone? It's massive!

To use technology effectively in daily life is to understand what it's for, not just what it is. Like choosing a screwdriver, it's not about owning the latest tool; it's about knowing which one fits the job. Flathead, Phillips or posidrive? Maybe even a cheeky Allen key? The same principle applies to emerging tech: from game engines to AI, from digital twins to blockchain infrastructure, the smartest tools don't just impress, they enable. Just as Bertie the Brain showcased hardware through gameplay, today's game tech, Unity, Unreal, Godot, cloud streaming is leveraged to demonstrate and de-risk business innovations from fashion to finance. These early demos weren't entertainment; they were product validation cycles. The metaverse follows suit.

That's why game technology has become one of the most powerful (and surprisingly underutilised) engines for productivity, simulation, creativity and engagement across industries (Anthropy and Clark, 2014). Unlike so many brilliant innovations that remain siloed within niche sectors, game tech has spilled over into education, healthcare, defence, retail and, of course, the metaverse.

So, if this intro has felt like a blueprint, that's intentional. You've now got a foundational operating system, a conceptual loadout, ready for whatever comes next. And we're only just getting started.

We're going to some interesting places together. Bring your favourite tool.

REFERENCES

Anthropy, A. and Clark, N. (2014) *A Game Design Vocabulary: Exploring the Foundational Principles Behind Good Game Design*. Upper Saddle River, NJ: Addison-Wesley.

Bogost, I. (2007) *Persuasive Games: The Expressive Power of Videogames*. Cambridge, MA: MIT Press.

Campbell-Kelly, M. and Aspray, W. (2004) *Computer: A History of the Information Machine*. 2nd edn. Boulder, CO: Westview Press.

Ceruzzi, P.E. (2003) *A History of Modern Computing*. 2nd edn. Cambridge, MA: MIT Press.

Copeland, B.J. (2006) *Colossus: The Secrets of Bletchley Park's Codebreaking Computers*. Oxford: Oxford University Press.

Edwards, P.N. (1996) *The Closed World: Computers and the Politics of Discourse in Cold War America*. Cambridge, MA: MIT Press.

Edwards, P.N. (2018) 'The Infrastructure of Modernity: SCADA, Smart Grids, and Critical Systems', *Technology and Culture*, 59(2), pp. 369–375.

Habbo Hotel. (2000). PC [Game]. Finland: Sulake Corporation.

Hodges, A. (2012) *Alan Turing: The Enigma*. Centenary edn. Princeton, NJ: Princeton University Press.

Kent, S.L. (2001) *The Ultimate History of Video Games: From Pong to Pokémon*. New York, NY: Three Rivers Press.

Lowood, H. (2009) 'Videogames in Computer Space: The Complex History of Pong', *IEEE Annals of the History of Computing*, 31(3), pp. 5–19.

Malloy, S. (2014) 'Bertie the Brain: The Forgotten Arcade Machine That Launched an Industry', *Canadian Historical Review*, 95(2), pp. 180–203.

Michael, D.R. and Chen, S.L. (2006) *Serious Games: Games That Educate, Train, and Inform*. Boston, MA: Thomson Course Technology.

Moore, G.E. (1965) 'Cramming More Components onto Integrated Circuits', *Electronics*, 38(8), pp. 114–117.

Prensky, M. (2001) 'Digital Natives, Digital Immigrants', *On the Horizon*, 9(5), pp. 1–6.

Randell, B. (1976) 'The COLOSSUS', in Metropolis, N. et al. (eds.) *A History of Computing in the Twentieth Century*. New York, NY: Academic Press, pp. 47–92.

Second Life. (2003). PC [Game]. USA: Linden Lab.

Stephenson, N. (1992) *Snow Crash*. New York, NY: Bantam Books.

WarGames (1983) Directed by John Badham. USA: United Artists.

Wolf, M.J.P. (ed.) (2008) *The Video Game Explosion: A History from PONG to PlayStation and Beyond*. Greenwood Press.

World Chess Champion Garry Kasparov Loses Game to Computer | February 10, 1996 (2025) *History .com*. A&E Television Networks. Available at: https://www.history.com/this-day-in-history/february-10/kasparov-loses-chess-game-to-computer (Accessed: 16 July 2025).

CHAPTER 2

Early Tech Stacks

THE LANGUAGE OF LOVE

Technology teaches us that there is nothing we can't do. A little bit of code goes a long way.

console.log("Hello, World!");

If you're a game developer and you are reading this: if you know, you know. However, if you're not a game developer and you haven't got a clue why I have just quoted "Hello World" in JavaScript, it's because it's the most common language. Games are written in other languages like Java. Jagex, the well-known Massively Multiplayer Online (MMO) studio of *RuneScape* fame, is named for being JAva Game EXperts (Donovan, 2010).

Hello World is a great way to get us thinking about how to build tech stacks for what will become our games and virtual platforms. It's always day one of coding school, and being able to produce this in any coding language is an achievement for beginners. How we first approach Hello World is usually indicative of the type of languages we might use as coders of the future. These languages are like any languages, they have to be learned and, as with all languages, they are culturally involved. That is to say that languages are contextual. We call them general programming languages, though we also have Domain-Specific Language (DSL) for targeted use cases. SQL, for example, is used for querying relational databases (Date, 2004).

Why did I first start writing code and programming? It was Christmas 1982. I was nine years old. My mum worked three jobs: as a cleaner, a shop assistant and a quality control operative for locally made underwear. My dad worked as an engineer. Together they bought me a Sinclair ZX Spectrum 16K. The ZX Spectrum, also known as the Speccy or the Spectrum, became my obsession. Just 16 kilobytes of RAM would open the world to what was possible. I could do anything. But first I would need to: read the manual (Smith, 2012).

I come from Nottingham, in the United Kingdom. It's a place with a very distinctive dialect that confounds most Shakespearean actors, and to everyone else, it is a nondescript sound from somewhere "up North." Just like how I pronounce the city of Leicester, Sinclair BASIC had its own dialect too, a variation on BASIC with its own quirks. BASIC is an abbreviation of Beginner's All-purpose Symbolic Instruction Code. With just 88

DOI: 10.1201/9781003615248-2

keywords, including commands, functions and logical operators, it lets us code not only games but our imaginations. *Mined-Out* (1983) by Quicksilva Games was written by Ian Andrew. When I say "written by" I mean he created the idea, logic and the code. This game, a proto-Minesweeper, was eventually ported to other formats (Kent, 2001).

So how did we get from the white-coated chess tinkerers of the Turing age, through *Bertie the Brain*, to *Mined-Out* and all that good Atari and Magnavox stuff in between? The common thread is that while the Spectrum was a home computer, it was part of the same legacy as those giant lab computers. Going from a computer the size of Leicester city hall to something plugged into a black-and-white TV in the family kitchen took a monumental leap in hardware design (Ceruzzi, 2003).

Big corporations relied on mainframes to manage everything from transaction processing to data storage. These systems were the motherboards of enterprise computing. They needed to be fast, stable and efficient. That pressure drove innovation in operating systems such as Lotus and Microsoft. Using these systems, coding techniques filtered down into BASIC, DOS games and Assembly (Edwards, 1996).

STACKING UP

A tech stack requires more thought for video games than for mainframes. That may sound surprising, but games need dynamic, layered infrastructures. The game tech stack is like a department store. You move through different floors (mechanics, modes, features), but the cash desk and toilets work on all levels. Everything is centralised. This is vital as game studios increasingly outsource or modularise development. We now build with shared protocols: monetisation, security, community, art pipelines. That means different pieces may be built or maintained by different teams, sometimes even the publisher (Anthropy and Clark, 2014).

I've worked on different Massively Multiplayer Online games (MMOs), sometimes more than once. In my experience, the coding language itself often makes little difference. The stack is designed for MMOs to handle player volume through something called instances (a duplicate version of gameplay hosted independently). Server tech offers the greatest flexibility in games and metaverse development. It lets us gate, manage and customise player experiences with minimal disruption (Michael and Chen, 2006).

Take non-Web3 metaverses like *Roblox* or *YAHAHA*. These platforms put experience design first. They're not necessarily about gaming per se, but the tech under the hood is still game infrastructure. A typical stack might look like this: user login, then landing area, changelogs or store skins, then playable experience. That first-time user experience (FTUE) is critical. Fail there, and you've lost your audience (Bogost, 2007).

As we begin to architect more immersive and persistent digital spaces, it's useful to compare the typical infrastructure behind these platforms. Table 2.1 shows a high-level overview of how Web2 and Web3 metaverse stacks differ in key areas.

And let's not forget regulation. In non-Web3 metaverses, especially those targeting users under 13, there are clear compliance expectations. These are tightly policed. In Web3, by contrast, regulatory guidance is murky at best. There's no global playbook yet for how decentralised experiences should operate (Zhouxiang, 2023).

TABLE 2.1   Web2 vs Web3 Metaverses

Layer	Web2 Metaverse (e.g. *Roblox* and *YAHAHA*)	Web3 Metaverse (e.g. *Decentraland* and *Sandbox*)
User Identity	*Platform login* (username + password, stored on company servers)	*Wallet-based login* using tools like *MetaMask* (cryptographic identity stored on blockchain) (2016)
Content Delivery	Centralised *servers* or Content Delivery Networks (*CDNs*) deliver assets to users	InterPlanetary File System (*IPFS*) (Benet, 2014) or blockchain-powered CDN alternatives distribute content peer-to-peer
Economy	Uses *platform currencies* (e.g. Robux) and *in-app purchases* – all controlled by the platform	Uses *crypto tokens* (e.g. *ERC-20* (Vogelsteller, 2015) for currency and *NFTs* for assets), with *on-chain* value and control
Moderation	Managed by the company (e.g. child-safety systems, flagging and bans)	Managed by the *community* through Decentralised Autonomous Organisations (*DAOs*) (Buterin, 2014); this varies by project
Compliance	Regulated: *COPPA* (US child protection law) (1998), *GDPR* (EU privacy law) (2016)	Largely unregulated or inconsistent across jurisdictions; compliance is still emerging
Ownership	Users *license* assets (e.g. avatar skins and games), but don't own them outright	Users *own* assets on-chain, typically via *NFTs*, meaning transferable and tradeable ownership
Persistence	Platform servers save state and host gameplay	*Blockchain state* and *distributed nodes* maintain world and asset persistence

Today's cloud servers outperform traditional on-premise (in-house physical server infrastructure) server rooms. But let me tell you a story. I once worked on a game that never launched. It was a textbook example of Darwinian mismanagement. Our server room was in the basement of a glass tower situated in a hot country. The dev team was at the top of the tower, six floors away. Cue biblical storm. Flooded basement. Wet servers. Not "a bit damp" but soaked. We dried them with hairdryers. The Chief Technology Officer (CTO) thought heat was our biggest risk, not rain. "People will pass out from the heat if we keep the servers upstairs," he said. But those servers never should have been downstairs. They almost killed the project. And while we did manage to salvage the data, the game never shipped.

Business Takeaway: Tech Stack Terms

- **CDN**: Content Delivery Network: a system of servers that delivers content to users based on their geographic location.

- **IPFS**: InterPlanetary File System (2014); a decentralised file storage protocol.

- **ERC-20**: A standard for fungible (interchangeable) tokens on the decentralised Ethereum (2015) platform.

- **NFT**: Non-Fungible Token: a unique digital item on a blockchain, used for ownership of art, items, wearables, etc.

- **DAO**: Decentralised Autonomous Organisation (2014); a community-run entity governed by token holders.

- **COPPA**: Children's Online Privacy Protection Act (1998); US law regulating online data collection from children under 13.

- **GDPR**: General Data Protection Regulation (2016); EU law governing personal data and user privacy.

- **MetaMask**: A popular browser-based crypto wallet used for interacting with Web3 platforms.

THE FINAL FRAME

Games and metaverse platforms don't emerge magically. They're the result of planning, iteration and collaboration. Build your studio around the game, not the other way around. Surround yourself with generalists and specialists. The curious, the technical, the communicative. Project managers and producers are the unsung heroes.

I've always been a generalist. That meant I could move between teams, roles and functions. From *Jetpac* (1983) to *Tomb Raider* (1996), the 1980s' and 1990s' game studios were often staffed by people jumping into whatever white space needed filling. We were driven by urgency and optimism.

As a Sinclair BASIC programmer, I learned early that language matters. Not just Sinclair, or English, or Nottingham dialect, but the languages of logic, interaction and systems. Over time, I've worked in many languages: German, French, Python, HTML, Japanese, JavaScript and even Maltese. Those bridges between cultures and code helped me spot patterns and solve problems across disciplines.

That's why, as we go deeper into this book, you'll see how game developers are perhaps the most qualified pioneers of the metaverse era. They know how to build not just experiences, but ecosystems.

REFERENCES

Anthropy, A. and Clark, N. (2014) *A Game Design Vocabulary: Exploring the Foundational Principles Behind Good Game Design*. Upper Saddle River, NJ: Addison-Wesley.

Benet, J. (2014) *IPFS – Content Addressed, Versioned, P2P File System*. Protocol Labs. Available at: https://ipfs.io/ipfs/QmR7GSQM93Cx5eAg6a6RduhG5cDsC9Y63eJuP3mFbiAC1F (Accessed: 16 July 2025).

Bogost, I. (2007) *Persuasive Games: The Expressive Power of Videogames*. Cambridge, MA: MIT Press.

Buterin, V. (2014) *DAOs, DACs, DAs and More: An Incomplete Terminology Guide*. Ethereum Foundation. Available at: https://blog.ethereum.org/2014/05/06/daos-dacs-das-and-more-an-incomplete-terminology-guide/ (Accessed: 16 July 2025).

Ceruzzi, P.E. (2003) *A History of Modern Computing*. 2nd edn. Cambridge, MA: MIT Press.

COPPA (1998) *Children's Online Privacy Protection Act*. Washington, DC: Federal Trade Commission. Available at: https://www.ftc.gov/legal-library/browse/rules/childrens-online-privacy-protection-rule-coppa (Accessed: 16 July 2025).

Date, C.J. (2004) *An Introduction to Database Systems*. 8th edn. Boston, MA: Pearson Addison Wesley.

Donovan, T. (2010) *Replay: The History of Video Games*. East Sussex: Yellow Ant.

Edwards, P.N. (1996) *The Closed World: Computers and the Politics of Discourse in Cold War America*. Cambridge, MA: MIT Press.

GDPR (2016) *General Data Protection Regulation (EU) 2016/679*. Brussels: European Union. Available at: https://eur-lex.europa.eu/eli/reg/2016/679/oj (Accessed: 16 July 2025).

Jetpac (1983) ZX Spectrum [Game]. United Kingdom: Ultimate Play the Game.

Kent, S.L. (2001) *The Ultimate History of Video Games: From Pong to Pokémon*. New York, NY: Three Rivers Press.

MetaMask (2016). *MetaMask Wallet*. Brooklyn, NY: ConsenSys Software Inc. Available at: https://metamask.io/ (Accessed: 16 July 2025).

Michael, D.R. and Chen, S.L. (2006) *Serious Games: Games That Educate, Train, and Inform*. Boston, MA: Thomson Course Technology.

Mined-Out (1983) ZX Spectrum [Game]. United Kingdom: Quicksilva.

Smith, A. (2012) *Sinclair ZX Spectrum: A Visual Compendium*. Brighton: Bitmap Books.

Tomb Raider (1996) Core Design. PlayStation [Game]. United Kingdom: Eidos Interactive.

Vogelsteller, F. and Buterin, V. (2015) *ERC-20 Token Standard: Ethereum Improvement Proposal 20*. Ethereum Foundation. Available at: https://eips.ethereum.org/EIPS/eip-20 (Accessed: 16 July 2025).

Zhouxiang, L. (2023) 'The Birth and Development of Sports Video Games From the 1950s to the Early 1980s', *Sport History Review*, 54(2), pp. 200–224. https://doi.org/10.1123/shr.2022-0037

CHAPTER 3

Game Engines and AI

GET LOADED

We've got a tank full of programmers, a design team and half a packet of managers: HIT IT!

Mainframes and supercomputers be damned! The minicomputer found its way into the arcade where we played. The problem was, early tech stacks, mainframes included, were difficult to squeeze into a single standalone device. Arcade machines sustained a couple of attempts to shove a mainframe into them. And though the mainframe chewed through data with ease, it was not agile enough for games. Gameplay worked way better on a Printed Circuit Board (PCB) using Very Large Scale Integration (VLSI). This humble board was the fundamental technology with which magic was created (Table 3.1).

Computer Space was a space-themed arcade video game released in 1971, created by Nolan Bushnell and Ted Dabney. Compared to earlier space games like *Spacewar!* and *Galaxy Game*, *Computer Space* had simpler, more accessible gameplay and impressive graphics, with a single player controlling a ship and shooting at enemy targets. Despite its importance in the evolution of video games, its difficulty and lack of clear instructions limited its commercial success compared to later titles like *Space Invaders* (Donovan, 2010; Kent, 2001a).

BOOM! Video games were born. And as we passed through the refinements of electronic gaming and arcade games toward consoles and home computers, the struggle became that much more real. How would we pack sophisticated graphics into PCBs? How might we move out of the beep era?

TABLE 3.1 Early Game Hardware Comparison

Feature	Mainframe	PCB (e.g. Computer Space)
Size	Room-sized	Cabinet-integrated
Input latency	High	Low (near real-time)
Cost to deploy	Very high	Commercially viable
Max simultaneous users	Multiple (batch)	1–2 (real-time)

DOI: 10.1201/9781003615248-3

Between 1971 and somewhere in the mid-1980s, everything was intrinsically tied to the PCB chips. That meant if you were to create a game, you'd need to create it again for each platform, whether a particular computer brand client or a specific arcade cabinet brand. Presumably, that's where we get the term *client* (borrowed from mainframe development), and presumably why porting back then was a full-on manual experience.

Design and code would be built from the bottom up, and each implementation would be singular. The levels were small or short, and the graphics were data-coded, hence their pixel or voxel style. What we take for granted today – that fine concoction of graphical data, gameplay and emotion-inducing soundscapes – was a near-impossible burden for the limited hardware and memory of the time.

But, undeterred, the early video games movement was strong. In fact, some of the legends of early game development are names you either haven't heard of, or have totally forgotten. These people are legends.

CONTINUE?

I was hooked on *Pole Position*. I would feed that arcade machine with pence in the UK and pesetas when we holidayed in Magaluf. In the early 1980s there was nothing to do as a British holidaymaker but tan and drink. I was nine years old; tanning and drinking were not my jam. But Namco gave me life.

I put the peseta in the Atari arcade machine, selected Fuji Speedway and pushed the button, grabbed the steering wheel and the gear shift, listened to the three short beeps, watched the light on the track turn green and I was off. That's a lot of graphical and sound data being parsed at the same time. A Zilog Z8000 CPU and two 16-bit processors did it all (Sheff, 1993). In truth, the hardware of the time that ran *Galaxian* (and other titles successfully) was simply too old-fashioned to run this whizzy new concept of the time. Also, the game development took three whole years (Kent, 2001b). That's a long time in technology. Some might say that's a short time, but we live in the future and we're not feeling that Moore's Law effect like we were in 1982, when it seemed as though there were new micro systems and cores every five minutes. Today, we're simply twiddling our thumbs, waiting on quantum computing to properly happen. And I guess until we get that, Moore's law doesn't exist for gamers outside of graphical processing unit (GPU) capabilities.

> **Business Takeaway:**
> *Pole Position* marked a turning point in the business of immersion: custom CPUs and graphical chips enabled real-time responsiveness and arcade dominance, foreshadowing the GPU wars of the 2000s and today's VR demands.

What *is* Moore's law? I keep talking about it. Moore's law was a prediction made by Gordon Moore, the co-founder of Intel, in 1965. It states that the number of transistors on a microchip would double every two years, while the cost per transistor would decrease (Moore, 1965). In simpler terms, this means that computer processors would become more powerful and smaller over time, while also becoming cheaper to manufacture.

TABLE 3.2   Moore's Law in Games

Year	Transistor Density Milestone	Game Milestone
1971	Intel 4004 (2,300 transistors)	Computer Space
1982	Zilog Z8000 used in Pole Position	Pole Position
1996	First 3D acceleration in consumer PCs	Tomb Raider
2002	GeForce4 launches with Direct3D	Morrowind
2025	AI-accelerated cloud engines	The metaverse

We'd practised Moore's law for several decades and it had been the driving force behind the incredible advancements we've seen in computing technology. It allowed us to create smaller and more powerful devices, from smartphones to supercomputers, and enabled us to process more data faster than ever before (Waldrop, 2016).

The profound impact Moore's law has made on the tech industry encouraged constant innovation and the development of new technologies to keep up with the exponential growth of computing power. However, there are physical limitations to how many transistors can be placed on a chip, and some experts believe that Moore's law may eventually reach its limit. Some say it already has (Markoff, 2016). Nevertheless, the principles behind the law continue to influence the development of technology. It remains a crucial factor in driving progress and innovation in the world of computing (Table 3.2).

What impact does Moore's law have on what we're creating today? Well, quite a bit. Our beloved game engines are built on *Galaxian* and *Pole Position*, if you think about it, and right through the ancestry of the modest GPU we find Moore's law continuing to determine how we access graphics (Smith, 2019). Given that there are so many game engines, the world is not built just on Unity and Unreal, so it's important to understand what we mean when we say game *engine*.

As with every element of game development, game engines come to us as part of the framework. It's something we buy in (like Unity and Unreal), it's something proprietary, academic or it's part of something more open and accessible. I can think of *Dungeons & Dragons (D&D)* being a proponent of this, but let's face it, the world and his dog has written about the awesome power of Gary Gygax and Dave Arneson (Peterson, 2012). Therefore if *D&D* is a gateway to, well, everything it's fairly obvious why in 2002, I fell in love, deeply, with a game called *Elder Scrolls: Morrowind*. Narrative aside (because that's the next section), the technology in this compared to *Daggerfall*, its previous title in the series, was like someone had opened a door to a new world for me. Not since 1996's *Tomb Raider* had I felt a game impact my sense of being in this way. And why? Mostly because of aesthetics. And what the hell does this have to do with *Pole Position*? Loads. Loads and loads. Think back to *Pole Position* if you can. Seeing Fuji Speedway's map on the entry screen, all the way to failing to make *Pole Position* and ultimately losing (sometimes), was at that time the most immersive experience I could feel as a gamer. And that was *more* than story.

PUTTING THE U IN UI

Gamers do not just need narrative to feel immersed. They need technology to get them there first. Everything else follows. Since *Daggerfall* was released in 1996, something was

TABLE 3.3   UI Control Evolution from 1996 to 2020

Game	Year	UI Capabilities	Player Control
Daggerfall	1996	Static UI/Menus	Limited
Morrowind	2002	Configurable UI/Journal system	Medium
RuneScape	2004	Browser-based, persistent UI	High
League of Legends/Amazing Cultivation Simulator	2009/2019	Real-time HUD/Modding options	High

changing in games. When *Morrowind* came along, we were finally free from the constraints of obscure, out-of-range errors that broke the experience and narrative. The kill screen in *Donkey Kong*, the chequered flags in *Pole Position* and the denouement of *Metal Gear Solid* all signalled the end of the world because the developer said so. But this player (that is me) was not ready. Not until *Morrowind*.

It gave us, the players, the freedom of User Interface (UI). That freedom carried through to *RuneScape* and beyond; from *League of Legends* (2009) to *Amazing Cultivation Simulator* (2019), we are in control (Schell, 2020). That was something new. In 2002, this kind of UI was an open door. It allowed players to feel immersed in a world that had not felt quite so present before. And because *Morrowind* was also an open world, I spent a long time wishing other games, like *Pole Position*, could be open world too (Table 3.3).

Even open-world games have their limits. When people ask me to describe *Red Dead Redemption* or its sequel, I say it is *Grand Theft Auto* on horseback. The Rockstar Advanced Game Engine is always the limiting factor in how far you can go in terms of actions inside a game (Rabin, 2010). Of course, *Morrowind* and my earlier aside about *D&D* lead us naturally to AI, which is coming up next. But for now, the immersion and emergent gameplay in *Morrowind* remain unparalleled for the time. Its aesthetic, user interface and user experience transcend game design and speak to the underlying technology driving combat and inventory.

Morrowind starts with easy onboarding: a simple melee attack. Just like *D&D*, where onboarding is also straightforward (Rollings and Morris, 2004). So, let us add that to the technical design document. I will pick this back up when we reach the game design section. The spirit of *D&D* lives inside *Morrowind*; Bethesda has never denied it. The player is on the *Hero's Journey* (Campbell, 1949). This freedom of design, in an endless, procedural sandbox, was revolutionary. Perhaps it even forced Bethesda to abandon their original engine, XnGINE. They needed something to support Super VGA resolution (800 × 600, which was a lot in 2002). They needed a bigger boat. Enter NetImmerse (now Gamebryo), a Direct3D-powered engine that offered more aesthetic freedom and transformation. It came with 32-bit textures and skeletal animation (Gregory, 2018). We were talking about Hollywood levels of visual quality. No coincidence this aligned with the release of Nvidia's GeForce4, the McLaren supercar of graphics cards at the time (NVIDIA, 2002).

By then, I had transitioned from PC to Xbox. The Xbox was essentially a closed box of assembly code, a game engine in its own right (Kline, Dyer-Witheford and de Peuter, 2003). Because every console was the same, there was no way to mod or upgrade the graphics card. Bethesda had to replicate the full *Morrowind* experience within that small black box.

What made *Morrowind* extraordinary on Xbox was how its graphics made me feel I belonged. That sense of belonging is crucial in player behaviour (Isbister, 2017). The game engine enabled this. Without the avatars, environments, items and summons working together in that space, we would not feel what we feel as players. That emotional pull starts with the experience, then deepens through the narrative.

The evolution of game engines also brought with it the Hans Zimmer effect: cinematic audio that transformed gameplay. And who better to elevate that than Jeremy Soule? Apart from Steve Vai shredding the guitar on *Halo 2* and *Halo 3*, or Nobuo Uematsu's orchestral-but-MIDI brilliance, few game soundtracks have moved me like *Morrowind* (Collins, 2008).

Audio quality must not be lost inside the game engine. To preserve that cinematic feel while still incorporating voice work into the narrative is no small feat. So, when publishers ask me to shrink my game into an app for iOS or Android, something under 20MB, I remind them how far we have come. If three years felt long for *Pole Position*, it took *Morrowind* around four to seven years to develop (Howard, 2003). It was likely conceived during the development of *Elder Scrolls II: Daggerfall*. That is no small accomplishment, especially given the beta-state access to hardware and software at the time.

IKIGAI

The Japanese really pushed the envelope during the PlayStation 2 days. Sure, early games took as long as they took because there was no competition. However, the rise of commerce and desire for new titles and experiences found us as game developers in constant development. You might say that was the beginning of the crunch, but when bigger game corporations started to fill the charts with games it was companies like Capcom who led the vanguard in bringing development times down (Kent, 2001a). Where *Devil May Cry* may have taken years to develop in a non-competitive marketplace, suddenly there were other hack and slash competitors that came to steal Dante's lunch (or Pizza if you're a superfan).

It is therefore no surprise that, as this chapter unfolds, the number of metaverses is growing globally and relentlessly. The metaverse is not a monolith but rather a collection of multiple ecosystems, each evolving in parallel, sometimes cooperating, sometimes competing and almost always coexisting. This is not unlike the early years of the internet or even the emergence of the modern video games industry, where diverse platforms, standards and business models flourished simultaneously before certain dominant frameworks emerged.

At the heart of this expansion lies a simple truth: the metaverse is both technological and cultural. It sits at the intersection of gaming, enterprise, entertainment and social infrastructure, and in doing so, it has already become a billion-dollar industry. Estimates vary wildly depending on definitions, but by 2030, projections range from several hundred billion to over $3 trillion in value (Analysis Group, 2022; Economist Impact, 2023; Research and Markets, 2025). The scale of the opportunity is not just financial, but structural, redefining how people work, create, socialise and transact.

Why, then, don't we see a single dominant metaverse platform? Why do we observe instead this sprawling jungle of platforms? In part, it is because of *democratisation*. The low barriers to entry for creators and companies driven by open standards, powerful game engines and

TABLE 3.4   Metaverse Platforms by Focus Area

Platform	Primary Focus	Engine Used	Monetisation
Decentraland	Web3 + NFTs	Unity	Token economy
YAHAHA	User-Generated Content (UGC)/Creative sandbox	Unity	Creator rewards
Oberhasli	Music integration	Unreal	Event tickets
The Otherside	NFT gaming	Proprietary	Asset sales
Breakroom	Enterprise collab	Unity	B2B SaaS

interoperable toolchains have allowed for a diversity of experiences to emerge organically. As Matthew Ball observes, the metaverse today resembles the gaming industry in its early stages: multiple genres, multiple user needs, multiple technological stacks. Instead of a single place, we have many destinations, each with its own genre specialism (Ball, 2022).

Each platform occupies a niche, much like how we see distinct genres in video games: MMORPGs, first-person shooters, sandbox builders, narrative RPGs each thriving because of their specificity, not in spite of it (Table 3.4).

Even at the level of development infrastructure, the diversity continues. Some of these worlds are built with Unreal Engine technologies, others with Unity and still others with Godot or proprietary stacks. If you speak with anyone working inside these platforms, you'll quickly realise that there is a remarkable agnosticism between them, because at their core, most of these experiences resolve to just two primary endpoints: mobile or desktop (Dionisio et al., 2013).

Later in this book, I'll return to this idea of *user experience convergence*, because while the front-ends may vary wildly, the back-ends increasingly intersect through shared protocols, standards and design patterns that shape the way we access and navigate these digital universes. As we begin to build these increasingly complex digital spaces, another invisible layer begins to take centre stage: artificial intelligence. If the metaverse is the infrastructure, then AI is becoming the cognitive layer that allows these worlds to feel alive, scalable and personal. Without AI, much of what we expect from dynamic content generation, user personalisation, automated NPC behaviour and even world moderation would simply not be feasible at the scale the metaverse demands. This is where machine learning, generative models and automated pipelines enter the conversation, not as abstract buzzwords, but as essential building blocks that allow the next generation of digital worlds to exist.

Business Takeaway: Form Factors for the Metaverse

Just like early arcade cabinets, today's metaverse platforms are built with varying hardware "form factors," each optimised for different business models.

What was the metaverse made for? There is a strong belief in the power of the metaverse being a 3D internet of the future powered by mobile. These believers find comfort in connecting to their personal choice of metaverse as they commute into their local town to visit the dentist's office or for long train journeys. They don't want to be chained to the desktop to do anything other than work. For others, the metaverse is work. Attending Metaverse

Fashion Week in *Decentraland* (2021) or exploring deep object definition in avionics parts for a health and safety simulation might require a desktop for the full experience.

Unreal Engine, Godot and Unity Technologies as well as Frostbite (2008) and CryEngine (2002) are a bit like gateways into bigger frameworks, infrastructures and tech stacks. In the games industry specifically, compared to non-games platforms which tend to be fairly proprietary, there's a tendency to use Unreal or Unity Engines as a template or an initial tech solution to prove out the feasibility of a use case (Gregory, 2018). These use cases might be art rendering or high-quality audio plugins. Using a bought engine solution like Unreal or Unity can make the development process more efficient and less time-consuming for non-game developers, as it offers a wide range of features and support that allow developers to focus on creating unique experiences for their clients. This approach avoids the cost and complexity of building and maintaining a proprietary engine and leverages the expertise of the engine's creators, who constantly improve the engine and add new features, ensuring that developers can stay up to date with the latest technologies and trends in the industry (Schell, 2020). They all deploy with plugins, and what that does is give us, on the tech side, the opportunity to build more native or proprietary systems if the games require it.

When I was involved in the (now defunct) development of *Transformers Universe* (2012), we used, during our early stages, the RuneTek Graphics Engine (specifically RuneTek 6), which is native to Jagex. We also used RuneScript for content. It was easy for our tech team who had trained in RuneTek and RuneScript, but actually quite a lot of stuff was built in Python and Lua. So, what does all this mean? Well, it means that sections of activity within specific experiences may not necessarily appear interoperable, but they still come together to make games happen. We always tell the younger generations to go off and learn C++, but there is some merit to idiots like me who learned BASIC and then Python. On *Transformers Universe* especially, in the end, we used quite a few bits and bobs from various engines, from Havok to early Cloudgine integration, thanks to our Lead Core Developer eventually becoming the CEO of Cloudgine (Unity Technologies, 2021).

Unity didn't launch for a whole six years after *RuneScape* launched in 2001. In that time, RuneTek and RuneScript were able to double down on perfecting and stabilising their flavour of JavaScript before rendering out to DirectX or OpenGL. That level of detail requires time, and for many developers, it's a labour of love. When I worked at Jagex, I found myself comparing Jagex to Nakamura Manufacturing Company (that's Namco!) or Taito Corporation (which though Japanese was founded by Ukrainian superhero Misha Kogan). There was always something DIY about Jagex. As someone who understands code, I want to be able to climb inside it. That's hard to do with a plug-in (Table 3.5).

> **Business Takeaway:** Proprietary versus Open
>
> Unity didn't launch until six years after *RuneScape* (2001), but RuneTek had already stabilised its pipeline for JavaScript rendering to DirectX.

Over the course of the last 15 years, at least, most game engines have filtered down into these two brands: Unity Technologies Unity Engine and Epic's Unreal Engine. The exposure

TABLE 3.5 Engine Feature Comparison

Engine	Proprietary	Graphics Power	Modding Support	Use Case
RuneTek 6	Yes	Medium	Low	MMO (RuneScape)
Unity	No	High	High	Cross-platform
Unreal	No	Very high	High	AAA + metaverse
Gamebryo	No	Medium–high	Low	Open-world RPG

that these two brands have had has propelled them into the fast-moving consumer goods of game development. Inevitably, in 2019 and 2020 and sometime just before the dreaded pandemic, both brands were looking at the possibility of serving other verticals. Using Unreal and Unity as two pillars of how game engines could develop, we can then look at how, for example, *Decentraland* builds its backend. And the truth is, *Decentraland* does use quite a bit of Unity technology (Decentraland Foundation, 2021). But does *Decentraland* allow for an immense amount of pixel streaming? And should it?

Pixel streaming allows developers to have many more procedurally generated environments compared to having to preload environments or spaces. In the good old days of cartridge or disc gameplay, environments in games were pre-loaded as static "levels" or a mise en scène before fading to black at the end of that process. These days, thanks to content delivery networks (CDNs), we have only the basic program on our PC or even mobile device. The generation of scenes and our entire experience builds from there like a snowball effect (Gomez et al., 2021). Both Unity and Unreal have invested heavily in pixel streaming over the years, allowing that sweet mobile-first joy of *Call of Duty Mobile* (or insert your favourite mobile game here).

This amorphous mass of different technologies works together towards the same end goal: user experience and enjoyment. In the metaverse, as consumers or players, we may not be aware of the underlying technologies that enable our digital experiences. But whether we see it or not, we are constantly interacting with systems that make the complex feel simple.

Take, for example, Web3 and blockchain technologies, which support decentralised transactions and ledger systems (Tapscott and Tapscott, 2016). In *Decentraland*, a popular metaverse platform, users can track their MANA balance (*Decentraland*'s native currency) as they move through the virtual world and even monitor it in real life if they choose. But how does *Decentraland* know how much MANA you have? How does your wallet, sitting in your browser or on your phone, connect seamlessly to the virtual world?

This is where APIs quietly do the heavy lifting.

At its core, an API, or Application Programming Interface, acts like a digital waiter between two systems. It takes your request ("What's my wallet balance?"), delivers it to the blockchain system where your data lives and brings back the response ("You have 250 MANA"). You don't need to know how the blockchain is structured, how the servers communicate or how the transactions are secured. The API abstracts all that complexity away and allows *Decentraland* to present a simple, seamless user experience.

Ultimately, the metaverse provides us with greater freedom to explore and interact with digital environments using trusted and transparent systems of transactions. But if we stake our claim that we're building something mobile first or desktop first, then our end of the bargain as tech people is to give our users freedom: freedom from friction, from confusion and from technical hurdles, and APIs are one of the invisible tools that help deliver that promise.

Look at pseudo-metaverses like *Fortnite* or *Minecraft*. These platforms have long prioritised cross-platform technology because it effectively doubles engagement (which for games is double the profitability in some cases). The experience needs to be as seamless as watching *Squid Game* on Netflix, shifting effortlessly from a desktop in the office to a living room TV, then onto a mobile phone in bed and to a tablet or any other device. If this space has taught us anything, it's that cross-platform technology moves us far beyond the limitations of early gaming, far from *Pole Position*, yet close to the same ikigai that has always driven developers: the pursuit of frictionless gameplay. From printed circuit boards to the cloud and beyond, the underlying purpose remains the same: to create frictionless, accessible experiences wherever users are. If the player has to decouple from the narrative or gameplay experience, the player is no longer playing and that's a death sentence for any experience.

GENESIS PLAZA IS FULL OF NOBODIES

Have you been inside *Decentraland* lately? In some areas of the platform, it is common to find only one or two non-player characters, or NPCs, present. For many people unfamiliar with the underlying design of digital worlds, this might feel surprising or even a little underwhelming. But this is entirely normal in today's virtual spaces, because NPCs quietly play a far bigger role across the digital landscape than many realise.

NPC stands for non-playable character. In games, this simply means characters that are not controlled by a human player but exist to populate, guide or enhance the world. Historically, video games could only support a limited number of human players at any given time, often one, maybe two or three. Early games like *Street Fighter* (Capcom, 1987), *Time Crisis* (Namco, 1995) or *Rainbow Six* (Red Storm Entertainment, 1998) were designed for small groups of players gathered around a single machine. These games could not accommodate millions of players all sharing the same world at once.

Today, metaverse platforms still face similar technical constraints. Servers, the computers that host these digital worlds, remain a key limitation. Even on modern metaverse platforms, many servers max out at just 500–700 users simultaneously. This may sound small compared to the record-breaking 91,311 players who connected to a single *World of Tanks* server back in 2011 (Guinness World Records, 2011), but supporting even a few hundred users in persistent, interactive worlds is still a remarkable technical achievement.

There are, of course, special cases. In April 2020, *Fortnite* hosted a virtual concert for Travis Scott that attracted over 12.3 million attendees (Epic Games, 2020). But it is important to note that these enormous events are not *live* in the traditional sense. The performers were not physically present in the game. Travis Scott and Marshmello, who previously attracted 10.7 million players, appeared as digital avatars, essentially advanced forms of NPCs designed for a mass audience.

NPCs, however, are not a recent invention. The term originated in tabletop role-playing games like *D&D* (Gygax and Arneson, 1975), where non-player characters were used by the Game Master to provide quests, information or obstacles for the players. In digital games, NPCs serve much the same purpose. They onboard players, give directions or create a sense of life within the world. Like a navigation system suggesting the best route or alerting users to obstacles ahead, NPCs act as guides, providing useful cues and context that help players engage with the environment.

As games have evolved, so too have NPCs. Early characters like Marc Gullite from *The Elder Scrolls IV: Oblivion* (Bethesda, 2006) followed scripted dialogue paths. Players could speak to him, but only within the limits of pre-written text boxes. In games like *Tomb Raider* (Core Design, 1996) or *Tekken 3* (Namco, 1997), dialogue was limited to brief text captions or cutscenes. But in recent years, artificial intelligence has allowed NPCs to engage in more natural and flexible interactions. Modern titles such as *The Last of Us* (Naughty Dog, 2013), *Dragon Quest XI* (Square Enix, 2017) and *Final Fantasy VII Remake* (Square Enix, 2020) incorporate sophisticated dialogue and behaviour systems. In some genres, like *Phoenix Wright: Ace Attorney* (Capcom, 2001) or Japanese dating sims, interaction with NPCs is the core of the entire gameplay experience.

One thing is certain: NPCs will remain a fundamental part of digital environments, from games to metaverse platforms. Their evolution represents a broader trend in digital world-building, creating rich, immersive spaces that feel alive, guided and socially engaging. As this book will explore in the following sections, NPCs also play a growing role in shaping narrative design, user experience and the social fabric of virtual worlds.

THE MACHINE QUESTIONNAIRE

I love reading the back pages of magazines. These days I read e-magazines and that means no back page. Some back pages of magazines have usually presented some lazy form of the Proust Questionnaire. Marcel Proust created a series of questions as a parlour game in 1885 to keep his guests from Oscar Wilde to Karl Marx entertained. He recorded these in a confession book. In 2023, I would add an addendum to the confession book and wonder what the answers would be if we input these questions into a machine, a computer. What might the answers look like if they were randomised? Would we be creating a Frankenstein's monster of Arthur Conan Doyle and Paul Cézanne, or if we use the Proust Questionnaire on the back pages of *Smash Hits* or *Grazia*, would we get an amalgam of Stella McCartney and Axl Rose? What I have just described here is a layman's approach to Natural Language Programming and Generative Pre-trained Transformers (Brown et al., 2020), which, at its heart, is Machine Learning and Artificial Intelligence.

During the pandemic, I started talking about machine learning because, though it was the buzzword of the time, I was working on a program to develop generative AI for 3D objects. I started exploring the possibilities of how, in 2020, generative AI would be able to help the games industry particularly (Ramesh et al., 2021). From working with customer service chatbots to image segmentation for cutscenes, machine learning can do it all. Practical use cases might be spam filtering, character recognition, search engines or computer vision; you would choose machine learning as your desired tool (Jordan and Mitchell, 2015).

It would be hubris to suggest I had anything to do with what happened next because I'm just an idiot from the games industry harnessing the awesome power of AI. To be honest, machine learning works for me because I'm lazy. But unlike some of my peers in other (cough, Venture Capital, cough) industries, I have to know what machine learning and AI do before I pontificate about how robots will steal our jobs. Even I know that this area is broken into two camps: questions and answers (Chollet, 2019).

Machine learning asks questions of everything (but we have to tell it what to ask). You remember the five Ws and H questions, don't you? It's the Clark Kent 101 of working at the *Daily Planet*. Who, what, where, when, why and how. Now apply that to machine learning and some AI and what we get are the concepts of examine, simplify, speed, learn and predict to provide a comprehensible explanation of the core elements of AI and ML (Domingos, 2015).

- *Examine* is about the analysis of data or a problem to determine the best approach to solving it. In the context of AI and ML, this involves examining the data and identifying patterns that can be used to train an algorithm.

- *Simplify* refers to breaking down something massive into smaller, more manageable pieces.

- *Speed* is about using efficient algorithms and hardware to process large datasets quickly, essential in real-time applications like autonomous vehicles or fraud detection.

- *Learning* is the act of training an algorithm to recognise and respond to patterns in data.

- *Predict* is the machine's capacity to anticipate an outcome or recommendation based on learned data (Goodfellow et al., 2016).

If the creation pipeline starts with the examination of things, we have to go deep. There is a human element to this step. Machine learning gives computers the ability to learn without being explicitly programmed (Mitchell, 1997). That means, in order to learn without programming, we have to tell the computer what we're looking for. In image segmentation, the creation pipeline examines objects by preparing explicit algorithms. We're telling the machine to look for particular things.

Vertex and object analysis is focused on metrology, and this is an area of research that gets little attention despite its impact on our day to day. If I say vertex and object analysis to you, you say *what*. Then if I talk about negative space, you might still say *what*. If I mention Rubin's vase (1915), or Dr Edgar Rubin, you might still be puzzled, yet you have some idea of an image of two faces in silhouette directly opposed to each other and all you can see in the middle is something that looks like a chess piece or a vase. Now do you know what

I'm talking about? Yes. Rubin's area of research was around visual perception, something he wrote his doctoral thesis about (Rubin, 1915). Diagnostic equipment requires metrology and negative space to work as the diagnoser.

Let's say a pair of shoes that we really love but somehow always seems to end up giving us blisters when we wear them. We can use ML and AI to determine the point, age or material that will blister our feet up in a pinch, literally.

Pipeline performance, this is quite a controversial point in an age where we're trying to put human employability high. However, machines that make product performance better by streamlining are the sure-fire hit of the decade. We live in the fourth industrial revolution, and, if you've read *The Augmented Workforce* by Cathy Hackl and John Buzzell, you will know that the "internet of things is [...] gradually impacting more of how we live, work and play" (Hackl and Buzzell, 2021, p. 16). What a statement to make at a time like this, but how true is it in an age of Stable Diffusion or Midjourney? It's very accurate.

Only recently I talked with an anonymous game studio founder who was building an entire art system with Stable Diffusion, because "in the end" as he put it, "art is development and that can be done quickly and cheaply by software developers." While on a cost-benefit analysis that may be true, I would rather have Steve Vai play the theme from *Halo 2* on his guitar than hear the MIDI or chiptune version of the theme. I want composition and soul. How soon before we get AI to do everything? In the case of art, I would love to invest in the core of an art team, but I want them to have the mind of a computer and that's a tough problem to solve.

In my previous role working with digital twins and 3D objects, we were operating our art provision at 50 per cent human capacity. That means that the other 50 per cent was AI. The machine was a high-end workstation computer (but not as big as a Manchester lab) to handle VGL files (a PC file format from Volume Graphics GmbH) and Digital Imaging and Communications in Medicine (DICOM, a medical imaging format from the National Electrical Manufacturers Association, 2019). A saving of 50 per cent in salary is a 100 per cent investment in AI.

In my previous job, I compared image segmentation to finding a print of an object, like via Xerox on a piece of A4 paper. Then, taking scissors, I chopped the image into strips and reconstructed the segments digitally. I also developed a rule for NFTs, a standard, which followed these principles:

1. I looked at the object as a physical entity and measured its dimensions, mass and volume.

2. I scanned the object using a Computed Tomography scanner. LiDAR could be used, but CT was more accurate for this use case (Lee et al., 2018).

3. The segments were processed using tomographic reconstruction algorithms to produce cross-sectional images (Siddon, 1985).

I used that information to finalise the object digitally. The bounding boxes and taxonomies were set. But metadata mattered too. Metadata is self-referential data describing the object's qualities, composition, ownership and value (Zeng and Qin, 2016).

For games, this method sped up development. Instead of downloading different assets, I stripped the object to the mesh and reused it across genres. The mesh remained constant; only the aesthetic changed.

To learn, the machine needs training data. We fed our machine 50 pomegranates, 50 pens, 50 phones and 50 hairdryers. These were not identical items but different variants, bruised, split, red and yellow. The machine examined these via segmentation and began to form hypotheses (LeCun, Bengio and Hinton, 2015). It rebuilt the object from its data fragments and began to learn the difference, constructing a model of what the "next" version could be. That's the generative AI at work.

The outcome defines success. If I need the shine of a metal surface to be accurate, the machine will learn how to reproduce it. That is the reward loop of AI.

DUMB STATE MACHINES

In game development, we may well use AI for asset creation (generative AI) as already described. But did you know that we can use AI for combat systems? I mentioned the vehicular features we used during the development of *Transformers Universe*, but how about melee attacks? Does it work for that? Of course, machine learning and AI work together to study how players behave but more importantly how NPCs might behave at the moment of attack. In a blog entry at *gamedeveloper.com*, Bart Vossen explores the three major areas of enemy design and AI: enemy AI, grouping and other enemy traits and behaviours (Vossen, 2022) (Table 3.6).

Vossen says that the design of enemies in AI patterns and responses is a complex task which is easily underestimated (Vossen, 2022). This is backed up by the incredible research that individuals such as Dr Tommy Thompson, computer scientist and academic lecturer at King's College London, assert in his *AI and Games* series on YouTube (Thompson, 2016). Each week Tommy selects a game or a franchise and deconstructs the AI from the gameplay to ascertain its meaning and usefulness.

Procedural generation is a current buzzword, but it's an old practice which has more recently been automated. Back in the day of me being a raw and unfiltered junior game designer, we might create or generate battles, levels or map selections as a team. One of us would have board game know-how, another would be strong on tech, and I would be more motivated by reasoning and the motivation of players. We would do this on a spreadsheet that mapped directly to the core engine, invoking new and exciting content for the player. Could we call it AI? Nope, definitely not. Can we do it now? Yes, because this infinite

TABLE 3.6 AI Behaviour Pillars in Combat Systems

Type	Purpose	Example (Game)	AI Technique
Enemy AI	Movement logic	*Elder Scrolls III: Morrowind*	Finite state machines(FSM)
Enemy grouping	Dynamic scaling	*Elder Scrolls IV: Oblivion*	Influence mapping
Enemy traits	Response variety	*The Last of Us*	Utility AI

TABLE 3.7   AI Automation in Game Dev Pipelines

Process	Traditional Method	AI Enhancement
Localisation QA	Manual language review	NLP-based translation + flagging
Bug identification	Manual testing	GPT-assisted bug lookup
Art asset scaling	Manual resizing	AI upscaling/inpainting
Environment generation	Manual level design	Procedural + generative AI

playlisting and selection of everything is exactly what the core engine does these days. All we do as game designers and developers is feed the beast with information.

Business Takeaway: Procedural or AI? You choose!

Procedural generation, once spreadsheet-driven, is now AI-powered. What used to take teams weeks can now be prototyped in hours, reshaping both budgets and creative scope.

Finally, for now, QA. Localisation, quality assurance, liveops automation, bug lookup and autofix (Table 3.7):

The list will most definitely go on because, and certainly for me as I write this, I can clean my code up using everything from Claude to ChatGPT, meaning that User Acceptance Testing is something more automated than it ever was before.

REFERENCES

Analysis Group (2022) *The Potential Global Economic Impact of the Metaverse*. Analysis Group. Available at: https://www.analysisgroup.com/globalassets/insights/publishing/2022-the -potential-global-economic-impact-of-the-metaverse.pdf (Accessed: 1 June 2025).

Ball, M. (2022) *The Metaverse: And How It Will Revolutionize Everything*. New York, NY: Liveright.

Brown, T., Mann, B., Ryder, N., Subbiah, M., Kaplan, J., Dhariwal, P., & Amodei, D. (2020) 'Language Models Are Few-Shot Learners', *Advances in Neural Information Processing Systems*, 33, pp. 1877–1901.

Campbell, J. (1949) *The Hero with a Thousand Faces*. Princeton, NJ: Princeton University Press.

Chollet, F. (2019) *Deep Learning with Python*. 1st edn. Greenwich: Manning Publications.

Collins, K. (2008) *Game Sound: An Introduction to the History, Theory, and Practice of Video Game Music and Sound Design*. Cambridge, MA: MIT Press.

Decentraland Foundation (2021) *Decentraland Documentation*. Available at: https://docs.decentraland.org

Dionisio, J.D.N., Burns III, W.G. and Gilbert, R. (2013) '3D Virtual Worlds and the Metaverse: Current Status and Future Possibilities', *ACM Computing Surveys*, 45(3), pp. 1–38.

Donovan, T. (2010) *Replay: The History of Video Games*. Lewes: Yellow Ant.

Domingos, P. (2015) *The Master Algorithm: How the Quest for the Ultimate Learning Machine Will Remake Our World*. New York, NY: Basic Books.

Dragon Quest XI: Echoes of an Elusive Age (2017) Playstation [Video Game]. Japan: Square Enix.

Economist Impact (2023) *Towards a Successful Metaverse: Building the Metaverse Economy*. Economist Impact. Available at: https://impact.economist.com/perspectives/sites/default/files/download/economist_impact_toward_a_successful_metaverse_final_28_june_2023_1.pdf (Accessed: 1 June 2025).

Final Fantasy VII Remake (2020) Playstation [Video Game]. Japan: Square Enix.

Fortnite: Travis Scott Concert (2020) PC [Online Event]. USA: Epic Games.

Gomez, M., Liu, J. and Shirmohammadi, S. (2021) 'Cloud-Based Pixel Streaming for Interactive 3D Applications', *IEEE Transactions on Cloud Computing*, 9(1), pp. 30–42.

Goodfellow, I., Bengio, Y. and Courville, A. (2016) *Deep Learning*. Cambridge, MA: MIT Press.

Gregory, J. (2018) *Game Engine Architecture*. 3rd edn. Boca Raton, FL: CRC Press.

Guinness World Records (2011) 'Most Players Online Simultaneously on One FPS Server', *Guinness World Records*. Available at: https://www.guinnessworldrecords.com/

Gygax, G. and Arneson, D. (1975) *Dungeons & Dragons*. Lake Geneva, WI: TSR.

Hackl, C. and Buzzell, J. (2021) *The Augmented Workforce: How AI, AR, and 5G Will Impact Every Dollar You Make*. New York, NY: Wiley.

Howard, T. (2003) 'Postmortem: The Elder Scrolls III: *Morrowind*', *Gamasutra*. Available at: https://www.gamedeveloper.com/design/postmortem-bethesda-s-the-elder-scrolls-iii-morrowind

Isbister, K. (2017) *How Games Move Us: Emotion by Design*. Cambridge, MA: MIT Press.

Jordan, M.I. and Mitchell, T.M. (2015) 'Machine Learning: Trends, Perspectives, and Prospects', *Science*, 349(6245), pp. 255–260.

Kent, S.L. (2001a) *The Ultimate History of Video Games: From Pong to Pokémon and Beyond*. New York, NY: Three Rivers Press.

Kent, S.L. (2001b) *The Ultimate History of Video Games*. Roseville, CA: Prima Publishing.

Kline, S., Dyer-Witheford, N. and de Peuter, G. (2003) *Digital Play: The Interaction of Technology, Culture, and Marketing*. Montreal: McGill-Queen's University Press.

LeCun, Y., Bengio, Y. and Hinton, G. (2015) 'Deep Learning', *Nature*, 521(7553), pp. 436–444.

Lee, C., Goo, H.W. and Lee, J.Y. (2018) 'Multidetector Computed Tomography and Imaging-Based Reconstruction in Pediatric Cardiology', *Korean Journal of Radiology*, 19(4), pp. 789–802.

Markoff, J. (2016) 'Moore's Law Running Out of Room, Tech Looks for a Successor', *New York Times*. Available at: https://www.nytimes.com/2016/05/05/technology/moores-law-running-out-of-room-tech-looks-for-a-successor.html

Mitchell, T.M. (1997) *Machine Learning*. New York, NY: McGraw-Hill.

Moore, G.E. (1965) Cramming More Components Onto Integrated Circuits. *Electronics*, 38(8), pp. 114–117.

National Electrical Manufacturers Association (2019) *Digital Imaging and Communications in Medicine (DICOM) Standard*. Rosslyn: NEMA.

Nvidia (2002) *GeForce4 Product Launch Overview*. Available at: https://www.nvidia.com/en-us/geforce/news/geforce4/

Peterson, J. (2012). *Playing at the World: A History of Simulating Wars, People and Fantastic Adventures*. San Diego, CA: Unreason Press.

Phoenix Wright: Ace Attorney (2001) PC [Video Game]. Tokyo: Capcom.

Rabin, S. (ed.) (2010) *Introduction to Game Development*. 2nd edn. Boston, MA: Cengage Learning.

Ramesh, A., Pavlov, M., Goh, G., Gray, S., Voss, C., Radford, A. and Sutskever, I. (2021) *Zero-Shot Text-to-Image Generation* [Preprint]. arXiv:2102.12092.

Research and Markets (2025) *Metaverse Industry and Companies Analysis Report 2025–2030*. Research and Markets. Available at: https://www.globenewswire.com/news-release/2025/04/25/3068346/28124/en/Metaverse-Industry-and-Companies-Analysis-Report-2025-2030-Are-We-Ready-to-Shift-from-WFH-to-WFM-Revenues-Set-to-Reach-US-1-1-Trillion-by-2030.html (Accessed: 1 June 2025).

Rollings, A. and Morris, D. (2004) *Game Architecture and Design: Learn the Best Practices for Game Design and Programming*. Indianapolis, IN: New Riders.

Rubin, E. (1915) *Synsoplevede Figurer: Studier i psykologisk Analyse*. Copenhagen: Gyldendal.

Schell, J. (2020) *The Art of Game Design: A Book of Lenses*. 3rd edn. Boca Raton, FL: CRC Press.

Sheff, D. (1993) *Game Over: How Nintendo Zapped an American Industry, Captured Your Dollars, and Enslaved Your Children*. New York, NY: Random House.

Siddon, R.L. (1985) 'Fast Calculation of the Exact Radiological Path for a Three-Dimensional CT Array', *Medical Physics*, 12(2), pp. 252–255.

Smith, G. (2019). *How Game Engines Work. Game Developer.* Available at: https://www.gamedeveloper.com

Street Fighter (1987) Arcade [Video Game]. Osaka: Capcom.

Tapscott, D. and Tapscott, A. (2016) *Blockchain Revolution: How the Technology Behind Bitcoin Is Changing Money, Business, and the World.* New York, NY: Portfolio.

Tekken 3 (1997). Playstation [Video Game]. Japan: Namco.

The Last of Us (2013) XBox 360 [Video Game]. USA: Naughty Dog.

Thompson, T. (2016–present) *AI and Games* [YouTube Series]. Available at: https://www.youtube.com/c/AIandGames [Accessed: 29 May 2025].

Time Crisis (1995) [Arcade Game]. Japan: Namco.

Tom Clancy's Rainbow Six (1998) PC [Video Game]. USA: Red Storm Entertainment.

Tomb Raider (1996) Playstation [Video Game]. United Kingdom: Core Design.

Unity Technologies (2021) *Unity Engine Documentation.* Available at: https://unity.com/

Vossen, B. (2022) The Three Pillars of AI in Enemy Design. *Game Developer.* Available at: https://www.gamedeveloper.com/design/the-three-pillars-of-ai-in-enemy-design (Accessed: 29 May 2025).

Waldrop, M.M. (2016) 'The Chips Are Down for Moore's Law', *Nature*, 530(7589), pp. 144–147.

Zeng, M.L. and Qin, J. (2016) *Metadata.* 2nd ed. Chicago, IL: ALA Neal-Schuman.

CHAPTER 4

Avatars, Digital Twins and Plug-Ins Part I

THE SKIN WE'RE IN

In the beginning, the avatar was not us. Avatars were Donkey Kong, Mario, Crash Bandicoot, Lara Croft or Soap MacTavish.

Then Avatars Became Us

Hello, I'm Southrey Dragonash. That's *my Second Life* (2003) handle/ID. "Mine's name is Tigra, and then she became Tigra Volkihar, after becoming a vampire lord via Serana biting her. Then they got married after slaying Harkon and the Dawnguard" (Unnamed Redditor, 2023).

Now, Avatars Offer Choices

In video games, avatars serve as the player's bridge into digital worlds: personal, immersive and endlessly customisable. Whether simple 2D sprites or hyper-detailed 3D models, avatars reflect preferences, skills and identity (Figure 4.1).

The term itself – *Avatar* – precedes gaming by millennia. In Sanskrit, avatar (अवतार) describes the earthly manifestation of a deity, most often Vishnu. Even then, the avatar was a projection of a higher self, a form sent into the world on behalf of something larger. That metaphysical foundation echoes through today's digital cultures.

> **Business Takeaway:**
> Avatars are digital identity proxies. Monetisation of appearance taps directly into social psychology, not just aesthetic preference.

DOI: 10.1201/9781003615248-4

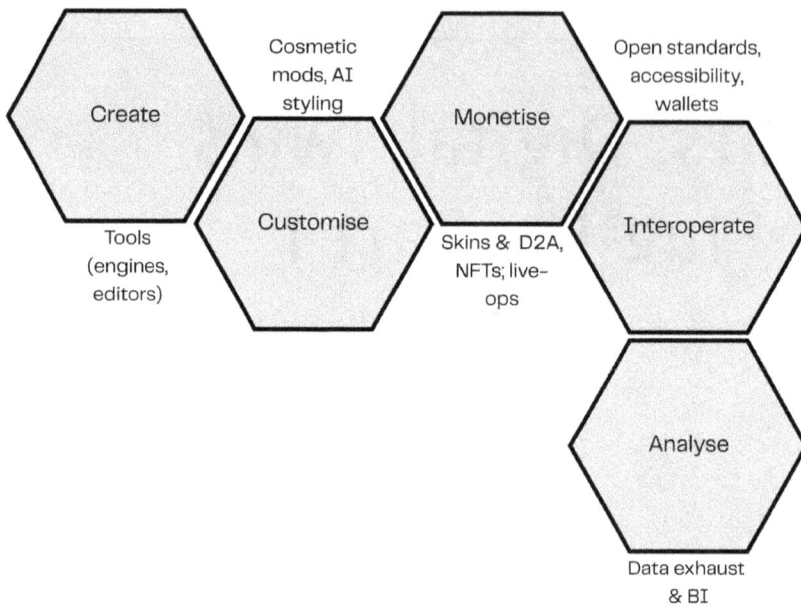

FIGURE 4.1   Avatar value chain.

In early computing, however, avatars were not divine – only practical. They began as simple icons: a paddle in *Pong* (1972), a spaceship in *Space Invaders* (1978), a hungry yellow disc in *Pac-Man* (1980). Players existed only through control of movement, not identity.

By the 1980s and 1990s, avatars began evolving into distinct characters. *Donkey Kong* (1981) introduced Mario, while *Ultima IV: Quest of the Avatar* (1985) explicitly used the term *avatar* in its narrative, asking players to embody virtues through their choices. Sophistication grew through the 1990s: Lara Croft in *Tomb Raider* (1996), Cloud Strife in *Final Fantasy VII* (1997), Solid Snake in *Metal Gear Solid* (1998); characters the player controlled, but did not fully own.

It was with the rise of customisable characters in RPGs and MMOs that avatars first began resembling their players. *EverQuest* (1999), *The Sims* (2000), *World of Warcraft* (2004) and *Second Life* allowed users to create digital extensions of themselves. No longer just game mechanics, avatars became public-facing representations of who we were, or who we wished to be in persistent digital spaces.

BEINGS

Today, we're entering a new phase: not simply building gravatars or virtual masks, but constructing persistent digital selves. The avatar is no longer just who we are; it's who we are becoming. Once again, it is video games that offer the clearest indicators of where this digital evolution is heading.

Avatars serve several fundamental functions inside digital worlds:

- *Emotional identification*: Players become invested in their characters and the environments they inhabit.

- *Role-playing and storytelling*: Avatars carry backstories, personalities and player-authored narratives.

- *Skill reflection*: A player's abilities, gear and achievements are visually expressed.

- *Social interaction*: Avatars serve as points of contact for friendships, rivalries and collaborations.

Avatars are central to the video game experience, creating immersive, engaging and highly personalised worlds. Yet not all avatars function equally. They are not always direct representations of the player's real-world identity, nor even their in-game self.

In some titles, such as *Sid Meier's Civilization*, players control entire factions or historical leaders rather than a singular, embodied avatar. Sports franchises like *NHL*, *FIFA* or *NBA 2K* place players behind real-world athletes whose likenesses are updated annually to reflect the latest sports data (Nieborg, 2011). Real-time strategy games like *Age of Mythology* and *Company of Heroes* cast the player as omniscient commanders managing units and resources, rather than controlling discrete digital bodies.

The tabletop world of *Dungeons & Dragons* first introduced the idea of highly personalised characters through a combination of classes, abilities and races, a system video games have enthusiastically adopted and expanded. In *The Elder Scrolls* series, for instance, players may select a class like Necromancer, specialising in death magic, and develop abilities across skill trees such as Grave Lord, Bone Tyrant and Living Death (UESP Wiki, 1995). Racial choices like the feline Khajiit, known for agility and stealth, further influence gameplay. Cosmetic features such as height, weight and facial structure enable players to shape deeply individualised digital identities.

Yet skill trees do not automatically create personality. A Necromancer might control the undead, or choose instead to be a peaceful merchant, a wandering scholar or the adoptive parent of three orphaned wood elves. The technical framework supplies the mechanics; the player provides the narrative.

> **Business Takeaway:**
> Skill-tree design is not just game balance; it's a blueprint for tiered pricing. Each perceived power plateau (visual, ability, social) is a new SKU.

In many ways, skill trees mirror career ladders or educational pathways in real life. The more a player learns, the more powerful and specialised they become, much like professional expertise leading to advanced roles or specialisations (Schell, 2020; Rollings and Adams, 2003). These progression systems also enable skill-based matchmaking, pairing players with similarly skilled opponents as they advance (Kim, 2022).

Titles like *Company of Heroes* and *Command and Conquer* use tech trees to simulate entire eras of technological development, while games such as *Rise of Kingdoms* allow players to influence system-wide stats and hierarchies, all without reliance on Non-Fungible Tokens (NFTs) or tokenomics (Newzoo, 2023).

Beyond gameplay, skill trees have become a metaphor for real-world learning itself. Gamification theorists have argued that applying progression mechanics: levelling systems, achievements, unlockable skills, can boost real-world motivation (Deterding et al., 2011; Kapp, 2012). Imagine learning sewing, coding or even knitting with visualised mastery and skill unlocks mapped onto gamified progression trees. In this way, avatars and their systems of advancement offer not only digital entertainment, but blueprints for personal development far beyond the screen.

By the 1990s, even as avatars became more detailed and customisable, their believability remained limited, not only by visual fidelity, but by how they moved. Animation technology was a primary constraint on the player's emotional investment in their digital selves (Bevilacqua and Rosenberg, 2017).

Early video games used simple frame-based sprite animations. Characters in side-scrollers like *Super Mario Bros.* (1985) or *Sonic the Hedgehog* (1991) were animated through sequential 2D frames, creating the illusion of motion via rapid cycling. But these avatars, limited by storage capacity, moved in staccato bursts: charming, but rarely lifelike.

Rotoscoping delivered one of the first major breakthroughs. By filming real actors and tracing their movements frame by frame, titles like *Prince of Persia* (1989) and Flashback (1992) introduced fluidity and realism previously unattainable in sprite-based systems (Rosen, 2004). Suddenly, avatars stumbled, flailed and fell with recognisably human motion, even as their faces remained pixel abstractions.

By the mid-1990s, full 3D character models introduced new challenges and opportunities. *Tomb Raider* (1996) leveraged skeletal animation systems that allowed Lara Croft to dynamically respond to player input; climbing, swimming, aiming all across three-dimensional space. Her famously angular geometry was a concession to polygon budgets, but the system enabled embodied, responsive control (Bevilacqua and Rosenberg, 2017). For many players, Lara wasn't simply controlled, she was inhabited.

Simultaneously, the film industry experimented with CGI breakthroughs that filtered into game development. *Jurassic Park* (1993) showcased skeletal rigs driving lifelike creatures, while *Toy Story* (1995) demonstrated fully computer-generated characters capable of nuanced emotional expression (Foley et al., 1990; Rosen, 2004). As consoles and GPUs advanced, these tools slowly migrated into interactive media.

The real frontier, however, was motion capture. Initially prohibitively expensive, early mocap experiments allowed developers to record real human movement and translate it directly into avatars. Titles like *Tekken 3* (1997) and *Virtua Fighter 3* (1996) employed primitive mocap rigs, offering smoother, more believable combat animations than traditional hand-keyed frames (Bevilacqua and Rosenberg, 2017).

Business Takeaway:
Every leap in animation fidelity resets aesthetic baselines and opens a pricing window for premium "next-gen" cosmetics. Budget accordingly for asset refresh cycles.

In many ways, the evolution of avatar animation maps directly onto players' growing identification with their digital selves. The more convincingly an avatar moved, the more immersive and emotionally resonant the experience became. Early avatars behaved like puppets; by the late 1990s, avatars felt like true extensions of player intent, fluid, embodied, increasingly personalised.

ME AND MY SHADOW

By 2009, however, even blocky 3D avatars were straining to meet rising expectations for realism. Motion capture was king, but facial capture remained an emerging frontier. Developers recognised that full facial customisation, beyond titles like *The Elder Scrolls IV: Oblivion*, required far more advanced tools.

Mortal Kombat had first pushed mocap into mainstream production for digital media in the 1990s. Facial capture, meanwhile, remained mostly cinematic. Richard Bohringer became one of the first virtual actors cloned on screen in 1993, while FaceRig and Faceware emerged as early tools for direct-to-game facial capture (Rosen, 2004). In academic labs, I experimented with similar tools. At the time, optical technologies like webcams consistently failed inclusive and equitable facial recognition benchmarks (Buolamwini and Gebru, 2018).

Still, some mapping pipelines began bridging facial movement into avatars. The arrival of Microsoft's Kinect and Lionhead's short-lived *Project Milo* hinted at what would become standard: camera-to-avatar pipelines combining facial capture, gesture recognition and full-body animation.

Today, facial rigging tools function more like modular plug-ins for broader production ecosystems, often built for specific engines. Epic's *Metahuman* has become an industry benchmark, particularly for virtual influencers and metaverse developers, for its realism and interactivity inside virtual environments (Epic Games, 2021; Gravina, Li and Fortino, 2022).

> **Business Takeaway:**
> Every leap in animation fidelity resets aesthetic baselines and opens a pricing window for premium "next-gen" cosmetics. Budget accordingly for asset refresh cycles.

Metahuman avatars resemble the player. Built atop fully customisable skeletal armatures, users can fine-tune body shapes, face types, eye colours and more. The pandemic only accelerated this drive toward hyper-personalisation, as users sought to define not just how they looked, but who they were, and what they owned, in virtual worlds.

When *Metahuman* launched in 2021, it was met with near rapturous excitement. What developers had struggled to achieve since *Mass Effect* and *Oddcast* was now possible. *Metahuman* combined advanced scanning, rigging and Artificial Intelligence (AI)-driven editing tools to produce avatars nearly indistinguishable from real humans, in appearance, motion and facial expression. And importantly, no computer science degree was required (Epic Games, 2021).

Photorealism matters. Along with emerging technologies, it is driving the broader evolution of virtual environments towards a video game-inspired metaverse: richly simulated, deeply immersive and data-intensive (Gravina, Li and Fortino, 2022). This realism enhances user immersion in VR training, simulations and educational environments where full engagement is crucial for skill acquisition.

It also transforms digital social interaction. In virtual meetings, Metahuman avatars allow colleagues to respond to subtle facial expressions, gestures and emotional cues, producing more natural, human-like exchanges.

Empirical studies confirm these effects. A 2019 study in *The Journal of Computer-Mediated Communication* found that realistic avatars significantly improved users' sense of social presence and interpersonal connection (Oh, Bailenson and Welch, 2018). Similarly, a 2020 study in the *International Journal of Human-Computer Interaction* found enhanced emotional expression and recognition in virtual interactions using photorealistic avatars (Park, Kim and Sohn, 2020).

Not every study finds equally strong effects, of course. Task type, context and user familiarity still shape virtual interactions. But overall, the ability of realistic avatars to improve communication and emotional connection is increasingly evident.

The adoption of facial capture tools marks a genuine step forward for virtual environments across sectors, from entertainment and education to healthcare and therapy. Avatars are no longer mere digital costumes; they are becoming sophisticated proxies for how we show up, communicate and engage inside virtual worlds.

THE MIRROR HAS TWO FACES

In many modern games, particularly competitive online titles, visual customisation has become central to both player identity and monetisation. These upgrades, known as *skins*, have shifted from simple cosmetics to core components of digital self-expression and commercial success (Table 4.1).

Originally, skins merely altered a character's appearance without affecting gameplay. Over time, however, they have become deeply entwined with identity, status and emotional

TABLE 4.1   Avatar Systems Across Major Platforms

Platform	Avatar Type	Customisation Depth	Monetisation	Interoperable
Roblox	User-generated + layered clothing	High: skins, animations, UGC items	Robux marketplace, DevEx	Partially (UGC avatars stay in ecosystem)
Fortnite	Branded + original avatars	Medium–high – cosmetics, emotes, gliders	Battle Pass, in-game store	No (Epic ecosystem only)
VRChat	Fully user-created avatars	Extremely high – often community-built from scratch	External (via Gumroad, Patreon)	Yes (via Unity upload pipeline)
Decentraland	NFT-based avatars + wearables	Moderate – NFT wearables, accessories	Crypto economy (MANA, NFT sales)	Yes (on-chain items)
Meta (Horizon)	Realistic human avatars	Low–moderate – clothing, facial features	Linked to Meta account + store	No (closed ecosystem)

engagement. No longer just aesthetic flourishes, skins function as personal investments into a player's avatar experience (Kim, 2022).

League of Legends exemplifies this evolution. Players select from pre-designed champions, then purchase skins that modify not only visual design but also animations, voice lines and effects (Kim, 2022). While these upgrades leave core mechanics unchanged, they significantly influence how players inhabit their characters. For many, favourite or rare skins amplify immersion, and some even report feeling more skilled when equipped with prized cosmetics (Kim, 2022).

Importantly, skins provide a form of soft progression, a kind of emotional "stat boost" tied to personal investment rather than mechanical advantage. Developers carefully balance gameplay to avoid pay-to-win models, but skins offer players opportunities for individual expression, fandom and digital prestige (Nieborg and Poell, 2018).

> **Business Takeaway:**
> Skins = emotional stat-boosts. The deeper the identity investment, the more elastic the price ceiling. Your job is to raise symbolic value without tilting into pay-to-win.

The business model has proven exceptionally lucrative. Today, 85% of US gamers aged 13–45 are familiar with skins, and many spend real money to acquire them. A smaller segment of "whales" drive disproportionate revenue, spending an average of $25 per month (Carmichael, 2013). Globally, the market is even more significant, with companies like Riot Games generating substantial revenue from Asia-Pacific regions, particularly China, which represents a major share of global skin sales (Niko Partners, 2022).

As monetisation tools, skins have become one of the most powerful engines behind gaming's current business models. But they are more than just revenue streams: skins function as complex cultural signals, blending personal taste, digital identity and social currency inside both gaming and metaverse economies (Nieborg and Poell, 2018).

While avatars offer profound opportunities for identity, creativity and self-expression, their evolution also invites complex ethical challenges. As avatars grow more persistent, portable and hyper-realistic, the risks of harm grow in parallel, blurring the line between virtual violation and real-world trauma.

Avatars today function far beyond simple game constructs. Increasingly, they serve as social proxies, financial assets and data-bearing identities capable of moving fluidly across platforms (IEEE, 2023). This interoperability opens powerful opportunities for commerce, but it also creates unprecedented exposure to harassment, exploitation and abuse.

By 2024, public debate sharply intensified around avatar abuse within metaverse platforms. Reports of harassment, stalking and simulated violence, including sexual assault, surfaced in platforms like *Horizon Worlds*, *VRChat* and *Roblox* (Sales, 2024). These incidents underscored an unsettling reality: when avatars operate as digital extensions of the self, attacks on avatars can carry genuine psychological and emotional consequences.

Researchers in embodiment theory have long warned of these risks. Studies demonstrate that users form strong cognitive and emotional attachments to their avatars, often experiencing real physiological stress when their avatars are violated or mistreated (Slater and Sanchez-Vives, 2016). The more persistent and personalised an avatar becomes, the more potent the psychological harm of avatar abuse (Wolfendale, 2007).

The fragmented state of avatar governance further compounds these vulnerabilities. While early standards like IEEE P3141 aim to define technical frameworks for avatar portability, no universal legal framework yet exists (IEEE, 2023). Instead, platforms remain siloed walled gardens, each with inconsistent safety protocols, monetisation models and enforcement mechanisms.

In response, some platforms have implemented technical safeguards such as personal space boundaries, consent-based touch systems and proximity blocking tools (Meta, 2022; VRChat, 2023). These design choices reflect a growing understanding that avatar interaction is not simply game mechanics but embodied social contact that demands consent-based governance.

Yet, regulatory gaps persist. As of 2025, no international legal standards govern avatar safety across platforms (Schneider, 2024). Where real-world harassment and assault are legally codified, avatar violations often fall into jurisdictional grey zones. Victims frequently face limited avenues for legal recourse or emotional support.

Interoperability raises additional challenges. Avatar portability means abuse can follow users across virtual borders. Psychological trauma experienced inside one VR platform may carry over into entirely separate virtual spaces, creating what some scholars describe as *platform-agnostic harm* (Cross, 2023).

This "second body problem," as Katherine Cross defines it, reflects the profound embodiment of the user experience in virtual spaces, particularly for women, LGBTQ+ users and other marginalised communities disproportionately targeted for avatar harassment (Cross, 2023). Unlike simple offensive speech, these embodied violations mimic physical assault, triggering real-world psychological damage.

The ethical dilemmas of avatar culture demand new collaborations between technology designers, policymakers, psychologists and legal theorists. Without comprehensive consent frameworks, interoperability standards and psychological safeguards, the next phase of avatar development risks amplifying harm even as it expands human potential.

In this sense, avatars sit precisely at the intersection of law, psychology, design ethics and platform governance. Solving the challenges of avatar abuse will demand highly coordinated action from platform operators, legislators, legal scholars, clinical psychologists and interaction designers, all working toward systems that embed consent, accountability and digital self-defence at their core (Schneider, 2024).

> **Business Takeaway:**
> Safety tooling is not a cost centre; it's churn mitigation. Platforms that cut harassment by 10 % see up to 5 % lift in-game spend (Meta, 2022).

As we shift toward increasingly interoperable metaverse platforms, avatars simultaneously unlock new forms of participation and expose users to new types of vulnerability. Trust in these spaces hinges on recognising avatars not simply as playful representations, but as deeply meaningful extensions of personhood, digital identities that require equally serious protections.

And yet, the avatar has always represented something larger than code or commerce. Today's digital avatars continue that tradition: not merely characters, but aspirational projections of selfhood, digital gods of our own creation, carrying both our fantasies and our fragilities into virtual space.

ORDINARY PEOPLE

The 1990s marked a kind of adolescence for both digital culture and digital identity, a decade where selfhood oscillated between empowerment and anxiety, between godhood and collapse. Much like the teenagers who eagerly adopted these new virtual frontiers, digital identity was elastic, chaotic and filled with both promise and dread.

Cinema captured this duality vividly. In *The Lawnmower Man* (1992), digital identity was both seductive and dangerous, casting cyberspace as an existential threat to humanity's boundaries. In *Hackers* (1995), young protagonists performed identity as spectacle, through handles, animated sequences and neon-infused rebellion, breaking into adult systems of control. The hacker became a digital trickster: neither criminal nor technician, but an avatar, playing god inside the machine.

This tension spilled into the visual culture of the era. Music videos such as The Prodigy's *Voodoo People* (1994), *Odyssey into the Mind's Eye* (1996) and Westbam's *Bostich Remix* (1992) were drenched in early digital animation and crude polygonal avatars, functioning as visualisations of psychological states, emotional intensity and techno-futurist dreams. They were not simply design experiments, they were early manifestations of human imagination projecting into nascent virtual worlds.

Teenagers, as always believing themselves invincible, embraced these experiments as opportunities to transcend physical constraints. The digital avatar was, even then, a godlike projection: a self that could be perfected, multiplied and released into gravity-free digital spaces. Yet behind this utopian impulse lurked a quieter fear of identity distortion, disembodiment and loss as human selves migrated into machines.

In many ways, this 1990s mythology laid the emotional foundation for everything avatars would become: not only vessels for play or commerce, but expressions of aspiration, anxiety and evolving selfhood.

As digital culture accelerated, video games amplified this transformation. Titles like *Wipeout 2097* (1996), *DOOM* (1993) and *Quake* (1996) created flow-state experiences, kinetic, immersive and intensely self-directed. These were not traditional avatars with fully articulated bodies but extensions of player intent: vessels for speed, agency and pure adrenaline.

Simultaneously, language itself evolved. Terms like *cyber*, *hacker*, *virtual* and *digital self* entered popular discourse. Corporate giants such as Microsoft, Sony and IBM consolidated control over hardware and protocols, while millions of users experimented with identity in chat rooms, IRC handles, Geocities pages, early message boards and the first-generation MMOs.

Literature paralleled this cultural shift. William Gibson's *Neuromancer* (1984) and Neal Stephenson's *Snow Crash* (1992) crystallised the avatar as an epistemological projection, a cognitive agent navigating sprawling virtual networks. In Gibson's cyberspace, a "consensual hallucination," avatars were not just proxies but complex narrative embodiments of human cognition, agency and identity.

Beneath both the utopianism and dystopian anxiety of these narratives lies a deeper theoretical current: Donna Haraway's *A Cyborg Manifesto* (1985). Haraway argued that the boundary between human and machine was already dissolving. Identity, in her view, was no longer singular but a continuous negotiation across biology, technology, gender and politics. Avatars, seen through Haraway's lens, function as hybrid sites, cyborg extensions of both resistance and complicity within technological systems of power.

Haraway's insights remain crucial for understanding avatars today, not as mere commercial decorations, but as complex cultural artefacts revealing how deeply technology shapes identity itself. As she writes, the digital self is "a condensed image of both imagination and material reality" (Haraway, 1985).

Even as corporations build increasingly sophisticated avatar economies, they continue to wrestle with the same unresolved tensions that first surfaced in the hyper-coloured, rebellious adolescence of 1990s digital culture.

I, ROBOT

In a keynote I delivered recently in South Korea (possibly the most metaverse country in the world), I described how avatars are evolving into our digital clones, no longer just playthings, but persistent proxies capable of handling tasks, transactions and negotiations in environments we may never physically visit. The implications are enormous. Yet alongside these commercial and social complexities lies significant promise: a growing body of research suggests that avatars may offer profound therapeutic and educational benefits, particularly for neurodivergent individuals.

Among the most promising developments is the use of avatars as cognitive scaffolds, tools for learning support, behavioural coaching and therapeutic guidance. Controlled studies have shown that children with ADHD demonstrate improved task performance, attention regulation and executive function when working with avatar-mediated systems rather than traditional classroom instruction (Kim et al., 2023). Rather than acting as mere distractions, these avatars serve as focused facilitators, providing structured visual prompts, consistent routines and adaptive guidance that help simplify complex tasks.

This consistency may in fact be one of the avatar's most underappreciated strengths. Unlike human instructors, whose tone, patience or delivery may vary, avatars can offer stable, predictable interactions and non-judgemental reinforcement, qualities that are particularly valuable for neurodiverse learners who may struggle with unpredictability or shifting social expectations (Parsons and Cobb, 2011). In this context, avatars function not just as projections of self, but as intelligent guides capable of flexing to a learner's individual cognitive style.

Virtual reality platforms have extended these capabilities even further. Pilot studies show that autistic children participating in VR-based social skills training, often represented by avatars, experience measurable gains in emotion recognition, conversational turn-taking and collaborative problem-solving (Ke and Im, 2013; Smith et al., 2019). The controlled virtual environment helps reduce sensory overload while allowing for repeated, low-pressure practice of complex social exchanges.

Taken together, these studies hint at an expansive future where avatars act as therapeutic companions, behavioural coaches and even cognitive prosthetics. Rather than replacing teachers, therapists or caregivers, avatars may serve as tireless intermediaries, helping individuals navigate challenging tasks at their own pace. Over time, some avatars may evolve into persistent co-regulators, modelling executive function, reinforcing healthy behaviours and delivering non-judgemental coaching precisely calibrated to each person's unique needs.

Yet this same therapeutic potential highlights one of the avatar's most difficult design challenges: flexibility. A truly effective avatar system must be highly *personalisable*, not only in terms of customisations such as physical appearance but also in interaction style, emotional tone, pacing and sensory feedback. What soothes one learner may overwhelm another; what motivates one person may discourage someone else entirely. In this way, avatar design enters the emerging field of adaptive cognition, creating digital identities that modify themselves in response to users' evolving cognitive profiles.

Beyond education, avatars are increasingly finding applications in clinical healthcare. For instance, early studies show that stroke patients engaging in avatar-mediated physical therapy exhibit higher adherence and motivation than those undergoing traditional rehabilitation (Cameirão et al., 2010). By visually projecting recovery progress onto an embodied avatar, patients report stronger emotional investment and psychological ownership of their rehabilitation journey, transforming repetitive exercises into personally meaningful narratives of recovery.

> **Business Takeaway:**
> Assistive avatars create incremental Annual Recurring Revenue (ARR) for EDU/health vendors. Bundled licensing beats per-seat when avatars act as multi-session companions.

Collectively, these developments suggest that avatars may not simply reflect who we are, but actively shape who we can become. In therapy, education and neurodivergent support, avatars are shifting from passive representations into active collaborators: digital scaffolding that expands capability, fosters emotional safety, and opens new pathways for personal growth.

If the first generation of avatars were designed to *represent*, the next generation may be designed to *assist*, augmenting our ability to learn, adapt and thrive across complex digital and real-world environments alike.

IT'S A GAS

I work in a world of digital economies. My career has been in video games for the last three decades, where the monetisation of everything from units and tools to skip timers and magic tea chests has been my daily bread.

But What About *Avatars*?

Are they just digital costumes? Are they investments? Or are they becoming something even more personal, such as containers that hold pieces of who we are? This question has been at the heart of my work as we begin to build the next phase of the internet: one where our identities travel with us.

It's thrilling and a little unsettling to watch this evolution unfold. Because we're not just creating new ways to play or work. We are now building systems where pieces of our personal identity, appearance, reputation, belongings, even memories live inside data structures that move between platforms, apps and economies. Avatars are becoming persistent identity containers that carry value socially, financially, even legally wherever we go in the metaverse.

At the centre of this transformation sits a huge question:

> Will we truly own our digital selves? Or will our avatars remain trapped inside the walled gardens of big tech companies who control access to our identities?

This isn't just a technical problem. It's a much deeper challenge that touches on:

- Who controls our personal data.

- Whether digital assets are property or licences.

- How platforms extract revenue from identity itself.

- How safe do we feel when we enter these spaces.

- Who gets to represent themselves freely, and who gets left out.

- And how we even define identity, agency and ownership in a fully digital world.

Let's explore how avatars are shifting from simple representations to programmable assets, and in time, to semi-autonomous agents that might act on our behalf. Avatars are becoming far more than just characters we play: they're becoming the passports we travel with inside digital economies.

And along the way, we'll see how this shift doesn't just impact developers or game studios. It affects regulators, business leaders, designers, artists and everyday users who are now bringing real pieces of themselves into these emerging virtual ecosystems.

NEW YOU

The next phase in avatar development towards something more tangible in a digital future is the rise of Direct-to-Avatar (D2A) commerce. Over the last few years, D2A has felt a bit like trying to make *fetch* happen, and if you've seen *Mean Girls* (2004), you'll know fetch still hasn't fully crossed the chasm (Moore, 1991). But make no mistake: it's coming.

Unlike traditional merchandise pipelines, where physical products are made first and later digitised for avatars, D2A flips the process entirely. Here, digital items are designed natively for virtual spaces, often with no intention of ever becoming physical products. The avatar, rather than the person, becomes the primary customer.

Business Takeaway:
D2A turns fashion from seasonal to perpetual. "Drop" cadence should follow patch cycles, not runway calendars.

Major fashion houses have already begun experimenting:

- Gucci partnered with *Roblox* to launch *Gucci Garden*, where some virtual items even exceeded real-world prices (Gucci, 2023).

- Balenciaga, Burberry and Louis Vuitton have each developed exclusive digital collections for titles such as *Fortnite, Honor of Kings* and *League of Legends*.

- Metaverse Fashion Week events inside platforms like *Decentraland* showcase entire runway shows detached from the constraints of physical manufacturing.

But this isn't limited to luxury fashion. Entire digital-first brands are emerging:

- Platforms like DRESSX, The Fabricant and RTFKT Studios (recently sunsetted by Nike) exist entirely to create virtual fashion exclusively for avatars.

- My own company, NAK3D, operates as a digital fashion engine capable of producing 30,000+ virtual fashion items per month, generating assets directly from URLs, text inputs or mood board inspiration into fully functional 3D platform-ready items.

- Independent creators are thriving too, using accessible 3D tools like Marvelous Designer, CLO3D and Blender to populate avatar marketplaces with original virtual wardrobes (Duan et al., 2021; Blender Foundation, 2024).

What D2A unlocks isn't simply more fashion, it's a radical reconfiguration of production and distribution models. Creators no longer require factories, shipping or inventory management. Digital fashion travels instantly, without logistics chains. Inventory is infinite, limited only by imagination, code and platform policy.

And while fashion leads the way, the model applies broadly to avatar commerce at large, from digital furniture to NFT sneakers, virtual pets to custom hairstyles. D2A represents a wider shift: Avatars have become standalone marketplaces, capable of generating and consuming their own digital economies.

Despite the creative explosion of avatar commerce, one critical question remains unresolved: who actually owns virtual assets?

In most mainstream platforms today:

- Skins and avatar items are licensed to users under restrictive Terms of Service agreements.

- Players have limited or no legal ownership rights over their purchased items.

- Assets are typically non-transferable, non-resalable and non-portable between platforms.

The legal ambiguity has already produced high-profile disputes over intellectual property inside virtual worlds. Blockchain-based models have attempted to address this with Non-Fungible Tokens (NFTs) proposing persistent, wallet-based ownership structures that would allow skins and assets to travel between games and marketplaces (Park and Kim, 2022). Yet adoption has been limited outside of Web3-native communities, in part due to speculative market volatility and regulatory uncertainty.

Perhaps the most famous Web3-native infringement between physical and digital assets so far is the MetaBirkin case (Hermès v. Rothschild, 2023). In this lawsuit, artist Mason Rothschild created a series of NFT artworks called *MetaBirkins*, referencing the iconic Hermès Birkin bag without Hermès' permission. Rothschild argued that his NFTs were artistic commentary, protected under free speech. Hermès countered that they constituted trademark infringement and dilution of its luxury brand in both physical and virtual markets.

The court ultimately sided with Hermès, awarding damages and affirming that virtual goods, even as NFTs, can still infringe on trademark rights, just like physical products. The ruling effectively recognised that virtual assets are not immune from real-world IP law, setting a precedent that may shape many future disputes over virtual goods, avatar fashion and metaverse commerce (Hermès International v. Rothschild, 2023).

The case highlights the broader tension that as virtual goods gain real-world economic value, they collide head-on with existing IP frameworks not designed for fully digital markets.

The idea of true interoperability, where avatars, skins and digital assets move fluidly between platforms, sounds simple. Technically, it's anything but. Commercially, it's a direct threat to how most major platforms generate revenue. And philosophically, it touches the raw nerve of who controls identity inside the metaverse economy.

If realised, interoperability wouldn't just allow a jacket purchased in *Fortnite* to appear in *Roblox*, or a skin bought in *Zepeto* to cross into *VRChat*. It would begin dismantling the very business models that keep users locked into walled gardens. Platform owners aren't afraid of shared file formats; they're afraid of shared customers.

Business Takeaway:
Open avatars threaten walled-garden ARPUs, but unlock network-level data monetisation. The choice is margin now vs. platform equity later.

As we continue building more immersive, persistent, and intelligent avatars, these therapeutic and developmental applications may prove to be among the most profound and far-reaching. They offer not just new ways to play, but entirely new ways to learn, to heal and to thrive, reframing how we think about identity, cognition and even human potential itself.

My avatars have always been *me*. Yet it was only recently that I fully grasped their deeper role within metaverse platforms. For many years, I simply stared at the back of my avatar's head, unaware that this digital projection would soon evolve into something far more persistent, meaningful and even commercial.

Because avatars are no longer just characters we inhabit temporarily. They are becoming persistent data objects: social proxies, financial assets, learning companions, cognitive assistants and integral nodes within vast, interconnected simulation ecosystems. They carry not only our visual likeness but fragments of our behaviour, preferences and histories. In time, they may speak for us, act on our behalf and form a durable part of our ongoing digital footprint, long after individual gameplay sessions have ended.

The avatar is no longer just a costume for digital play. It is becoming an economic structure. The skin you design for your avatar today may very well negotiate your employment tomorrow. The virtual identity you cultivate today may continue to earn, negotiate and represent you long after you're gone.

This is the avatar economy we are building: an economy where digital selves aren't just reflections of who we are, they're active participants in global financial, legal and social systems. And as we hand increasing control over to these programmable identities, we must ask ourselves not only how we find ourselves in these worlds, but how we avoid losing ourselves entirely.

This evolution marks the true arrival of the avatar age, not as a single product or platform, but as a fundamental shift in how human identity will operate across digital systems in the coming decades. This persistent digital identity transforms further as avatars merge with ownership models, commercial economies, and platform governance. Is it shaping the architecture of the emerging avatar economy? Or merely muddying the waters of our psyche?

REFERENCES

Bevilacqua, R. and Rosenberg, R. (2017) 'Motion Capture and Its Importance in Video Games', *Journal of Media Studies*, 32(2), pp. 75–89.

Blender Foundation (2024) *Blender 4.0 Release Notes* [Online]. Available at: https://www.blender.org (Accessed: 29 May 2025).

Buolamwini, J. and Gebru, T. (2018) 'Gender Shades: Intersectional Accuracy Disparities in Commercial Gender Classification', *Proceedings of Machine Learning Research*, 81, pp. 1–15.

Cameirão, M.S., Bermúdez i Badia, S., Duarte, E. and Verschure, P.F.M.J. (2010) 'The Combined Impact of Virtual Reality Neurorehabilitation and Its Interfaces on Upper Extremity Functional Recovery in Patients with Chronic Stroke', *Stroke*, 41(7), pp. 1477–1484.

Carmichael, S. (2013) 'What It Means to Be a 'Whale' – and Why Social Gamers Are Just Gamers', *VentureBeat* [Online]. Available at: https://venturebeat.com/games/whales-and-why-social-gamers-are-just-gamers/ (Accessed: 29 May 2025).

Cross, K. (2023) 'The Queer Avatar of Failure', *Making and Breaking* [Online]. Available at: https://makingandbreaking.org/article/the-queer-avatar-of-failure/ (Accessed: 1 June 2025).

Deterding, S., Dixon, D., Khaled, R. and Nacke, L. (2011) 'From Game Design Elements to Gamefulness: Defining Gamification', in *Proceedings of the 15th International Academic MindTrek Conference*, ACM, pp. 9–15.

Duan, Y., Cao, S., Liu, J. and Li, Z. (2021) 'Research on Digital Fashion Design System Based on CLO3D Virtual Fitting Technology', *Journal of Physics: Conference Series*, 1748(3), p. 032012.

Epic Games (2021) 'Introducing Metahuman Creator: High-Fidelity Digital Humans Made Easy', *Unreal Engine* [Online]. Available at: https://www.unrealengine.com/en-US/metahuman (Accessed: 29 May 2025).

Foley, J.D., van Dam, A., Feiner, S.K. and Hughes, J.F. (1990) *Computer Graphics: Principles and Practice*. 2nd edn. Boston, MA: Addison-Wesley.

Gibson, W. (1984) *Neuromancer*. New York, NY: Ace.

Gravina, R., Li, Q. and Fortino, G. (2022) 'Human Avatar Generation for Virtual Reality Applications: A Survey', *IEEE Communications Surveys & Tutorials*, 24(1), pp. 1–30.

Gucci (2023) 'Gucci Garden on Roblox: Luxury Fashion Enters the Metaverse', *Gucci Vault* [Online]. Available at: https://vault.gucci.com (Accessed: 29 May 2025).

Hackers (1995) Directed by Iain Softley [Film]. USA: United Artists.

Haraway, D. (1985) A Cyborg Manifesto: Science, Technology, and Socialist-Feminism in the Late Twentieth Century', in Haraway, D. (ed.) *Simians, Cyborgs, and Women: The Reinvention of Nature*. New York, NY: Routledge.

Hermès International v. Rothschild (2023) United States District Court, S.D. New York. 22 Civ. 384.

IEEE (2023) 'P3141 Standard for Digital Avatars: Draft Overview', *IEEE Standards Association* [Online]. Available at: https://standards.ieee.org (Accessed: 29 May 2025).

Jurassic Park (1993) Directed by Steven Spielberg [Film]. USA: Universal Pictures.

Kapp, K.M. (2012) *The Gamification of Learning and Instruction: Game-based Methods and Strategies for Training and Education*. San Francisco, CA: Pfeiffer.

Ke, F. and Im, T. (2013) Virtual-Reality-Based Social Interaction Training for Children with High-Functioning Autism', *Journal of Educational Research*, 106(6), pp. 441–461.

Kim, H. (2022) 'Monetization and Visual Identity in Online Games: The Case of League of Legends', *Games and Culture*, 17(3), pp. 345–364.

Kim, H., et al. (2023) 'Avatar-Assisted Interventions for Children with ADHD: A Randomized Study', *Journal of Child Psychology and Psychiatry*, 64(1), pp. 45–53.

Toy Story (1995) Directed by John Lasseter [Film]. USA: Pixar Animation Studios.

The Lawnmower Man (1992) Directed by Brett Leonard [Film]. USA: Allied Vision.

Meta (2022) 'Horizon Worlds Personal Boundary Update', *Meta Newsroom* [Online]. Available at: https://www.meta.com (Accessed: 29 May 2025).

Moore, G.A. (1991) *Crossing the Chasm: Marketing and Selling High-Tech Products to Mainstream Customers*. New York, NY: HarperBusiness.

Newzoo (2023) 'Global Games Market Report 2023 (Free Version)', *Newzoo* [Online]. Available at: https://newzoo.com/resources/trend-reports/newzoo-global-games-market-report-2023-free -version (Accessed: 3 June 2025).

Nieborg, D.B. (2011) *Triple-A: The Political Economy of the Blockbuster Video Game*. PhD thesis. University of Amsterdam.

Nieborg, D.B. and Poell, T. (2018) 'The Platformization of Cultural Production: Theorizing the Contingent Cultural Commodity', *New Media & Society*, 20(11), pp. 4275–4292.

Niko Partners (2022) 'China PC, Mobile, & Console Games Market Was $45.5 Billion in 2022; Now Forecasted to Surpass $57 Billion in 2027', *Niko Partners* [Online]. Available at: https:// nikopartners.com/news/china-pc-mobile-now-forecasted-to-surpass-57-billion-in-2027/ (Accessed: 29 May 2025).

Odyssey into the Mind's Eye (1996) Presented by Odyssey Productions [Video]. USA: Image Entertainment.

Oh, C.S., Bailenson, J.N. and Welch, G.F. (2018) 'A Systematic Review of Social Presence: Definition, Antecedents, and Implications', *Journal of Computer-Mediated Communication*, 24(1), pp. 79–98.

Park, S. and Kim, J. (2022) 'Blockchain-Based Decentralized Gaming Platforms: Current Research and Future Directions', *Telematics and Informatics*, 68, p. 101872.

Park, S., Kim, S. and Sohn, J. (2020) 'The Effects of Avatar Realism on Emotional Communication in Virtual Reality', *International Journal of Human-Computer Interaction*, 36(9), pp. 851–861.

Parsons, S. and Cobb, S. (2011) 'State-of-the-Art of Virtual Reality Technologies for Children on the Autism Spectrum', *European Journal of Special Needs Education*, 26(3), pp. 355–366.

Rollings, A. and Adams, E. (2003) *Andrew Rollings and Ernest Adams on Game Design*. Indianapolis, IN: New Riders.

Rosen, P. (2004) *Change Mummified: Cinema, Historicity, Theory*. Minneapolis, MN: University of Minnesota Press.

Sales, N. (2024) 'A Girl Was Allegedly Raped in the Metaverse. Is This the Beginning of a Dark New Future?', *The Guardian* [Online]. Available at: https://www.theguardian.com/commentisfree/2024/jan/05/metaverse-sexual-assault-vr-game-online-safety-meta (Accessed: 29 May 2025).

Schell, J. (2020) *The Art of Game Design: A Book of Lenses*. 3rd ed. Boca Raton, FL: CRC Press.

Schneider, T. (2024) 'Synthetic Identity Rights and the Metaverse', *Journal of Law and Emerging Technologies*, 12(1), pp. 45–72.

Second Life. (2003). PC [Game]. USA: Linden Lab.

Slater, M. and Sanchez-Vives, M.V. (2016) 'Enhancing Our Lives with Immersive Virtual Reality', *Frontiers in Robotics and AI*, 3, p. 74.

Smith, M.J., et al. (2019) 'Virtual Reality Job Interview Training and 6-Month Employment Outcomes for Individuals with Schizophrenia Seeking Employment', *Schizophrenia Research*, 208, pp. 33–39.

Stephenson, N. (1992) *Snow Crash*. New York, NY: Bantam Books.

The Prodigy (1994) *Voodoo People* [Music Video]. United Kingdom: XL Recordings.

UESP Wiki (1995) Online: Classes [Online]. Available at: https://en.uesp.net/wiki/Online:Classes (Accessed: 29 May 2025).

Unnamed Redditor (2023) 'r/ElderScrolls. To Those That Play as a Khajiit, How Do You Usually Go About Naming Them?' [Online]. Available at: https://www.reddit.com/r/ElderScrolls/comments/17e9yf3/to_those_that_play_as_a_khajiit_how_do_you/ (Accessed: 17 July 2025).

VRChat (2023) 'Safety and Trust Systems', *VRChat Documentation* [Online]. Available at: https://docs.vrchat.com/docs/safety-and-trust-system (Accessed: 29 May 2025).

Westbam (1992) *Bostich Remix* [Music Video]. Germany: Low Spirit Recordings.

Wolfendale, J. (2007) 'My Avatar, My Self: Virtual Harm and Attachment', *Ethics and Information Technology*, 9(2), pp. 111–119.

CHAPTER 5

Avatars, Digital Twins and Plug-Ins Part II

FACSIMILE

If avatars are the personal face of the metaverse, digital twins are its industrial nervous system.

We often imagine digital twins as flashy, real-time holographic replicas of real-world cities, factories or human bodies. But at their core, digital twins are much more pragmatic, and much more powerful. They are the data models that transform simulation into infrastructure – the scaffolding that allows entire economies to run predictive models in real time. While avatars wrestle with questions of identity, ownership and selfhood, digital twins confront a different challenge entirely: how do we virtualise the world itself?

In his essay, *The Sophist*, Plato speaks of two kinds of image-making. The first is a faithful reproduction, in an attempt to facsimile the original. The second is a deliberate distortion to coerce the viewer into believing what they see is real. Plato suggests that Greek statues were much larger on the top than on the bottom so that at eye level we would accept what we saw. The truth, however, would always lie in the scaling (Plato c.360 BCE, 1997; Eco, 1986; Baudrillard, 1981). In designing the metaverse, we're looking for simulacra, and digital twins provide several benefits to the metaverse by enabling more efficient and effective operations, better user experiences and improved decision-making. There is a lot to the world of 3D and it's had a long life believe it or not. As we try to find a fit for faster development, we have tried to build tools that follow that deliverable demand. The digital twin is not a new concept. The simulacrum has been described in texts as early as Ancient Greece and yet, we're still trying to explore better ways of creating images rather than code or text because we mostly eat with our eyes.

The 3D object came before both the digital twin concept and the volumetric pixel, and the development of 3D computer graphics and modelling dates back to the 1960s and 1970s

DOI: 10.1201/9781003615248-5

with the creation of wireframe models and the development of algorithms to render 3D objects on computer screens (Foley et al., 1990).

The concept of digital twins emerged much later, in the early 2000s, as a way to create virtual replicas of physical objects or systems and simulate their behaviour in real-time (Grieves, 2002; Tao et al., 2019). Digital twins are more than just 3D models; they incorporate real-time data, sensors and simulation capabilities to enable a deeper understanding and analysis of the physical counterpart.

Voxels, a portmanteau of *volumetric* and *pixels*, are a representation of 3D space that subdivides it into small volumetric elements, similar to how pixels divide a 2D image. Volumetric pixels have been used in medical imaging and scientific visualisation since the 1980s (Kaufman, 1991), though they are not directly related to the concept of digital twins; they play a large part in how objects will develop as digital twins for us as technology advances.

Outcast (1999) developed by Belgian studio Appeal is considered a pioneering title in open-world gaming and is known for its innovative use of voxel technology (Appeal, 1999; Rollings and Adams, 2003). Voxels were used as the foundation for its terrain and object rendering. Voxels represent a three-dimensional point in space and, unlike traditional polygon-based graphics, which use flat surfaces to construct objects and landscapes, voxels might offer a more detailed and realistic representation of the game world.

The pioneering aspects of the game's development were just bonkers for their time. The game's environments were generated using voxel-based algorithms. This approach allowed for a highly detailed and dynamic terrain, with realistic features and deformations. Voxels also enabled complex physics simulations and interactions within the game world. Objects could be destroyed or deformed realistically, and the terrain responded dynamically to player actions, such as explosions or environmental changes (Rollings and Adams, 2003).

Voxel-based lighting models in Outcast provided more realistic and dynamic lighting effects, including realistic shadows cast by objects and characters in the game world. Where we are shifting towards photon tracing today, back then we used ray tracing, where we only throw viewing rays into the scene and trace the objects with light. Photon tracing is a lighting technique that happens after mapping the object with a two-phase rendering approach: first we map the ray that has been used to trace the objects with illumination and then the way it has been mapped (Pharr et al., 2016). Photon tracing is used in game engines, notably Unreal Engine's more recent iterations where TV series like The Mandalorian have used photon tracing to add more dynamism to environments through light (Stump et al., 2020).

Outcast demonstrated the potential of voxel technology in game development and influenced subsequent titles that explored similar voxel-based approaches. Its use of voxels remains notable in the history of video games and showcases the creative possibilities of leveraging alternative rendering techniques for immersive open-world experiences while keeping the use cases of technology meeting real-world objects on the bleeding edge (for its time).

Volumetric technology is alive and well in 2023. Companies such as Microsoft, known for their mixed reality hardware, and Reflector, which famously created Augmented Reality

(AR)-visible representations of different Madonnas for the Billboard awards in 2019, are continually exploring what volumetric technology can offer end users (Billboard, 2019; Microsoft, 2023) making fans of us all. Some businesses even use voxels to create real-time holographic conference calls. That's really pushing the technology towards digital twins, if a little rough around the edges.

The concept of digital twins originated in the early 2000s and was first coined by Dr Michael Grieves at the University of Michigan in 2002 (Grieves, 2002). However, the development and application of digital twins have evolved significantly since then, especially with the advancements in Internet of Things (IoT), cloud computing and Artificial Intelligence (AI) technologies (Fuller et al., 2020; Tao et al., 2019).

NASA has been actively involved in the development and application of digital twin technology for its space missions, to enhance the design, development and operation of spacecraft and systems. By creating virtual replicas of physical assets, such as satellites or rovers, NASA can simulate and analyse their behaviour in various conditions, test different scenarios and optimise their performance (Glaessgen and Stargel, 2012).

Digital twins enable NASA to monitor and analyse real-time data from space missions, detect anomalies and make informed decisions for maintenance and troubleshooting; they also support mission planning, training simulations and risk assessment. By leveraging digital twin technology, NASA aims to improve mission success rates, reduce costs and enhance overall space exploration capabilities, something that excites the metaverse voyager hugely as they embark on their missions to find brave, new, digital worlds.

- Digital twins can be used to create highly realistic, interactive virtual environments that provide users with a more immersive and engaging experience. By incorporating real-time data and feedback from the physical world, digital twins can enhance the authenticity and richness of the metaverse, making it more appealing to users (IBM, 2023).

- Resource management might be put to better use with digital twins by virtue of modelling and simulating the behaviour of physical objects and systems in real time, allowing for more efficiencies in Digital Asset Management (DAM). This can help optimise energy usage, reduce waste and improve overall sustainability within a metaverse setting compared to its physical origination (Kritzinger et al., 2018; Fuller et al., 2020).

- Monitoring and the analysis of the behaviour of virtual objects and systems can be improved, I think, with digital twins. They might enable the detection of potential security threats or patterns of anomalies. This can help ensure the safety and security of the metaverse and its users (Fuller et al., 2020).

- As a data fan myself, digital twins will definitely improve real-time data. By providing real-time data and insights, digital twins can support better decision-making within the metaverse. For example, they can be used to optimise traffic flow in virtual cities, predict the performance of virtual infrastructure or identify areas for improvement in virtual environments (Tao et al., 2019; IBM, 2023).

TABLE 5.1   Digital Twins vs Sushi

Twin Type	Description	Example	Business Use
Component	Smallest part	Grain of rice	Predictive maintenance
Asset	Individual unit with data	Maki roll layer	Ownership/NFT tracking
Process	Action logic	Recipe/process	Automation, training
System	Full ecosystem	Sushi shop	City-wide simulations

Do you think that digital twins could help to create a more efficient, immersive and secure metaverse? In describing digital twins, IBM suggests similar KPIs for how digital twins exist in this uncharted territory of Building Information Model (BIM) and assets. We want to give our users more realistic and engaging experiences, while also improving resource management, sustainability and decision-making (IBM, 2023).

I was once presented with the opportunity to create digital sushi for a rave taking place in a Swiss ski resort called Laax. In creating this installation, I started to think about how I could map the experience to the development of the digital twin's functionality across their different layers. If we think of a simple maki roll, we can actually break it down into its constituent parts, and by doing so, we explain exactly how digital twins are built (Table 5.1).

Component twins represent the most granular level of a digital twin, individual parts or elements that, when aggregated, form the foundation of more complex systems. These digital representations can be derived from physical counterparts through technologies such as 3D scanning, photogrammetry, CAD modelling or even high-resolution imaging techniques like MRI and CT scanning. For example, in the context of a digital sushi roll, a component twin might correspond to a single grain of rice or a slice of fish: an individual unit that retains its structure, provenance and distinguishing characteristics even when separated from the original.

Also referred to as "parts twins," these models are essential building blocks for more comprehensive digital twin applications. While all component twins serve to digitise specific physical elements, parts twins may refer to less critical or non-core components in a system, though they still play a role in the overall fidelity and functionality of a digital twin (Tao et al., 2019).

The utility of component twins lies in their versatility and precision. Engineers and designers can use them to:

- Simulate and optimise the performance of larger assemblies before they are physically manufactured.

- Conduct stress tests or scenario modelling without material waste.

- Monitor wear and degradation of specific components over time, enabling predictive maintenance and reducing system downtime (Kritzinger et al., 2018).

These applications are already critical in industries such as aerospace and defence, where precision is non-negotiable. In such contexts, digital twins ensure that replacement parts are not just functionally equivalent but structurally identical to their physical predecessors, a key requirement for both safety and performance (Fuller et al., 2020).

In practical terms, component twins can represent everything from industrial drill bits to micro components in luxury timepieces. Their relevance is not limited to mechanical systems. Within Building Information Modelling (BIM) frameworks, component twins may also represent architectural details such as piping networks, electrical conduits or even individual fasteners, all with embedded metadata that supports traceability, simulation and reusability (Eastman et al., 2011).

This granular, data-rich representation forms the bedrock of interoperability and intelligent design across both physical and virtual environments, including the metaverse, where fidelity and traceability of digital assets become paramount.

When we zoom into that grain of rice, our component twin, we start entering the domain of the *asset twin*. Magnify it 60x and suddenly it's not just rice anymore. We're looking at surface textures, imperfections, even trace mineral deposits. This is where things get interesting. At this scale, data emerges: where it was sourced, how it was grown, whether it was irrigated or rain-fed. If you really wanted to, you could even map its genetic makeup.

That's the point. Asset twins aren't just about geometry, they're about story. They're the digitally enriched representations of physical objects, embedded with everything needed to track, analyse and reuse them intelligently. These are data-dense, high-fidelity twins built using 3D modelling, Augmented Reality (AR)/Virtual Reality (VR) interfaces, simulation layers and often machine learning analytics, not just to visualise the asset, but to operate and improve it (Autodesk, 2023; IBM, 2023).

Asset twins form a single source of truth: a live, evolving record of a physical item's specifications, tolerances, service history and even ownership rights. Whether it's a turbine blade or a luxury handbag, an asset twin helps us answer the real questions:

- Where did it come from?

- What state is it in now?

- What do we need to do next?

In many of the systems I work with, especially in gaming, digital fashion and emerging metaverse economies, asset twins behave like NFTs, but with actual functionality. Not speculative JPEGs, but tokens with utility baked in: traceability, rights management, reuse permissions, even resale conditions. The aesthetic layer? That's just the surface. The power lies in the metadata: supply chain, conditions of use, repair history and embedded logic for transferability (Park and Kim, 2022).

Asset twins also act as integration hubs. When tied into Building Information Models (BIMs), they connect individual parts of infrastructure (like windows, Heating, Ventilation and Air Conditioning (HVAC) systems or wiring junctions) to broader operational strategies, performance monitoring, energy modelling and predictive maintenance. They don't just look smart. They behave smart.

When I think about creating sustainable digital assets, garments, props, products, I think in terms of asset twins. That's what gives them *reusability*, *interoperability* and *value over time*. In a world of endless digital content, asset twins are what make objects matter.

Then comes the *process twin*, the logic layer. If component twins are the ingredients and asset twins are the fully annotated pieces, then process twins are the recipes. They capture *how* something is made, not just *what* it is. Think of sushi: it's not just about having rice and fish. It's about knowing how the rice is prepared, how tightly to roll the nori and the precise order in which ingredients are layered. That sequence, that *assembly knowledge*, is what the process twin replicates.

The process twin is a digital model of a real-world process, anything from manufacturing workflows to emergency protocols. These twins don't just visualise the flow; they actively simulate it. They're used to monitor, control and optimise complex operations in real time. And in industries like aerospace, energy or logistics, they're critical for:

- Health and safety validation

- Disaster recovery and business continuity planning

- Efficiency modelling and predictive optimisation
(Tao et al., 2019; Fuller et al., 2020)

Process twins rely on real-time data inputs, from sensors, logs, user inputs or machines, to create a continuously updated model that can test variations, flag inefficiencies and model "what if" scenarios without ever interrupting the physical process. They're the digital rehearsal space where mistakes cost nothing and insights come fast (Kritzinger et al., 2018).

I've seen these applied in everything from virtual car assembly lines to simulation training for VR-based learning environments. In the metaverse, process twins are the backbone of dynamic interaction. They power immersive training experiences, where users learn not by reading manuals, but by *doing*, inside highly realistic digital environments. One of the best large-scale examples is Japan's Project Ryugukoku, a nation-scale digital twin that includes not just objects and systems, but workflows, governance and service delivery models (Tan et al., 2018).

What excites me about process twins is how they extend simulation into rehearsal. Whether it's training a workforce, onboarding users in a complex game economy or simulating supply chain shifts in a virtual city, process twins let us anticipate, iterate and improve in ways that static systems never could.

Finally, we arrive at the *system twin*, the environment where everything comes together. Think about walking into a sushi shop: I place my order. The chef selects individual components (component twins), each with its own properties and provenance (asset twins). They execute a familiar process, wash the rice, layer the nori, roll the fillings (process twin). And then? Out comes a full meal, a seamless orchestration of preparation and delivery. That, in essence, is the system twin.

In digital terms, a system twin brings together every layer, components, assets and processes into one coherent, operational model. It doesn't just simulate individual parts or their interactions. It simulates *everything*, live and in motion (Grieves, 2002; Tao et al., 2019; Fuller et al., 2020).

Sometimes referred to as unit twins, system twins represent entire functional ecosystems. This might be an aircraft in operation, a smart factory floor or an urban transportation network. Crucially, they show how products and processes behave as part of a broader environment, revealing friction points, inefficiencies and new opportunities that would be invisible at lower levels of analysis (Fuller et al., 2020; Tao et al., 2019).

Real-world applications are already impressive:

- In aviation, system twins are used to predict optimal engine maintenance intervals.

- GE's digital wind farm project pioneered the use of real-time system simulation to optimise energy production across a whole grid (GE, 2016).

- Siemens has applied system twins to factory environments, modelling production at scale to optimise throughput, workforce allocation and machine uptime (Siemens, 2022).

System twins rely on massive, continuous streams of operational data from thousands of inputs across a network. They're often represented as real-time dashboards or spatial models that can zoom from the macro (a city) to the micro (a pipe fitting) and back again, always within context.

And in the metaverse, system twins are the dataset of entire worlds. These are not static builds or simple game levels. They are dynamic, data-responsive simulations, capable of adapting, scaling and reflecting real-world conditions. Platforms like Meta's Horizon Workrooms rely heavily on user data, behaviour tracking and interaction telemetry, but here, the simulacrum is built *from* the data, not *on top of* it (Meta, 2023). It's not just visual fidelity, it's system logic, rendered live.

The sushi metaphor continues to serve us well here. Like digital twins, sushi is assembled layer by layer: component precision, asset context, process choreography and finally plated and served as a complete experience. The system twin doesn't just *represent* that dish. It simulates the whole restaurant: from supply chain to chef's workflow, to customer experience, to energy consumption and staff schedules.

And in an interoperable metaverse, this kind of systemic simulation is gold. It gives us not just visual spectacle, but live, navigable truth, truth that can be rendered, repurposed, sold, shared, simulated and optimised over and over again.

If you're here looking for handsets, headsets and other wearable tech, I'll cover that in the user experience section, but that's not to say that we don't acknowledge this ethos as actual technology. Wasn't it Nintendo's Virtual Boy that heralded the age of VR? This portable video game console was released by Nintendo in 1995. It was hailed as the first console capable of displaying stereoscopic "3D" graphics (Nintendo, 1995). The player uses the console like a head-mounted display, placing the head against the eyepiece to see a red monochrome display. It was one of the few financially failed products of Nintendo. Other peripherals or devices such as the Power Pad, Power Glove and Zapper bring us up to date from NES to the Wii, and yet, we may not look at the *Time Crisis* Light Gun or the *Guitar Hero* wireless controller with the same nostalgia as the Virtual Boy. Is that the reason why VR came back? And will the Gibson G-45 or the Les Paul make a return? I hope not.

HANDLING THE TRUTH

In my career I've made loads of context switches between specialisms and fields – programmers hate it, executive producers love it, but I've always thought it was a necessary skill in truly understanding how every element of the games industry works as we move closer to an industry that is hopefully more open. I could follow this up with a heavily politicised statement, but I'll leave you to make your own conclusions. What the games industry started and what I hope will continue is a system of communication. After all, that's exactly what entertainment and technology are doing and should do: communicate.

In an earlier part of this chapter, I talked about digital twins servicing the metaverse with an emphasis on single sources of truth. I'm pretty passionate about this. If we're working in a simulation which requires real-time data, why would we use off-the-shelf objects with limited information?

Autodesk recognised the potential of Building Information Modelling to revolutionise the architecture, engineering and construction industries by offering a more efficient and collaborative approach to building design and construction (Eastman et al., 2011; Autodesk, 2023). Autodesk's flagship BIM software, Autodesk Revit, was first released in 2000, and it played a significant role in popularising the BIM for a variety of use cases. Though it has played a crucial role in the development and promotion of BIM technology, the BIM theory itself is a collaborative process and methodology in practice that involves various stakeholders, including software developers, architects, engineers, contractors and building owners, of course. It represents a paradigm shift in the way buildings and infrastructure projects are designed, constructed and managed.

Why would I use the story of the BIM to exemplify the digital twin and its role in video games and the metaverse? Largely because that's exactly how we've reached this apex. A collection of interested engineers, passionate creatives and truth seekers are applying the same methodologies to first, video games and now the metaverse.

BIMs as digital representations and collaborative processes for designing, constructing and managing buildings and infrastructure open a bunch of workflow possibilities for a variety of use cases.

- Modelling and Data for creating 3D plus models that do more than just look pretty:

  - Collaboration and work-sharing, I'm a big, no, huge fan. Collaborative workflows enable multiple team members to work on the same project simultaneously. Like a really visual Slack. This way, models can be divided into work sets or use cloud-based collaboration tools to exchange information, coordinate tasks and manage changes.

  - We use similar language across verticals, but the extraction of quantities from the model (materials etc.), facilitating cost estimation and project budgeting, might fill in the blanks for, say, cost databases in generating accurate cost estimates and tracking changes throughout the design process (Eastman et al., 2011).

- Users can create and define any building's components, from walls to windows. This data is intelligent to capture properties, relationships and behaviour – it's called parametric data.

- BIM software allows users to assign and manage data associated with building components, such as material properties, dimensions, performance characteristics and manufacturer information. This data is stored within the model and can be extracted for analysis and reporting (Autodesk, 2023).

- Generating construction documents (with software of course) is a big BIM strength, from floor plans to deeper dives. Because the 3D model is the central source of information, changes made to the model automatically update the associated documentation, ensuring consistency and accuracy.

- BIM systems and software offer various interoperable visualisation and analysis tools to enhance collaboration and decision-making, and project understanding:

  - Various analysis capabilities, including structural analysis, energy analysis, lighting analysis and clash detection tools, help identify potential design issues, optimise performance and improve sustainability.

  - Importing and exporting industry-standard file formats, such as Industry Foundation Classes, which facilitate interoperability with other BIM tools and software used by different project participants.

  - Cloud-based collabs enable project teams to collaborate, share models, manage document workflows and conduct virtual design reviews.

What I want to be able to see through the haze of technology is how these things can come together. Each vertical has its own challenges and its own standards, yes, its own standards, so anyone who can wave a magic wand in this direction to point to a single source of truth that isn't a physical entity, gets the thumbs up from not just me over here in the video games industry, but me in the metaverse, the fashion industry and many other places that can as easily operate an open policy on tracking, because that's what we're talking about here, the data of objects as a single source of truth and interoperability.

Currently, this theory is not too dissimilar from how Digital Asset Management (DAM) and Product Information Management (PIM) behave as they work to service digital objects, images and data (Williams, 2017; Tao et al., 2019). One might argue that this is a step down from a BIM, but I think it has better use cases when the DAM and the PIM live together for things like game inventory and e-commerce merchandise systems. I couldn't convince a single person in my organisation that this was the way to go regarding the universality of digital objects, so I wrote a paper. Here's the abstract:

A single source of truth is the practice of structuring information models and associated data schema so that everything is stored/mastered in one place. These systems provide data that are genuine, suitable and provide reference to the end user.

(VERO, 2021)

But the DAM and PIM are two distinct systems that serve different purposes within an organisation. Digital Asset Management (DAM) stores, organises, retrieves and distributes digital assets such as images, videos, documents, audio files and other media files. DAM software already provides a centralised repository where organisations can manage their digital assets efficiently. Assets get ingested, categorised into lookup data/tables with filters and tags before spewing out into sharing systems or via APIs and plug-ins. Version control is the centre cog in this design because the DAM ensures the latest version of an asset is readily available. Versioning is also great for handling expiration and deletion policies.

Product Information Management (PIM) enriches product data by collecting the backstories and extra detail that the DAM will have missed. From data integration and collection to data management and distribution, the PIM is a product lifecycle management essential (Williams, 2017). I'm obsessed with anything that serves data in this way because in everything I make I require consistency, accuracy and completeness of product information. Where governance and workflow are more rigid and when collaboration is key, PIMs are great at fitting the needs of the product; so when faced with the prospect of being part of a bigger machine where the DAM and the PIM come together like a BIM to make digital twins, er, sparkle and shine, this is where we can really go places with objects and assets. The ante will be upped, but the appeal of managing assets is only overstepped by the appeal of exploring and developing new ways to define, implement and ultimately scale objects; first for video games, then for everything else. Because it's here that we, as game developers, can really flex our creativity beyond the aesthetic and cross over into technology, and still call it art.

The bedrock of BIMs is about creating data from objects or for objects. Voxel-based development is parallel to this sophistication of object management. I see digital twins of the future as being a structural blending of the best of both states: rich data formats and rich rendered visuals.

Step forward the Universal Scene Description (USD) format for ever-changing models. Developed by Pixar Animation Studios for efficiently creating, editing and sharing 3D computer graphics data, this is an open format (Pixar, 2016; Bouville, 2022). It provides a scalable and versatile solution for managing complex scenes and assets in various stages of production, from modelling and animation to rendering and simulation. The USD is intrinsic to this changing world of video games to metaverses, from e-commerce to g-commerce, as it introduces a new approach to object development by offering a myriad of key features.

- Imagine replacing complex polygonal scenes with USD? This standard represents objects and assets as "prims" (short for primitives). Prims can be thought of as the building blocks of a scene, representing individual objects, geometry or collections of other prims. These can be organised hierarchically, creating a scene graph structure that defines relationships and transformations between objects (Pixar, 2016).

- USD employs a layered authoring approach, enabling collaboration and versioning in a production pipeline. With USD, multiple artists and technical developers can work on different layers simultaneously. Each layer contains changes or additions to the scene without modifying the underlying data, ensuring non-destructive editing. This layering system makes it easier to manage different versions or variations of a scene across a global workplace without constantly committing (producers and QA will love and pull their hair out in equal measure) (Pixar, 2016).

- Referencing assets is a feature of USD, where one asset can be linked to multiple scenes or shots without duplicating data. This referencing mechanism improves efficiency by reducing data duplication and simplifying updates across different instances of the same asset. USD also supports variants, which enable the representation of different versions or variations of an asset within the same scene or layer (Bouville, 2022).

- The data queen that lives inside me is screaming with joy at this one because USD provides a compact, high-performance file format for serialising scene data. The data can be saved in a binary format (USD .usd) or a textual format (USD .usda). These formats are designed to be fast to load and save, enabling efficient data interchange and streaming across different applications and platforms.

- The scalability and performance as well as the interoperable nature of the USD have been "built" to handle large-scale data management. The extensible framework also allows developers to create custom schemas, plug-ins and workflows to tailor the system to specific production needs (Bouville, 2022).

By employing a Hydra rendering architecture, which is an imaging system based on a scene abstraction and transformation pipeline, and a renderer abstraction and execution pipeline (Pixar, 2024). This allows for efficient display and rendering of scenes by leveraging the capabilities of modern GPUs. USD also supports a level-of-detail system, allowing for efficient handling of large datasets and optimising performance during interactive workflows as well as supporting integration with various industry-standard tools and formats, such as Alembic, OpenColorIO and Python, ensuring compatibility and interoperability within existing production pipelines (Pixar, 2016).

The problem with polygons is that they need to go on a diet (don't we all?) mainly because polygons literally house useless data within their quads (squares) and tris (triangles, both of which make up polygons). The direction of travel in video games and the metaverse, and everything in between, is more sophisticated than that – that word again: *sophistication*. Anyway, we can pack more into our objects and environments and finally tell the truth about what the eye really sees and what the brain really knows.

Polygonal technologies won't die tomorrow. They will not expire overnight or instantly disappear in some dinosaur extinction event. Polygons give us the depth and breadth of exploration. We can dive into meshes, and fix artefacts, which are unintended visual bugs on the object made by the digital process, analytically as part of the artistic process rather than trying to bandage a hedgehog. The unique symbiosis of mesh and texture allows it to go deep, no, deeper in that which we can almost feel, taste or hear as we create visions to enlighten your senses; for VR, this is absolutely the way. As we edge closer to haptics, we will refine this state between actual synaptic responses against phantom or placebo reactions.

The glue sticking all of this together is the Level of Detail (LOD). LOD is critical in polygonal object design as it balances performance, memory usage and visual fidelity. By providing different levels of detail at appropriate distances, LOD optimises rendering, improves efficiency and enhances the overall user experience in real-time applications. Adaptive LOD systems in games such as Out Cast allowed the use of voxels to enable objects and landscapes to change their level of detail dynamically based on the player's proximity (Rollings and Adams, 2003; Pharr et al., 2016). This optimisation technique helped maintain performance while preserving visual quality. And that's where we're headed towards even more of a Mirrorworld, a term coined by Yale University computer scientist David Gelernter in the 90s (Gelernter, 1991); something which the metaverse community back in 2019 and 2020 at least, loved to quote but really saw it as a Matrix analogy rather than a data truism.

Your next obsession in games and metaverse knocks the humble pixel stream into a cocked hat. Neural Radiance Fields (NeRF) enhance procedural generation in video games by using advanced machine learning techniques to create highly detailed and realistic 3D environments, objects and characters. It generates dynamic and interactive worlds with accurate lighting and physics, offering procedural variation and a high level of detail. NeRF enables real-time rendering, allowing for seamless gameplay experiences in visually stunning virtual worlds that can be generated on the fly. In *Tom Clancy's Ghost Recon* (2012), scenes were pre-rendered to allow for processing times and hardware capabilities, which for their time were not as limited as an arcade machine in an amusement arcade in the 1980s' Spain. However, traditional procedural generation methods such as *Tom Clancy's Ghost Recon* typically rely on predefined algorithms and rulesets, which can result in repetitive patterns and less variation in the generated environments. NeRF offers procedural variation by training on datasets and generating unique environments that can be dynamically created on the fly. This provides a high degree of diversity and uniqueness to each generated scene (Mildenhall et al., 2020). It is here that the dinosaur extinction event will ultimately happen and I can't wait to watch in awe and lament in equal amounts like the designers, developers and pioneers have with each generational shift from video games to this beautiful metaversal future.

This section was nowhere near exhaustive, but it gives a voice to early game systems and how we might apply them to modern server-driven platforms and worlds, which are simply virtual motherboards and PCBs, right? The more we try to assume that there is a fork in the road of games and the metaverse, the more that we will find a confluence between the two states (Ball, 2022; Kapp, 2012). The rise of Web3 gaming, especially, will change that; its emergent technology of immersive game design with interoperable assets and financial technologies supported by distributed ledgers brings together the traditional nature of gameplay with the sustainable future of automation, mechanisation and applied industrial techniques (Park and Kim, 2022; Lemley, 2022).

REFERENCES

Autodesk (2023) *Building Information Modelling (BIM)* [Online]. Available at: https://www.autodesk.com/solutions/bim (Accessed: 3 June 2025).

Ball, M. (2022) *The Metaverse: And How It Will Revolutionize Everything*. New York, NY: Liveright.

Baudrillard, J. (1981). *Simulacres et Simulation*. Paris: Galilée.

Billboard (2019) 'Madonna Hologram Performance at Billboard Music Awards 2019', *Billboard*, 1 May.

Bouville, B. (2022) 'Universal Scene Description (USD): A New Standard for 3D Content Creation', *Journal of Computer Graphics Techniques*, 11(4), pp. 27–44.

Eastman, C., Teicholz, P., Sacks, R. and Liston, K. (2011) *BIM Handbook: A Guide to Building Information Modeling for Owners, Managers, Designers, Engineers and Contractors*. 2nd edn. Hoboken, NJ: John Wiley & Sons.

Eco, U. (1986). *Travels in Hyperreality*. New York, NY: Harcourt Brace Jovanovich.

Foley, J.D., van Dam, A., Feiner, S.K. and Hughes, J.F. (1990). *Computer Graphics: Principles and Practice*. 2nd edn. Boston, MA: Addison-Wesley.

Fuller, A., Fan, Z., Day, C. and Barlow, C. (2020) 'Digital Twin: Enabling Technologies, Challenges and Open Research', *IEEE Access*, 8, pp. 108952–108971.

GE (2016) 'GE Creates World's First Digital Wind Farm', *General Electric Newsroom*, 28 May.

Gelernter, D. (1991) *Mirror Worlds: Or the Day Software Puts the Universe in a Shoebox... How It Will Happen and What It Will Mean*. Oxford: Oxford University Press.

Glaessgen, E. and Stargel, D. (2012). The Digital Twin Paradigm for Future NASA and U.S. Air Force Vehicles. *53rd AIAA/ASME/ASCE/AHS/ASC Structures, Structural Dynamics and Materials Conference*. Honolulu: American Institute of Aeronautics and Astronautics.

Grieves, M. (2002) *Product Lifecycle Management: Driving the Next Generation of Lean Thinking*. New York, NY: McGraw-Hill.

IBM (2023) *Digital Twin Technology: A Guide* [Online]. Available at: https://www.ibm.com/topics/digital-twin (Accessed: 3 June 2025).

Kapp, K.M. (2012) *The Gamification of Learning and Instruction: Game-based Methods and Strategies for Training and Education*. San Francisco, CA: Pfeiffer.

Kaufman, A. (1991). 'Volume Visualization', *IEEE Computer*, 24(8), pp. 51–64.

Kritzinger, W., Karner, M., Traar, G., Henjes, J. and Sihn, W. (2018) Digital Twin in Manufacturing: A Categorical Literature Review and Classification', *IFAC-PapersOnLine*, 51(11), pp. 1016–1022.

Lemley, M.A. (2022) 'Property, Intellectual Property, and Metaverse Real Estate', *Journal of Law and Innovation*, 5(1), pp. 1–34.

Meta (2023) Horizon Workrooms: VR Collaboration Redefined [Online]. Available at: https://www.oculus.com/workrooms (Accessed: 3 June 2025).

Microsoft (2023) Microsoft Mixed Reality Solutions [Online]. Available at: https://www.microsoft.com/en-us/mixed-reality (Accessed: 3 June 2025).

Mildenhall, B., Srinivasan, P.P., Tancik, M., Barron, J.T., Ramamoorthi, R. and Ng, R. (2020) 'NeRF: Representing Scenes as Neural Radiance Fields for View Synthesis', *European Conference on Computer Vision (ECCV)*, pp. 405–421.

Nintendo (1995) *Virtual Boy* [Hardware]. Kyoto: Nintendo Co. Ltd.

Outcast (1999) PC [Video Game]. Belgium: Infogrames.

Park, S. and Kim, Y. (2022) 'Self-Sovereign Avatars in the Metaverse: Blockchain-Based Identity Ownership and Interoperable Assets', *Journal of Metaverse Studies*, 1(1), pp. 1–19.

Pharr, M., Jakob, W. and Humphreys, G. (2016) *Physically Based Rendering: From Theory to Implementation*. 3rd edn. San Francisco, CA: Morgan Kaufmann.

Pixar (2016) *Universal Scene Description (USD) Specification*. Pixar Animation Studios.

Pixar (2024) *Hydra Getting Started Guide – Universal Scene Description API Documentation*. OpenUSD.org [Online]. Available at: https://openusd.org/dev/api/_page__hydra__getting_ _started__guide.html (Accessed: 3 June 2025).

Plato c.360 BCE (1997) *The Sophist* (Trans. White, N.P.). Indianapolis, IN: Hackett Publishing.

Rollings, A. and Adams, E. (2003) *Andrew Rollings and Ernest Adams on Game Design*. Indianapolis, IN: New Riders.

Siemens (2022) Digital Twin Solutions: Industrial Applications [Online]. Available at: https://www .siemens.com/digital-twin (Accessed: 3 June 2025).

Stump, E., et al. (2020) 'The Virtual Production of The Mandalorian', *SMPTE Motion Imaging Journal*, 129(4), pp. 16–28.

Tan, G., Ma, J., Liu, Y. and Xie, Z. (2018) 'A City Digital Twin Driven by 5G and AIoT: Architecture, Challenges and Applications', *IEEE Internet of Things Journal*, 5(6), pp. 4310–4320.

Tao, F., Qi, Q., Liu, A. and Kusiak, A. (2019) 'Digital Twins and Cyber–Physical Systems Toward Smart Manufacturing and Industry 4.0: Correlation and Comparison', *Engineering*, 5(4), pp. 653–661.

Vero, K. (2021) Luxury and Art: A Common Framework for Metadata in Practice, LinkedIn. Available at: https://www.linkedin.com/pulse/luxury-art-common-framework-metadata -practice-kelly-vero/?trackingId=Gzh%2F3GPmQyOiInx5%2FxpdxQ%3D%3D (Accessed: 17 July 2025).

Williams, D. (2017) *Digital Asset Management: Content Architectures, Project Management, and Creating Order out of Media Chaos*. 2nd edn. Burlington: Focal Press.

CHAPTER 6

Introduction to Narrative and Design

BLOTCHY SPIDERS, HIDDEN OBJECTS

The remix of Suboceana is one of my favourite things about *Tom Tom Club* (1998), but this section really belongs to their other famous song: *Wordy Rappinghood* (1981), because it's all about what words are worth. In video games, words are worth everything to the writer, something to the player and almost nothing to the rest of the development team. They're worth even less in the metaverse.

And yet, everything starts with them, not just story, but structure (Bal, 2017). In the DNA of any interactive experience, story is born with its closest sibling: design. And if you've ever been a sibling, you know that siblings love to fight.

This section is for the designers, developers, product leaders and narrative architects who are building experiences, in games, in metaverses, in emerging digital products, that need to mean something. That needs to keep people not just engaged, but emotionally invested.

Game design is messy. Beautiful. Brutal. It's not just where stories are told, it's where they're tested. If you want your audience to stay in your world, you'll need to master more than clever dialogue or beautiful UX. You'll need a creative compass:

WHO, WHAT, WHERE, WHEN, WHY and HOW.

- What are you making?

- Who is it for?

- Where will it live, and where is it set?

- When does it happen, and when does it launch?

- Why this, and why now?

- How will users experience it, emotionally, practically, playfully?

DOI: 10.1201/9781003615248-6

These aren't just questions for storytellers, they're vital to anyone building products that live at the intersection of content, interaction and community. This is where design thinking, game thinking and narrative thinking meet and occasionally collide (Kovach and Rosenstiel, 2007).

Before we break down user experience and content strategy in the pages ahead, let's start with a touchstone: two games that almost every designer has learned from, even if they've never played them. A franchise that doesn't just show you how design thinking works, it shows you where it falls short.

The Legend of Zelda (Nintendo, 1986) and *Super Mario* (Nintendo, 1983)

The Legend of Zelda series is known for its user-centred design approach. The games are designed with the player in mind, with a focus on delivering an immersive and engaging gameplay experience. The games are also designed to be accessible to players of all skill levels, with a gradual learning curve that allows players to learn and master the game mechanics at their own pace. Similarly, Shigeru Miyamoto's (1998) design process always started with observing users. He would watch people playing games, taking note of their behaviours and reactions. By doing so, he was able to identify the pain points that players experienced and the aspects of games that they found most enjoyable (Yee, 2020). This approach allowed him to design games that were more intuitive and engaging for players.

Another key element of *The Legend of Zelda* series' design thinking is its iterative design approach. The series has evolved over time, with each new game building on the successes and mitigating/fixing failures of the previous games. This iterative approach has allowed the series to stay fresh and relevant, while still maintaining the core elements that make the games so beloved by fans. And not to be left out, Miyamoto's design process also included iterative design. He would create rough sketches and prototypes of levels and game mechanics, then test them with players to see how they responded. He would then refine and iterate on those designs until they were polished and ready for release. This approach allowed him to create games that were finely tuned and well balanced.

Miyamoto's design philosophy was rooted in empathy for the user. He believed that games should be accessible and intuitive for all players, regardless of their skill level. He also believed that games should be fun and engaging, with a sense of surprise and wonder around every corner. This empathy for the user allowed him to create games that were both challenging and rewarding, yet still accessible to a wide range of players.

The Legend of Zelda series is also known for its attention to detail. From the intricate puzzles to the beautifully crafted environments, the games are designed to be immersive and engaging. The games are also filled with Easter eggs and hidden secrets, which add to the sense of exploration and discovery that is at the core of the series.

Miyamoto's design approach included meticulous attention to detail. He believed that every aspect of a game should be carefully crafted, from the level design to the sound effects to the character animations. This attention to detail is evident in the *Super Mario* series, which is filled with charming and memorable moments that have become iconic in gaming history.

More than *Super Mario* (*sorry Miyamoto-san*), *The Legend of Zelda* series has a timeless quality because it explores themes that are universal but also because the world that Link lives in is both relatable and pure fantasy at the same time. Themes like courage, friendship and the struggle between good and evil resonate with players of all ages and backgrounds. These themes are woven into the gameplay and story, creating a sense of depth and meaning that goes beyond mere entertainment. Of course, the transition from game to screen has so far been successful for Super Mario (with one notable exception), since the *Super Mario Bros.* movie has become the highest grossing animated film of all time (Childress, 2023).

When I first started playing games, it was *Horace and the Spiders* that caught my attention the most, and it was I who asked the 5Ws and H question about how I felt as a player back then. I am going to assume that no one has ever heard of the *Horace* series. The diehard gamers who are anomalous in the multitude of verticals and industries hoping to find their audience through this new development space will know exactly why I cite Horace as being a game changer, pun intended, for me as a player.

William Tang developed the *Horace* video game series for Sinclair Research in the 1980s (Sinclair Research, 1982) and though quickly suffocated by the *Jetpac* (1983), *R-Type* (1987) and the *Manic Miner* (1983) titles, the Horace series was known for its innovative gameplay mechanics, fun (which is a really loose concept I'll explain later) and charming character design. Each game in the series had its own unique set of challenges and puzzles, requiring players to use their problem-solving skills and quick reflexes to progress through the levels. The games also featured a mix of platforming and puzzle-solving elements, which kept players engaged and challenged throughout. But who is Horace and what were his games? A lovable little robot with a big heart and a penchant for adventure. His design was simple yet endearing, making him an instant favourite among players.

Hungry Horace (Beam Software, 1982), mmm, what could this be about? Food pellets dotted around a cyan-walled maze leave little to the imagination. Horace was definitely Pac-Manning his way around the TV screen.

Horace Goes Skiing (Beam Software, 1983), okay, okay, it was *Frogger* (Sega, 1981) on skis. Slipping through the slalom of our screens, Horace needed to cross a busy road to get to the piste.

In *Horace and the Spiders* (Beam Software, 1983), the titular rogue finds himself in a cave filled with arachnids and to escape he has to avoid them and the holes in the perfectly platformed webs as he escapes this *Donkey Kong*-esque series of levels.

The *Horace* series was also known for its sense of humour. The games were filled with puns, jokes and references to pop culture, making them universal and inclusive: anyone could play these games. The humour also helped to balance out the difficulty of the games, making them more approachable and enjoyable for players.

But for me it's the innovative use of technology and design. The games were among the first to use colour graphics and digital sound, which helped to create a more immersive and engaging gameplay experience. The games also pushed the limits of what was possible in hardware at that time, showing the potential of the early home computer market.

The game series was not stuck in a formula; what I loved about it as a player was that each title was completely different from the last. As William Tang experimented with genre, he also, and probably inadvertently, experimented with design and narrative, giving life to Horace and diverse game mechanics to players, which are seldom seen in gameplay these days. I might also be brave enough to state that a continuous IP or character-driven development should be the very foundation of a metaverse; but because developers and creators rely upon their players to "make" or "choose their own adventure," the experience peters out or dies really quickly. The metaverse "gamified experience" is completely baseless without solid directional design, which it barely has.

In popular games today, players are often kept within a linear format of storified gameplay, let's call it a cycle or a loop; outside of that, we have other styles of gameplay, which would perhaps be non-linear. That means that the story must be reconstructed as a whole as the player plays, and that's a design consideration. So, a main quest in any *Elder Scrolls* game might be stark in contrast (storywise) to side missions or crafting tasks (Bethesda Game Studios, 1994). A hidden object game isn't a walking simulator with collectibles; it puts finding hidden objects front and centre in its game context. Currently, this style of what we call mechanics doesn't feature in the metaverse as a naturally occurring experience for the end user. It should! Therefore, it must be a consideration when approaching building a bespoke metaverse or even a metaversal experience for a specific audience. Players wandering around with nothing to do will eventually stop visiting your platform and engaging with your experience. Let's fix it together.

REFERENCES

Bal, M. (2017) *Narratology: Introduction to the Theory of Narrative*. 4th edn. Toronto: University of Toronto Press.

Childress, E. (2023) 'Weekend Box-Office Results: Super Mario Sets Record in Its Second Weekend', *Rotten Tomatoes*, 17 April. Available at: https://editorial.rottentomatoes.com/article/weekend-box-office-results-super-mario-sets-record-in-its-second-weekend (Accessed: 8 July 2025).

Frogger (1981) Arcade [Game]. Japan: Konami/Sega.

Horace and the Spiders (1983) ZX Spectrum [Game]. United Kingdom: Beam Software/Sinclair Research.

Horace Goes Skiing (1983) ZX Spectrum [Game]. United Kingdom: Beam Software/Sinclair Research.

Hungry Horace (1982) ZX Spectrum [Game]. United Kingdom: Beam Software/Sinclair Research.

Jetpac (1983) ZX Spectrum [Game]. United Kingdom: Ultimate Play the Game.

Kovach, B. and Rosenstiel, T. (2007) *The Elements of Journalism*. New York, NY: Three Rivers Press.

Manic Miner (1983) ZX Spectrum [Game]. United Kingdom: Bug-Byte.

Mario Bros/Super Mario Series (1983) Arcade [Game]. Japan: Nintendo.

Miyamoto, S. (1998) 'Designing from the Player's Perspective', Game Developers Conference talk, March.

R-Type (1987) Arcade [Game]. Japan: Irem

The Elder Scrolls Series (1994) PC [Game]. USA: Bethesda Game Studios/Bethesda Softworks.

The Legend of Zelda Series (1986) Famicom Disk System [Game]. Japan: Nintendo.

Tom Tom Club (1981) *Wordy Rappinghood*. Tom Tom Club [Album]. Jamaica: Island Records.

Tom Tom Club (1988) *Suboceana*. Boom Boom Chi Boom Boom [Album]. Jamaica: Island Records.

Yee, N. (2020) 'Player Segments Based on Gaming Motivations: An Analysis of 400,000 Gamers', Game Developers Conference talk, August.

CHAPTER 7

Design and Game Thinking

DESIGN HAS EVERYTHING TO DO WITH YOU

Making something functional is like conducting an orchestra: from ideation to execution, you're balancing multiple considerations. This is where design thinking methodologies shine, but they're not always enough. For products that evolve like games or metaverse experiences, I find they're significantly strengthened by *Game Thinking* (Kim, 2019).

The classic "Empathise, Define, Ideate, Prototype, Test, Implement" model doesn't always suit dynamic, player-centric products. In 2019, on a long train ride from Gamescom in Cologne, I read Amy Jo Kim's *Game Thinking*. It crystallised my lived experience working in games: deep engagement isn't accidental, it's designed. Her Player Behaviour Model (Kim, 2019, pp. 18–19) offers a proactive way to hypothesise the perfect player, before development even begins.

Where we once relied solely on empathy to define our players, Game Thinking reframes that process as a hypothesis to be tested. This isn't abstraction, it's a pre-pre-production screening technique rooted in behavioural science. Collaborators like data scientist Jak Marshall have pushed this further. Jak has used hypothetical user identification and role-playing scenarios to stress-test assumptions during pre-dev (Marshall, 2015). These methods go well beyond traditional empathy tasks.

Designers must first consider players as people. People we might already know, within specific, relative demographics. The idea is to understand their wants and needs without prematurely resorting to user testing or focus groups. It's too early for that. The hypothesis must be neutral. It can't be shaped by ego.

In games, and arguably in the metaverse, the moment we prioritise what we want, or worse, what the CEO wants, we undermine the purpose of the development model. Design driven by ego or revenue masquerading as user need has become common. Many post-pandemic metaverses exist not because of player demand, but because someone in charge needed a COVID-era story or exit strategy.

Game Thinking instructs us to learn from early missteps. That means constantly iterating questions, refining ideas and testing implementation. As designers, we have to step out

DOI: 10.1201/9781003615248-7

of our own comfort zones. Hypothesis-led development isn't just strategic, it's therapeutic. It redirects us away from the idea and back to the user.

Instead of developing finite surface products, we're crafting immersive narrative ecosystems. Why do players get hooked? Why do some stay loyal to an Intellectual Property (IP) for decades? Because great game design is invisible. And because great designers build worlds around the wants and needs of their users, not their own.

We begin by asking everyday questions: What does a day in our player's life look like? What do they need? Where does their time go? And more cynically, how do we get them to spend that time, and maybe even money, with us?

Only after that do we reintroduce empathy. Now, empathy validates the needs we hypothesised. That's when we conduct surveys, interviews or focus groups. Suppose we're developing a mobile game. Research might reveal that players want something easy to learn, difficult to master and socially connected. That insight sharpens the product vision.

Take *BTS Universe Story*, developed by Netmarble (2020). The studio knew that music knows how to find its audience. HYBE (formerly Big Hit) (2020) had already cultivated a global fanbase by refining their demographic data across artists like 2AM and Changmin. They combined hypothesis testing and empathy validation to understand their audience, and the result was a game that knew exactly who it was for.

The popularity of *BTS Universe Story* isn't just about IP. Yes, BTS's massive fanbase is key, but the game creates a narratological feedback loop. It invites fans into a virtual world, lets them interact with their idols and constantly reinforces the brand's story. High production values and sandbox-style mechanics deepen immersion.

Netmarble understood their audience well enough to build a world no fan wanted to leave. That compelling tension between narrative and interaction is the very essence of fandom. It's why ARMY members stay by Jungkook or V's side virtually for hours.

The game ranked consistently among the top-grossing mobile titles in South Korea, the US and Japan. It generated millions in revenue while also attracting a diverse player base. Not just K-pop fans, story fans. That's reach. That's design.

But most players aren't K-pop superfans. So we still have to ask the right questions. And here's what we can't afford to do:

- Lead or control user focus outcomes

- Screen too broadly or indiscriminately

- Assume "if we build it, they will come"

Even as a huge fan of rapid prototyping, I don't get excited by micro-iterations driven by a developer unwilling to adapt their idea. Good design demands humility. Bad designers go after the lowest-hanging fruit in ideas, in data and in execution. They avoid discomfort. They avoid failure. And in doing so, they avoid the work.

As a storyteller in games, I can tell you: this principle applies to the creative team too. I've worked with more than a few entitled creative directors. They didn't ship anything meaningful because they couldn't let go of control.

FOLLOW THE STARS

What you are looking for are patterns. Patterns of play, patterns of time and habitual behaviours. As a developer or designer, you must be forensic and relentless in uncovering the truth. This means listening to how players behave and recording what changes.

Celia Hodent, User Experience (UX) designer behind *Fortnite*, offers a foundational approach to understanding the gamer brain. She simplifies the player psychology loop into three key components: Perception (input), Influencing Factors and Memory (synaptic modification). These feed into what she calls Information Processing (Hodent, 2017). This input to output cycle is what forms habits, not just in gaming, but in everyday decisions. When we ask users things like "Where do you buy your coffee?" or "What are you listening to right now?",we're uncovering pathways into that behavioural loop.

And sometimes, the most telling pattern is silence. If a player doesn't answer a question, if they pause or drift away, that too is a signal. It means they have opinions. Perhaps they're not ready to share them, or perhaps we've asked the wrong question. Either way, silence is data. And silence has a pattern.

Once you have empathy in place, the next step is to define the problem. This is not a vague aim, but a focused, actionable prompt. For example: *How can we create an experience that is easy to pick up, challenging to master and rich in social features?*

Too often, developers pitch solutions looking for problems. I've sat through countless presentations built around this flawed idea. Some would argue that the metaverse itself is a giant solution in search of a problem. I don't agree, and I'll explain why later, but many of these products simply haven't been built on hypotheses or validated empathy. They're guesswork dressed as vision.

During early empathy phases, players may describe what frustrates them, what blocks their progress or where they lose interest. This is where another principle becomes critical: the Pareto Principle, or the 80/20 rule. It suggests that 80% of your results will come from 20% of your actions.

In games, this means that a minority of missions, skills or features are likely to yield the majority of rewards. Take a Role-Playing Game (RPG) packed with side quests. Most of your loot, Experience Points (XP) and meaningful outcomes probably come from a few highly rewarding ones. The same applies to First-Person Shooter (FPS) games. Roughly 80% of your success will depend on a few core skills: aim, movement and game sense.

As designers, we should identify these high-impact features and lean into them. More importantly, we should examine why players avoid other mechanics. What's stopping engagement? Is it difficulty, design or disinterest?

The same goes for the often misunderstood "steep learning curve." While the phrase implies difficulty, it technically refers to a fast learning rate. In design, we often confuse curve steepness with the barrier to entry. But what really matters is how fast players pick up the basics and where they hit friction. Recognising those patterns, both of learning and dropout, is central to delivering value.

This is the point where game design becomes analytics. You begin preparing for meaningful engagement analysis. You look at everything the game is generating and start to spot what matters. I'll explore this more in the data section, but suffice it to say: data is currency.

With a clearly defined problem, the next step is ideation. This is the brainstorming stage, wild ideas welcome. One tip I picked up from Jak Marshall is to refer to your user by your own name when coming up with features. If I say, "Kelly loves this mechanic," it grounds the idea in someone real. It personalises the user journey.

During *Transformers Universe*, we ideated in agile groups: coders, QA, artists and marketers. That mix created a rich, multi-perspective design. Because we were working within a well-established IP, we could draw ideas from the show's lore or Hasbro's back-story. I often start with a story action, a micro-narrative, to spark the process. Whether it's designing a gameplay puzzle or a toy-inspired mechanic, these brainstorms link back to our hypothesis. In *Transformers Universe*, we had a grey box prototype that let us test real player actions. This is standard in games and should be standard in metaverse development too. These prototypes are where the vision gets stress-tested. What we build next depends entirely on what these tests reveal.

FEEL THE PAIN

Let's take a breath and ground this next phase. You've hypothesised your user, you've spotted their patterns and defined a clear problem. Now comes the messy but vital phase: building.

When I say "grey box," I'm referring to an unpolished, low-fidelity prototype of your experience. This is your first real Proof of Concept (POC). It's rough, but that's the point. It's not about aesthetics. It's about function. If you can test your idea with users in this primitive form and it holds their attention, you're onto something.

Even better, take a step back and try a tabletop prototype. All you need is a grid, a few coins, maybe some markers. It's game design theatre. Explore rules, mechanics, player flows without committing to code. You'd be surprised how many metaverse projects have skipped this step entirely. That's a shame, and a missed opportunity for fast, cheap learning.

This is one of the most fun phases of development. Forget the jam board for a moment. Pick up tokens. Simulate the loop. Play.

Once your grey box or prototype is up, it's time to validate against your original hypothesis. Ask yourself:

- What do users already have, or need, to engage consistently?

- What else are they interacting with when they're not using your product?

- Where do they go when their device is offline?

- How much time might they actually spend with your product each day?

This is how we start identifying pain points.

In games, pain points are those controller-throwing moments. Think of a platformer with maddening jumps or a boss fight that feels unfair. Or maybe it's sluggish User Interface (UI), long loading times or obtuse navigation. These are friction points, moments where your user wants to give up. But pain points exist in everyday life too: waiting for a bus, navigating airport security or trying to reset a password. When we as designers tune into these frustrations, we become more sensitive to removing them in our own products.

I call it QA-ing life. In games, quality assurance (QA) is the phase where everything gets pushed to breaking point. That mindset, testing the stress of every system, should carry over into your prototyping. I look for friction in everyday experiences the same way I look for design bugs. Because if your Minimum Viable Product (MVP) doesn't address those pain points, it's a waste of everyone's time. This is where the Build-Measure-Learn loop comes in handy. Amy Jo Kim and Celia Hodent both stress that Game Thinking is ultimately about product-market fit. You are not just building a thing. You are designing fit, culture, rhythm.

Let me break it down with a metaphor. Making a game is like baking a cake:

- *Build*: Gather ingredients and mix the batter.

- *Measure*: Bake and taste it.

- *Learn*: Adjust the recipe and bake again.

That's the tweet! This is the cycle. You build a prototype, release it to a small group, collect feedback, iterate and loop. The faster you can do this, the more likely your final product will resonate.

Let's say you build a new level. You give it to ten testers. They all get stuck at the same point or say it's too long. Great, now you have direction. You shorten the level, reduce the difficulty and retest. That's the loop. It's not glamorous, but it's critical.

Now, what if you're not ready for launch? Enter the vertical slice.

Your MVP is your skeleton, a playable version of the product that proves your core mechanics work. It's the beach sandcastle before the moat and towers. The vertical slice is what you show the world. It's polished. It's pretty. But it must still work.

Think of it like this:

- *MVP*: Functional prototype that validates fun.

- *Vertical slice*: Showcase segment that demonstrates polish and potential.

Use the vertical slice at conferences, on social media or for internal flexes. But know that when it's live, you're exposed. It has to work. The best vertical slices showcase every part of your system, level design, UX, audio, player feedback, in miniature.

There's a popular framework called *The Mom Test* (Fitzpatrick, 2013). It's about asking the right questions when validating an idea, but in product design it's evolved into a guiding principle for accessibility and inclusivity. Simply, Robert Fitzpatrick asks the designer (that's you): Can someone outside your demographic use it? They don't have to love it. But can they complete a task? Understand the interface? Access its value?

When I design games or apps, especially in areas that attract a female demographic such as Femtech, I *always* apply The Mom Test. Not just for usability, but for discoverability, cost, language and time. I ask:

- Can my user afford this?

- When do they have the time to use it?

- Do they have children? How old are they?

- Do they have a university degree? Or did their education end earlier?

- Are they part of a support network, online or offline?

Design should never require a degree to use. And assumptions about "free time," especially for new parents, are often wildly off base. Many Femtech creators assume that mothers are idle. They're not. They're multitasking survivalists.

The Mom Test is about respecting the user. Making your experience inclusive without dumbing it down.

When I first started designing games, the NES was the console to beat. Nintendo mastered accessibility through gameplay, but their localisation often left non-Japanese users behind. The inverse also holds true. If we expect Japanese players to understand our Western mechanics without adapting the narrative or cultural framing, we'll lose them.

If you want a masterclass in localisation, check out *Legends of Localization* (Mandelin, 2019). It shows how good translation is about intent, not just words. So, does *Pit Fighter* for the Sega Genesis pass The Mom Test in Japan? Probably not. But the gameplay? That must be universal. These principles carry through everything I build. Whether I'm designing a menstruation tracker, a game narrative or a metaverse prototype, I'm always testing for universality.

Because good design doesn't gatekeep.

It invites everyone in.

DEATH BY DESIGN

Before diving deeper into storytelling, let's pause to reflect on the product itself. Productivity, practice, learning and challenge, all of it becomes easier when your end user becomes your strategy. Whether it's HR or core gameplay mechanics, user-centred thinking creates conditions for flow throughout your studio (Kim, 2019).

Some of my favourite game studios are in Denmark and Sweden. Denmark, in particular, has something akin to the Japanese concept of Ikigai. They call it *arbejdsglæde*, that Sunday evening feeling of looking forward to work. The Swedes do it too. In my experience, Nordic studios don't design products off the tops of their heads. They apply everything we've covered in this chapter: empathy, hypothesis, iteration and feedback. It's no surprise that Danish, Swedish and Finnish studios rank among the most successful in the world.

They also do coffee empires. Smoothie bars. Boutique retail. But what about loyalty? Do they do it as well as Starbucks? That's debatable.

Starbucks has long been the poster child for user-focused loyalty design. Its programme, Stars, is a great case study in gamified progression: points, rewards, levels and incentives. It's a functional core loop. Here's how it works:

- *Sign up*: Via the app, website or physical card. That inclusivity is no accident.

- *Earn Stars*: Two Stars per dollar spent, plus occasional bonuses.

- *Redeem rewards*: Stars can be exchanged for drinks, food or merchandise. Simple, tangible feedback.

- *Level up*: Green, Gold and Welcome tiers offer escalating perks. This encourages deeper brand engagement.

- *Pay with app*: Stars accumulate with every digital transaction. Seamless, frictionless, habitual.

The Starbucks core loop? Buy coffee. That's it. But wrapped around that is a thoughtful system of rewards and progression. It's indulgent, repeatable and optimised for retention. We'll return to this when we discuss UX later in the book. Of course, no loyalty programme is perfect. And Starbucks is no exception:

- *You have to spend to earn*: This may alienate price-sensitive customers.

- *Reward options are limited*: You might want more than a drink.

- *It's complicated*: Multiple levels and tiers confuse some users.

- *Rewards expire*: Miss the window, and you lose your Stars.

- *Privacy matters*: Signing up means giving personal data, which some users resist.

These are *real* pain points. Ones I'll address again when discussing ethical design.

So what has this got to do with NFTs? In 2021, Starbucks launched an NFT-based rewards platform (2021) in South Korea. The pitch: customers could purchase digital tokens and redeem them for drinks or perks. Sounds innovative, right?

Reddit users called it a "cash grab." Others labelled it "soulless." Here's why it didn't work anywhere but South Korea:

- *Lack of clarity*: Most users didn't understand NFTs.

- *Limited appeal*: NFTs weren't broadly desirable.

- *Technical friction*: Bugs and access issues plagued the rollout.

- *Cultural mismatch*: South Korea's consumer behaviours differ from other regions. NFTs didn't fit.

Worse still, many markets don't recognise NFTs at all. And if you have to explain it repeatedly, and it still doesn't land, then it's not good UX. It's not loyalty. It's confusion.

The lesson here is important. The worlds of games and the metaverse are not so different from any other digital product. What changes is the cadence. We've moved from 2-player to LAN, from LAN to co-op, from multiplayer to metaverse. We're designing for persistence and fluidity. We have to anticipate player needs while never leaving users behind.

In Fast-Moving Consumer Goods (FMCG), the approach is often: build it, market it hard and hope for the best. But metaverse products can't be one-shot. They must evolve with the user. That means using traditional, iterative methods: paper prototyping, behavioural testing, hypothesis loops. It can't be given up on when all hope is lost. This approach must be ubiquitous. Think about the brands you loved in childhood that didn't adapt. Where are they now? Absorbed by megabrands? Out of business entirely?

Designing for loyalty means designing for growth. Not your growth, *theirs*: the user's, the player's, the citizen's, the metizen's.

REFERENCES

Fitzpatrick, R. (2013) *The Mom Test: How to Talk to Customers & Learn If Your Business Is a Good Idea When Everyone Is Lying to You*. CreateSpace.

Hodent, C. (2017) *The Gamer's Brain: How Neuroscience and UX Can Impact Video Game Design*. Boca Raton, FL: CRC Press.

HYBE Corporation (2020) About Us. Available at: https://www.hybecorp.com/eng/

Kim, A.J. (2019) *Game Thinking: Innovate Smarter & Drive Deep Engagement with Design Techniques from Hit Games*. Palo Alto, CA: Game Thinking Press.

Mandelin, C. (2019) 'Games with Famous Bad Translations INTO Japanese', *Legends of Localization*, 1 May. Available at: https://legendsoflocalization.com/games-with-famous-bad-translations -into-japanese/ (Accessed: 16 April 2023).

Marshall, J. (2015) No Brainer IAPs – Presentation. Industry Examples of Offering Value to Players. Personal communication.

Netmarble (2020) BTS Universe Story [Mobile Game]. Netmarble Corp.

Reddit (2021) r/CryptoCurrency Discussion on Starbucks NFTs. Available at: https://www.reddit .com/r/CryptoCurrency/comments/xcbhi6/starbucks_details_its_blockchainbased_loyalty/

Starbucks (2023) Starbucks Rewards Terms and FAQs. Available at: https://www.starbucks.com/ rewards

CHAPTER 8

Good Stories

THE CHICKEN AND THE EGG

Before we tell good stories, we need to understand how they might land. Stories, in games especially, demand good design. Colleagues of mine who come from non-games writing backgrounds often experience culture shock when entering the games industry. Many assume that story comes first. It does not. In game development, design always comes first, and everything else, including the narrative, is crafted in response to that design logic.

This might sound controversial to writers, but it is liberating for designers. If you are a natural storyteller and learn the fundamentals of game design, you will never be without work. The most effective designers are those who understand how to construct a story, then deconstruct and reconstruct it as needed, adapting it to gameplay loops, technical constraints and player choice. Good stories in interactive media are modular and flexible. They are engineered to fit specific narrative beats, player actions and platform contexts.

In this section, I am not setting up a false dichotomy between story and experience. Instead, I want to explore how both elements reinforce each other. I have written successfully for both story-first and experience-first frameworks. Both can elevate or destroy an experience depending on execution. With great power comes great responsibility, and yes, I've got the t-shirt.

As a small child, I was obsessed with *Choose Your Own Adventure* books. My reading process was unusual but methodical:

1. Read the book cover to cover, linearly.

2. Re-read the "intended" path.

3. Then play through all the non-linear branches, usually as the villain.

That non-linear logic is what first excited me about game storytelling. Many of my favourite in-game stories are side quests, narrative arcs tucked into the corners of large worlds. For instance, in *The Elder Scrolls IV: Oblivion* (Bethesda Game Studios, 2006), the quest

DOI: 10.1201/9781003615248-8

A Brush with Death begins with a simple prompt in Cheydinhal: help a distraught wife find her missing painter husband. The quest takes a surreal turn as you are drawn into a magical painted world. Similarly, in *Crisis Core: Final Fantasy VII Reunion* (Square Enix, 2022), the arc *Doors to the Unknown* lets protagonist Zack unlock his full combat potential by raising his damage limit to 99,999. That is not just a gameplay upgrade, it is a narrative reward that feels earned.

Not every subplot is about competition. Some are about discovery, emotion and narrative payoff. That principle is often lost in early stage metaverse development. Many metaverse creators seem hesitant to gamify their experiences, either fearing they will become sports-like or simply lacking the knowledge of how to do it.

When working with brands, which is a common situation in today's metaverse landscape, the experience must be story-driven. Narrative gamification is not just a gimmick, but a proven loyalty driver. If it works for AAA games like *The Elder Scrolls* and *Final Fantasy VII*, then it can also work for Walmart or Gucci. The more urgent question is why so many brands continue to misread what it means to tell a story on an interactive platform.

THE CHORUS

The video game industry has consistently pushed the boundaries of storytelling in ways that traditional media could never fully achieve. In games, story is not a passive sequence delivered to an audience. It is an interactive experience where the player is not merely a viewer, but a participant. Every player action has consequences that can reshape the narrative, and in turn, the evolving story reshapes player behaviour. This reciprocity is what makes storytelling in games not only unique, but structurally different from film or literature (Bal, 2017).

One of the most common vehicles for delivering story in games is the cutscene. These pre-rendered or scripted sequences occur between gameplay segments, offering narrative cohesion, world-building and emotional beats. Cutscenes can also serve as pacing tools, allowing the player time to absorb information and deepen their investment in the characters or setting.

This technique of combining narrative and rhythm has an ancient analogue in the chorus of Greek theatre. The chorus was a group of performers who sang, danced and delivered collective commentary. They served as a bridge between audience and actor, translating the emotional and moral stakes of the drama. They were not protagonists, but they were vital intermediaries. Their purpose was to reflect, amplify and interpret the action for the audience, and to provoke ethical reflection. In Aristophanes' *Lysistrata*, the chorus is split into two gendered halves, both offering perspective and comic disruption while reinforcing the stakes of war and peace (Aristophanes, c.411 BCE).

Brecht later modernised this idea through his theory of dramaturgy, using the chorus and direct address not simply to support the action, but to critique it. His plays such as *The Caucasian Chalk Circle* and *Mother Courage and Her Children* encourage the audience to evaluate their moral positions, rather than passively consume entertainment. In this way, the chorus becomes a vehicle for intellectual challenge and civic engagement (Brecht, 1964).

In more recent times, the chorus has evolved again in popular culture. The *Rocky Horror Show* and its cinematic adaptation, *The Rocky Horror Picture Show* (1975), demand not only the audience's attention but also their active participation. Audiences shout responses, throw objects and even dress as the characters, becoming a literal chorus that blurs the lines between spectator and performer. This is an example of dramaturgy as collective ritual and live reinterpretation.

We can observe a similar collective response in contemporary video games, especially in shared environments like *Minecraft* (2009) or even meme-driven experiences such as *Skibidi Toilet* on *Roblox*. These games have ignited wide social participation and user-generated content. The *Skibidi Toilet* phenomenon, for instance, began as a surreal in-game meme and evolved into a full YouTube series and cultural movement that retained its reactive, chaotic chorus throughout its transition to screen. According to BBC Newsround, the phenomenon has captured global youth attention and shows no signs of slowing (BBC, 2024).

The aesthetic presence of the Greek chorus, through elaborate masks, synchronised movement and choreographed rituals, created a rhythm and atmosphere that mirrored the narrative itself. This is strikingly similar to how cutscenes, ambient sound or non-playable characters function in modern games. Think of how a narrator, background score or ambient player chat on platforms like *Fortnite* or *Breakroom* creates emotional resonance and social context. These features act like a chorus by managing tone, pace and collective interpretation.

The rhythm of ancient theatre, carried by choral odes, served a second structural function: it broke the action into digestible intervals. Similarly, well-designed games alternate between action and reflection, combat and contemplation. The breaks in gameplay are not filler. They are there to let the narrative breathe. In this way, both ancient theatre and interactive entertainment use tempo to manage emotional intensity.

One of the most obvious modern uses of a "chorus" in video games can be seen in *Hades* (Supergiant Games, 2020). The player, as Zagreus, is accompanied by the Fates, three narrators who comment on his progress, foreshadow choices and reflect on themes of family, rebellion and mortality. They do not drive the plot, but they deepen its meaning. Their commentary reinforces the cyclical nature of gameplay and myth, while their voices and music add rich texture to the game's aesthetic.

This structural device could be powerful in metaverse design. Brands and developers often miss the opportunity to use chorus-like mechanics, such as narrative guides, ambient non-playable characters (NPCs) or Artificial Intelligence (AI) voiceovers, as a way to build community and context. As with the Greek chorus, these narrative instruments do not lead the experience, but they give users orientation, reflection and belonging.

The chorus offers more than a metaphor. It is a storytelling strategy with ancient roots and digital potential. It can be used to narrate, contextualise and harmonise a user's journey through complex, co-created worlds. In the metaverse, where coherence and engagement are hard-won, the chorus is not just aesthetic. It is strategic.

WHISPERS ON THE WIND

In-game dialogue is a vital tool in game development and story progression. A conversation between characters or narration by the player character can be the difference between accepting a quest and taking an arrow to the knee. Dialogue helps immerse players in the game world, reinforces character identity and creates emotional stakes. When done well, it transforms gameplay into a narrative experience. Yet when done poorly, it can alienate players.

The role of dialogue is to help normalise the player's presence in a digital environment. It bridges the uncanny divide between human and machine. During the first two decades of video game development, storytelling was almost entirely player-driven. With little or no plot to follow, the player often invented their own narrative based on in-game actions or character interpretation. They were not just participants, but the storytellers themselves. Today, the landscape has shifted. Games feel more cinematic and emotionally charged, delivering crafted narratives that resonate on a visceral level. Successful examples include the branching interactions in *Skyrim* (Bethesda Game Studios, 2011), the cinematic emotional depth of *Heavy Rain* (Quantic Dream, 2010) or the environment-reactive quips in *Grand Theft Auto V* (Rockstar Games, 2013). These experiences feel authentic because the dialogue is not just present, but responsive and believable.

There are three primary methods of dialogue delivery in games and metaverses:

- *Pre-scripted Dialogue*: This is the most common method, where voice actors deliver lines triggered by specific events. The player interacts with it by selecting from a fixed set of responses. Games like *Devil May Cry* (Capcom, 2001) and many other AAA franchises use this approach to create memorable one-liners and lore delivery. In metaverse environments, this often becomes a monologue. Non-playable characters (NPCs) offer guiding dialogue without expecting meaningful input, except triggering the next waypoint.

- *Dynamic Dialogue*: This approach introduces variation based on player choices or environmental conditions. Algorithms or branching scripts create context-aware responses. It features prominently in games like *Life is Strange* (Dontnod Entertainment, 2015), *Phoenix Wright: Ace Attorney* (Capcom, 2001) and *The Elder Scrolls III: Morrowind* (Bethesda Game Studios, 2002). This format is essential for agency and replayability.

- *Live Dialogue*: In multiplayer environments or virtual platforms, players speak to each other via voice or text in real-time. This "battle speak" creates spontaneous storytelling and communal energy. For example, the North American servers in *League of Legends* (Riot Games, 2009) are filled with chaotic vocal exchanges. Platforms like *Spatial* (2020) extend this further, creating global live dialogues between avatars, sometimes with video. These interactions are unscripted and unpredictable, but they become part of the shared narrative.

Historically, HCI (Human Computer Interaction) was grounded in repetition and mechanical coordination. Dialogue was static, interfaces were limited and immersion relied on player imagination. But expectations have changed. Today's players demand responsiveness and depth, not just functionality. Developers have tried to meet these demands by over-delivering narrative complexity, sometimes outpacing what technology can sustainably support.

This arms race has exposed flaws. Many game studios and publishers still struggle to implement scalable narrative engines or branching dialogue systems. These are resource-intensive, and without proper planning, they often collapse under their own ambition. The metaverse inherits this burden, but with fewer storytelling traditions to rely on. While metaverse experiences may look similar to video games, they often lack the narrative maturity or executional depth that games have spent decades refining (McKee, 1997). McKee, in his foundational work on story structure, emphasises the importance of character-driven dialogue and narrative economy in maintaining emotional engagement (McKee, 1997). Likewise, Tom Clancy's military thrillers, which later became successful video game franchises, traverse the often-difficult book to game or movie to game perimeter with ease, highlighting the power of concise, high-stakes storytelling that translates well into interactive formats (Clancy, 2002).

In both cases, the challenge remains the same: dialogue must create resonance, not redundancy. If dialogue feels natural and reactive, it anchors the player in the experience. If it feels wooden, missing or illogical, the world loses credibility.

NARRATOLOGY AND THE LIVES OF THINGS

The third major approach to storytelling in video games is environmental narrative. Rather than rely on dialogue or cinematic exposition, this form of storytelling uses the world itself to convey meaning. Architecture, artefacts, lighting and spatial layout can all deliver narrative cues. A well-crafted environment can tell a story without using a single word.

This approach is highly applicable to metaverse experiences. When done well, environmental storytelling enables branded content to feel native and immersive. The user or metaverse citizen does not need to be explicitly guided. Instead, they engage in interpretive play, much like a visitor in a museum. The user constructs meaning by exploring the spatial arrangement, aesthetic motifs and object interactions within a digital world.

Returning to the earlier discussion of the chorus, environmental storytelling may be its most silent iteration. It is ambient rather than audible. Yet it performs a similar function by offering moral or thematic commentary through non-verbal cues. Think of the desolate, irradiated landscapes of *Fallout 3* (Bethesda Game Studios, 2008) or the flooded corridors and art deco ruins of *BioShock* (Irrational Games, 2007). These spaces do not just set a mood. They act as narrators.

To understand how this works from a narratological perspective, we can draw on Mieke Bal's concepts of focalisation and narrative levels. Focalisation refers to the lens through which a story is perceived. In video games and metaverses, focalisation is shaped by the camera angle, movement controls and user interface. A close, over-the-shoulder camera tells a different story than a top-down isometric view. In *Inside* (Playdead, 2016), for example, the tight 2.5D framing forces the player to experience tension and constraint firsthand. The game world is sparse, but every object has a narrative function.

Bal's concept of narrative levels, meanwhile, helps us to understand how environmental storytelling often operates in layers. There is the primary narrative level (such as completing a quest or reaching a destination), but there may also be embedded or symbolic layers. Consider *Journey* (thatgamecompany, 2012), where the ruins of a fallen civilisation are scattered throughout the landscape. There is no spoken dialogue, but the layering of relics, glyphs and remnants of technology tells a tragic and spiritual tale (Bal, 2017).

Environmental storytelling has parallels in dramaturgy as well. The German playwright Heiner Müller spoke of space as "a character in its own right" (Müller, 1995). Similarly, modern production designers in theatre and film consider how stage and setting offer narrative clues even before a character speaks. In video games, this is reflected in level design that uses colour theory, line of sight and object placement to communicate with the player. In *The Last of Us* (Naughty Dog, 2013), the presence of children's toys in abandoned apartments tells stories of absence and loss without needing exposition.

When designing metaverses, these dramaturgical and narratological concepts become crucial. If we treat the digital environment as a semiotic system, every object and layout decision becomes a storytelling opportunity. The museum metaphor is useful here. Hanging a Rembrandt next to a Titian creates its own curatorial narrative. The player becomes both curator and audience, assembling personal meaning through movement, interpretation and attention.

Finally, HCI reminds us that this information transfer is bidirectional. Every design decision is a signal, and the player or user decodes that signal in context. In metaverses, this can be amplified through ambient music, responsive lighting or avatar gesture systems. The environment becomes a dynamic narrator, not a static backdrop.

HIGH-IMPACT STORYTELLING

To understand high-impact narrative in video games, we must revisit the foundations of cinema. Early silent films and early sound pictures offer rich lessons in visual storytelling. Films such as Tod Browning's *Freaks* (1932) relied on mood, facial expression and atmospheric cues rather than dialogue. The horror of its presentation, especially for 1930s audiences, forces the viewer to engage emotionally and viscerally. This is storytelling *felt* before it is *understood*. Similarly, Roger Corman's *A Bucket of Blood* (1959), or the introspective horror of Terence Malick and John Boorman, use visual and emotional language to provoke meaning. More recent works such as *True Romance* (1993) and *12 Years a Slave* (2013) reflect this same drive to ask urgent narrative questions. The question that resonates across all these works, and within the best games, is: why this story, and why now?

Games must evoke emotion to be memorable. If a game fails to move us, why play it rather than watch a film or read a novel? To rise above mechanical interaction, games adopt cinematic tools that heighten immersion, scale and empathy. These tools are not yet widespread in the metaverse, where technical limitations and inconsistent design often dilute narrative impact.

Cinematic Cutscenes: Video games frequently use cinematic cutscenes to deliver key story beats. These pre-rendered sequences mirror film direction: dramatic camera angles, dynamic lighting, and advanced animation create tension and focus. Hideo Kojima exemplifies this approach in *Metal Gear Solid* (1998) and *Death Stranding* (Kojima Productions, 2019), both of which combine Hitchcockian suspense with philosophical intrigue (Kojima, 2019).

Action Sequences: Games such as *Rainbow Six Siege* (Ubisoft, 2015) and *The Division* (Ubisoft, 2016), based on the works of Tom Clancy, employ action sequences with cinematic flair. These sequences rely on choreographed movement, slow-motion shots and dynamic environmental effects. A notable precursor to this style is *Shenmue* (1999), which introduced Quick Time Events (QTEs). QTEs created reactive cinematic moments, where player interaction determines narrative outcomes (Figure 8.1).

Character Development: As with film, strong character development deepens player engagement. Voice acting, facial motion capture and narrative branching all contribute to layered protagonists. The *Elder Scrolls* series (1994–2011) presents a world filled with distinct voices and mannerisms, allowing for a living, breathing environment populated by nuanced individuals.

Music and Sound Design: Audio design plays a critical role in narrative construction. A game's score and ambient sound can elevate an emotional moment beyond what visuals alone can convey. In film theory, we distinguish between diegetic sound, audio that exists

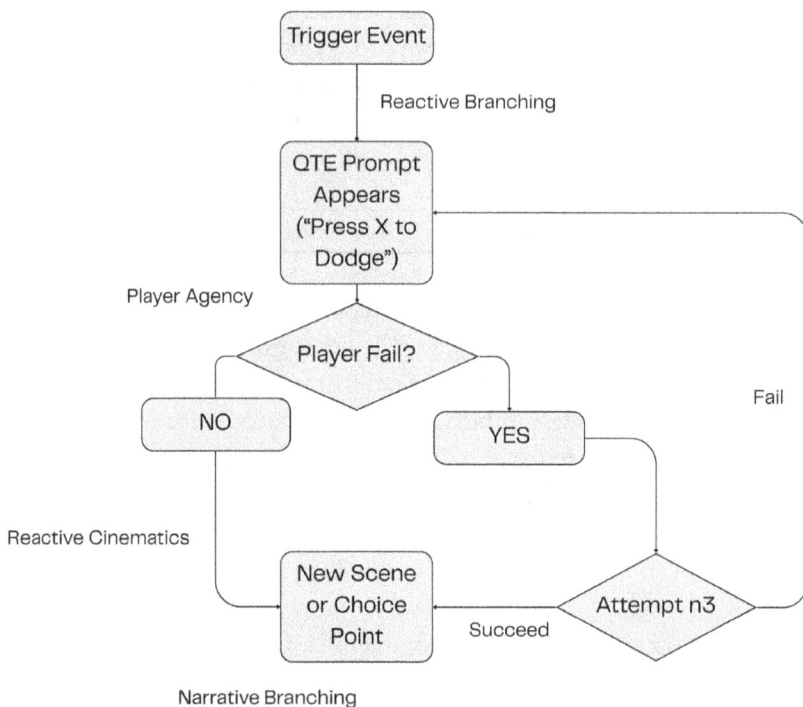

FIGURE 8.1 First introduced in Shenmue (1999), QTEs are now core to titles like God of War, Resident Evil 4 and Heavy Rain, each adapting the mechanic to their unique narrative tone.

within the world of the characters, such as footsteps or dialogue, and non-diegetic sound, which includes music and effects added for audience perception. Games similarly employ this spectrum to enhance emotional depth and world-building.

Hideo Kojima's *Death Stranding* (2019) uses non-diegetic music tracks from bands like Low Roar to evoke isolation and existential reflection as the player moves across desolate landscapes. Hitchcock, too, mastered the strategic use of silence and sound to amplify tension, especially in *Vertigo* (1958) and *Psycho* (1960), where sound becomes its own character (Truffaut, 1985). In *Journey* (2012), the absence of dialogue is counterbalanced by a powerful orchestral score that adapts to player movement and pacing, acting as an emotional narrator.

A more specific example can be found in the *Halo: Combat Evolved Anniversary* soundtrack (2016), which features a reimagining of the iconic theme *Arborea Above* by O'Donnell and Salvatori. Contributions from Brian Trifon, Lennie Moore, Paul Lipson and Tom Salta reshape earlier motifs, giving new emotional resonance to the Master Chief's lonely journey across scorched earth and forgotten places.

Dynamic Camera Angles: Cameras in games are no longer static. They guide, obscure, reveal and sometimes disorient. This cinematic control over perspective can shape meaning in subtle ways. In *Little Big Planet* (Media Molecule, 2008) and *Fable* (Lionhead Studios, 2004), playful and strategic camera angles foster agency and discovery. Camera work in these titles enhances narrative tone by placing visual storytelling within the player's hands.

These techniques, drawn from the grammar of film, create emotionally complex games that are capable of delivering experiences comparable to the best of cinema. While the metaverse has yet to master this style of high-impact storytelling, video games continue to show the way forward.

INFRASTRUCTURE

A compelling story in video games must do more than simply exist alongside gameplay. It must be interwoven with mechanics, enhancing and being enhanced by them. Well-developed characters are essential to this process. They must be believable and relatable, with clear motivations. For instance, we must believe that Martin Septim is truly the last hope of a dying dynasty (*Elder Scrolls IV: Oblivion*, 2006). Likewise, *The Elder Scrolls III: Morrowind* (2002) requires emotional investment in righting the wrongs committed by Dagoth Ur. Even seemingly light-hearted games like *Candy Crush Saga* depend on our buy-in to characters like Tiffi and Mr Toffee to maintain engagement through repetitive gameplay that the match-3 games require.

Good storytelling demands more than just compelling characters. It also requires a clear and intentional structure. While traditional dramatic arcs such as the three-act structure or the *Hero's Journey* (Campbell, 2004) continue to serve as templates, video games have evolved to include non-linear, branching paths more akin to *Choose Your Own Adventure* narratives. Players can embrace morally ambiguous roles or explore the world endlessly without touching the main quest. This dynamic form of storytelling supports the growing trend toward persistent digital worlds, including the metaverse.

To sustain engagement in these complex environments, game narratives must be carefully constructed. If the story is the roof, then plot and character are the pillars and bricks that hold it up. The plot builds chronology and contains subplots that form the storylines. Characters provide the emotional warmth that keeps players invested. Story structures vary widely, from three acts to 16-point circular journeys, but all require consistent care and cohesion.

A strong example of traditional structure can be found in *Max Payne* (2001), where Sam Lake presents a classic film noir in video game form. The game opens with gripping exposition and carries the player through escalating crises toward a high-stakes climax. However, not all games deliver this effectively. Overused plot devices like the "crashed ship" or a mystery-laden inciting incident can feel derivative when unsupported by meaningful content.

Games like *Metal Gear Solid* (1998) or *Shenmue* (1999) occasionally struggle under the weight of the three-act structure, requiring players to follow the story rather than shape it. In these cases, narrative designers often rely on content, like lore entries, fetch quests or repetitive missions, to stand in for story. While content is important, it should not be a substitute for coherent narrative structure.

Massively Multiplayer Online (MMO) games such as *Final Fantasy XIV* (2010), *RuneScape* (2001), *Guild Wars 2* (2012) and *World of Warcraft* (2004) present a different storytelling model. These games blend narrative architecture with participatory and emergent storytelling. Designers must balance player freedom with overarching plot, and this is a skill to be learned in order to deliver, well, anything. From brand stories to transmedia design, the understanding of these elements is vital.

Outside of traditional MMOs, platforms like *Roblox* have emerged as dynamic storytelling spaces. While originally focused on user-generated mini-games, *Roblox* now hosts expansive, episodic and even cinematic universes. Examples like *The Mimic* (MUCDICH, 2021), an episodic horror game with dense lore, or *Dreams of Valor* (Kubo Studios, 2023), an anime-inspired RPG with moral decision-making, showcase the breadth of storytelling possible on *Roblox*. Meanwhile, games like *Springs Rock High School* allow for spontaneous emergent storytelling shaped by community tropes and social performance. In *Timmeh!* (Wonder Works Studio, 2021), creators have pushed into meta-narratives that blend livestream culture with player identity. These examples illustrate how *Roblox* functions as a dynamic transmedia platform where stories emerge collaboratively and modularly, signalling a shift toward distributed, participatory storytelling that is especially resonant with Gen Z and Gen Alpha.

How *Roblox* Storytelling Works:

Roblox is a user-generated platform where creators use the Roblox Studio engine to build games, experiences and interactive narratives. Storytelling can take many forms – from linear quests and episodic content to emergent, player-driven drama shaped through roleplay or multiplayer interactions. Tools such as scripting, dialogue modules, animations and in-game objects allow creators to embed lore, design custom cinematics or facilitate social storytelling. Players act as co-authors, using avatars, emotes and community-generated content to deepen the story. This modularity allows *Roblox* to function like a transmedia hub, where games, machinima, livestreams and social commentary converge into living, evolving narratives.

The *Final Fantasy* Series original game designer Hironobu Sakaguchi and *Final Fantasy XIV* director Naoki Yoshida have both explored the idea of MMOs as proto-metaverses. Yoshida notes, "In a way, FFXIV is already its own metaverse [...] if you add the Blockchain mechanism it would be the metaverse these people envision" (Found in Translation, 2023). He also suggests that integrating real-world locations into the game such as Venice could expand immersion. Sakaguchi focuses more on the communication potential and server architecture as the technical basis for metaversal play.

To understand the structure behind these expansive worlds, it helps to divide narrative development into two categories: *Narrative Design* and *Context Creation*.

Narrative Design includes the storytelling of objects, locations and player experiences. It governs tasks like procedural missions, branching dialogue and experience management. It is often closer to project management than creative writing. The story of a rare party hat in *RuneScape* is a good example of environmental lore rooted in player economy and culture.

Context Creation, on the other hand, manages the overarching narrative. It oversees story arcs, player motivation, character relationships and major dialogue sequences. For media creators, this means shaping the emotional and thematic spine of the experience. Context creation is not just about what happens, but why it matters. It involves ensuring that every piece of dialogue, each character arc and every mission aligns with a coherent narrative vision. This is where narrative ambition lives, in defining what the player's journey means on a symbolic and structural level, and in how that journey is remembered, interpreted and shared by the audience.

The Hero's Journey, Joseph Campbell's essential story framework, maps transformation across twelve stages. Games like *Final Fantasy XIV* adopt this template, casting the player as the Warrior of Light who overcomes adversity and evolves into a powerful figure. The game provides enough flexibility for players to explore open-world or player versus player (PvP) options while maintaining a clear sense of narrative progression.

The Hero's Journey complements traditional three-act structures, though some argue that it offers a more expansive or layered approach. As players grow stronger, complete moral challenges and face ultimate foes, they participate in an archetypal story that transcends medium. Even Steven Spielberg has remarked on the changing nature of storytelling: "People have forgotten how to tell a story. Stories don't have a middle or an end anymore. They usually have a beginning that never stops beginning" (Speilberg, 1978). This reflects the logic of live games and persistent worlds rather than film. Justin Wyatt's concept of high-concept filmmaking, films based on a clear, *marketable* idea, translates readily into games like *Portal* (2007), *Journey* (2012), *Bioshock* (2007) and *The Last of Us* (2013). These titles each start with a strong, singular concept and build narrative richness around it (Wyatt, 1994).

High-concept storytelling has also driven transmedia development. When the Writers Guild of America went on strike in 2007–2008, the disruption led to a rise in unscripted programming like *Jersey Shore* and *Keeping Up with the Kardashians*. But it may also have opened space for risk-taking in other areas. As traditional media pipelines were blocked, studios and publishers turned to new franchises and formats. This timing arguably helped projects like the Marvel Cinematic Universe gain traction. While not caused directly by the strike, the disruption may have created opportunities for unconventional IP to flourish.

Video games were also affected, particularly in their storytelling and writing teams. Although many game writers were not WGA-affiliated, the strike underscored the precarious status of creative labour in transmedia development. Delays and scaled-back narratives affected projects that relied on unionised voice actors or writing talent, especially in AAA titles and licensed properties.

More recently, the 2023 WGA strike has also begun to ripple through media industries. While its full effects are still developing, early indicators suggest that scripted content delays and shifts in production schedules will impact TV and film well into 2025 and 2026. The strike, which also addressed the use of AI in creative writing, has reignited debate about ownership, authorship and labour protections across creative disciplines. Video game studios, particularly those with close ties to television and film IPs, are beginning to re-evaluate their narrative production models in response.

While not directly governed by WGA rules, the games industry will likely see secondary impacts over time, especially in areas like narrative design, cinematic writing and transmedia storytelling. The rise of user-generated story content serves as a reminder of how deeply entwined our industries have become, and how shifts in one can radically affect the creative ecosystems of others. What remains clear is that story infrastructure matters. Whether in a linear shooter or in *Roblox*, story must be treated with the same rigour as any other system. It must be constructed, maintained and, crucially, believed.

DEPTH OF FIELD

King from *Tekken* (1997) is one of my favourite characters in video games. While he may appear to be a standard luchador with a jaguar mask and a chiselled physique, his backstory offers much more. He is not just a fighter but also a character with a complex past. Originally a street brawler, King is taken in by Marquez monks in Mexico after being left for dead. His life is transformed when he recovers and establishes an orphanage, dedicating his winnings from wrestling to help disadvantaged children. After being killed by Ogre, the god of fighting, his mantle is picked up by King II, a former orphan inspired to honour his mentor by continuing both his fighting career and charitable mission.

This type of high-concept pathos resembles narrative arcs in superhero franchises, where motivation often stems from personal loss or redemption. The *Marvel Cinematic Universe* (2008) frequently uses these narrative devices in characters such as *Iron Man* (2008) or *Black Widow* (2021), anchoring larger-than-life figures in deeply human emotions. In games, this kind of emotional grounding is vital for transforming action-based mechanics into meaningful engagement.

Character backstories, when designed with depth and purpose, can shape the entire player experience. They do not simply serve the character, they support immersion, affect how we engage with the environment and even guide how we navigate narrative choices.

Immersion: Well-developed backstories allow players to step into a world with emotional stakes. In the case of King, the knowledge that he fights to fund an orphanage adds emotional gravitas to his in-game actions. Players become more invested because the stakes transcend pixels and stats (Isbister, 2006).

Player Empathy: When players understand a character's suffering, choices and goals, empathy naturally follows. This is especially potent in narrative-driven games where moral dilemmas are shaped by character backstory. In fighting games like *Tekken*, this connection deepens our engagement with repeated battles, transforming each win or loss into a personal journey (Fernández-Vara, 2015).

Narrative Depth: Backstories also fill in the narrative gaps between gameplay loops. They allow us to contextualise events, enemies and environments. For instance, King's past provides a narrative foil to characters like Heihachi Mishima, whose motivations are rooted in domination and violence. Their rivalry becomes more than competition; it becomes thematic conflict.

Character Development: A rich backstory gives characters space to evolve. It anchors emotional arcs across sequels or reboots. King's transition from brawler to protector and ultimately mentor frames his story as a legacy, one that players can follow and inherit. This is a key element of character longevity in long-running series (Rogers, 2014)

World-building: A character's backstory also contributes to the environmental and cultural depth of a game. King's Mexican heritage, wrestling influences and ties to the orphanage ground *Tekken* in a layered global context. His design reportedly draws on real-world figures like Fray Tormenta, a Mexican priest-wrestler, and Satoru Sayama, a Japanese wrestler known as the original Tiger Mask (Schreier, 2017).

Conversely, poor character design can undermine even the most visually stunning games. One-dimensional characters risk alienating players or reducing complex narratives to cliché. In AAA development, this is not just a creative issue, it is a commercial risk. Characters that shift motivations abruptly or reinforce harmful stereotypes can lose audiences and attract criticism, weakening franchise loyalty (Isbister, 2006).

This becomes even more relevant in metaverse contexts, where avatars and NPCs are expected to carry emotional and narrative weight. In digital storytelling, every character, whether brand mascot or user avatar, must be thoughtfully constructed or at least *designed* to be developed by the player or the brand. If brands are treated as characters, they need internally consistent motivations, tone of voice and narrative growth. Similarly, when users project themselves into avatars, they expect worlds to respond to them meaningfully. Flat or generic character logic breaks immersion and betrays player trust.

Character depth is not optional. It is a core infrastructure of narrative design, emotional engagement and commercial viability. Games and metaverses that succeed long-term are often those that understand this. Characters are not merely part of the game; they *are* the game.

Consider the range of character expression across media: from Alan Moore's psychologically layered depictions of Batman (1988), where trauma and moral ambiguity become the story engine, to Donnie Yen's nuanced performance as the Monkey King in *Journey to the West: Conquering the Demons* (2013), which reframes an archetype through emotion and physicality. These characters resonate because they are culturally and emotionally textured.

In video games, this same emotional architecture is felt viscerally. We don't just observe characters, we animate them. The depth we feel when playing as Joel in *The Last of Us* (2013), or as Aloy in *Horizon Zero Dawn* (2017), is not just because of what they say or do, it's because we *are* them in moments of high tension and quiet vulnerability. That embodiment of narrative is where games exceed traditional media.

In persistent social platforms like *Roblox, Minecraft, or Fortnite*, the power of character becomes communal. A player's avatar might be a meme, a hero or a self-crafted identity, but it is still embedded with narrative meaning – crafted in part by the individual and reinforced through community interaction. These platforms, while not narrative in the traditional sense, foster participatory storytelling that is powerful and persistent. Identity becomes iterative. Characters become vessels of shared mythology and lived experience.

As we imagine the future of the metaverse, characters, whether brand-created or user-generated, will be the emotional infrastructure of these worlds. If we are to design stories that matter, we must start with the characters who carry them, not just because they are protagonists, but because they are mirrors, guides and avatars of everything we believe to be true.

SHOW, DON'T TELL

Pacing is a vital component for a good story. The Goldilocks approach of not too fast and not too slow applies to many media products, including the metaverse. To be honest, I'm not entirely sure why so many people hang around in The Sandbox were it not to catch a glimpse of Snoop Dogg. Therefore, pacing should be just right to keep the player engaged. I'm a big believer that products providing any kind of metrics must be measured. I'll cover that a little more in the user experience section of this book. But pacing and balancing are important in story for video games. If you take a look at games such as *Neverwinter Nights* (2002), early (pre-FFVII) *Final Fantasy* games, *Tabula Rasa* (2007) and even *EVE Online* (2003), you will find that the story is pegged to specific metrics and measurement. It's a joke between players and developers alike that we call *EVE Online* "Spreadsheets in Space" because that's what players are doing: they're building spreadsheets of data – data about themselves, the enemy, logistics or anything really.

Game balancing and storytelling are both important aspects of video games, and they can work together to create a compelling and engaging experience for players. Balancing the gameplay mechanics and difficulty levels can help to pace the game effectively and keep players engaged in the story. Balancing refers to the process of adjusting various game mechanics, such as character abilities, weapons and environmental factors, to create a level playing field for all (Rogers, 2014).

The pacing of a video game's story can be influenced by the level of difficulty and the player's progression through the game. As the player advances through the game, the challenges should become progressively more difficult, but not so difficult that they become frustrating or impossible to overcome. This creates a sense of tension and excitement that is essential for keeping players engaged. On the other hand, if the challenges are too easy, the player may become bored and lose interest in the story. The game balance must be carefully designed to keep players challenged and invested in the story, while also allowing them to progress at a reasonable pace. If a game is not balanced, certain characters or strategies may be overpowered, making it difficult for other players to compete.

This can lead to frustration and a lack of enjoyment for those who are at a disadvantage. In addition, the game's story and the gameplay mechanics should complement each other to create a cohesive experience. The game's difficulty and mechanics should be designed to support the story and the player's journey through the game. This can involve adjusting the difficulty level of specific sections of the game to create a sense of tension, or allowing the player to use specific abilities or items to overcome challenges and progress through the story. I talked about the steep learning curve earlier; it's as important to get this right. If the player experiences all the story in the first five minutes of gameplay, what will the player do for the other 35 hours?

We often hear the term "show, don't tell." This term works for marketing as much as it works for telling a good story. *Show, don't tell* works as a principle to emphasise the importance of using visual and interactive elements to convey information to the player rather than relying solely on dialogue or text (McKee, 1997). To apply this principle, consider using environmental storytelling, where the game world and its elements tell a story without relying on text or dialogue. For example, you could use level design to convey a sense of mood or atmosphere or use sound effects to create tension or excitement. Games like *Journey* (2012) and *Hollow Knight* (2017) demonstrate this form with remarkable elegance.

The ultimate response to any game or gamified experience is "yes, and…" rather than "no, but…" to your product and, more importantly, story. (Leonard and Yorton, 2015) In their book "Yes, And: How Improvisation Reverses "No, But" Thinking and Improves Creativity and Collaboration," Kelly Leonard and Tom Yorton use a super trick to foster deeper connections across all states of business operations. I'm fascinated by how improvisation and storytelling on the fly, as it were, open ideation and product development to a wider audience with faster results.

Business Takeaway: Using Improv to Power Narrative Design

- Collaborative world-building: Teams build richer narratives by building on ideas instead of shutting them down.

- User-centred design: Characters (like users) have wants, needs and arcs that evolve, treating them as co-authors.

- Conflict as catalyst: Narrative tension mirrors design challenges, both move the story forward.

- Audience as performers: In metaverses, users aren't spectators, they're part of the show. Let them shape the story.

These insights position improvisation not just as a theatre tool, but as a blueprint for building meaningful, participatory digital experiences.

Show, don't tell is a difficult technique to master, so it's good to explore how this works through content creation. Content is as important as storytelling in developing engagement, and if you can make engagement happen, you can balance and measure, and that's the holy grail for everything from investment to acquisition. Using the "call to adventure" technique and "show don't tell" principle can enhance the content of your video game by immersing players in the game world, engaging them emotionally, and creating a memorable experience. Let's take a deeper dive into how this might work for your game or experience.

The "call to adventure" is a storytelling technique that involves introducing the player to the game's world and setting up a narrative that draws them in. To apply this technique, consider introducing the end user to a central conflict or challenge that they must overcome. This can be done through cutscenes, dialogue or other interactive elements that set up the story and provide context for the player's actions. Remember the crashed ship trope from earlier? It's that (Campbell, 2004).

To enhance the emotional impact of your product or experience, consider using narrative techniques such as character development, plot twists and dramatic tension. By building a connection between the player and the game's characters and story, you can create a sense of investment and engagement that will keep players immersed in the game. King is so well-rounded as a character it's hard to see why he isn't King of the Iron Fist Tournament every single time.

Interactive storytelling is a technique that allows players to make meaningful choices that affect the story's outcome. To apply this technique, consider incorporating branching narratives, dialogue trees or other interactive elements that allow the player to shape the story according to their choices. *Boyfriend Dungeon* (Kitfox Games, 2021) does this effortlessly and with the best results.

Business Takeaway: How Boyfriend Dungeon Works *with* the Player, Not against Them

- *Tight Feedback Loop*: Relationship progress grants mechanical upgrades, and combat success deepens relationships, creating a seamless gameplay-narrative loop.

- *Player Agency*: Through both combat and dating decisions, the player actively shapes the experience.

- *Emotional Engagement*: The use of symbolic combat and emotional storylines makes Boyfriend Dungeon feel like a game where your feelings matter as much as your skills.

RESISTANCE IS FUTILE

Earlier in this section, Hironobu Sakaguchi and Naoki Yoshida, titans of the RPG and MMO worlds, offered a design and story perspective of the metaverse. My inference is that their resistance comes from a place of being not quite ready for decentralised tools and applications. But I think that this is the only way to take that step between these two worlds. Our thinking is not quite joined up yet, and that's ok; we have the time, but we should be embracing the immersive aspect of world-building as a foundational theory or principle in creating the metaverse, as obvious as that seems. (Found In Translation, 2022).

Let's imagine that we are leveraging the latest advancements in technology to create fully realised metaverses that players can explore and interact with in a more intuitive and natural way. Extended Reality (XR) is an umbrella term that encompasses all immersive technologies that merge the physical world with the digital world. This includes Virtual Reality (VR) where the goal of VR is to completely immerse the user in a simulated environment that feels as real as possible. Augmented Reality (AR) technology recognises and tracks objects in the physical world and then overlays digital content onto them, creating an augmented experience, and Mixed Reality (MR) typically involves the use of a headset

TABLE 8.1   Narrative as a Device in Video Games

Application	How It Enhances Narratology	Narrative Impact	Examples
Artificial Intelligence (AI)	Makes characters and environments responsive to player choices and behaviours.	Enables branching storylines and emotional realism in NPCs, deepening immersion.	Dynamic NPCs in *Middle-Earth: Shadow of Mordor* (Monolith Productions, 2014); adaptive dialogue in *The Sims 4* (Electronic Arts, 2014).
Social interaction	Real-time voice/text/video chat lets players co-create stories with others.	Supports emergent storytelling and shared authorship.	Player-led events in *VRChat* (VRChat Inc., 2014) and *Roblox* (Roblox Corporation, 2006).
Open-world design	Empowers players to forge their own paths through expansive, non-linear environments.	Encourages narrative agency and exploration-driven storytelling.	*The Legend of Zelda: Breath of the Wild* (Nintendo, 2017); *Elden Ring* (FromSoftware, 2022).
Environmental storytelling	Uses design, objects and setting to convey plot and backstory.	"Show don't tell" technique that deepens world-building and lore.	*Journey* (thatgamecompany, 2012); *Bioshock* (2K Games, 2007).
Dynamic dialogue systems	Allows dialogue to shift based on past choices or behaviours.	Gives players ownership over character arcs and plot branches.	*Life is Strange* (Dontnod Entertainment, 2015); *Mass Effect* series (BioWare, 2007–).
Community tools and modding	Players extend or alter storyworlds through custom tools.	Enables transmedia-like narrative expansion.	*Skyrim* modding community (Bethesda Game Studios, 2011).
Persistent worlds (MMOs)	Continuously evolving story arcs shared across thousands of players.	Fosters living narratives and long-term character development.	*Final Fantasy XIV* (Square Enix, 2013); *World of Warcraft* (Blizzard Entertainment, 2004).

or smart glasses, which overlay digital content onto the physical world. The key difference between AR and MR is that in MR, the digital objects are anchored to the real world and can interact with physical objects in real-time. (Milgram and Kishino, 1994).

This is only half the story if we're talking about adoption. I'll explain user acquisition in more detail in the next section, but what we can be confident in our convictions of right now is all these things together would be too much. Though these extrinsics would assist in accessibility or inclusivity, they also make or break a studio budget. Extended realities in all their forms are a bit like MSG (flavour enhancer); you'll be hungry in about 30 minutes if you don't get the nourishment you want. So, to enhance experience more, we need some intrinsic application to the story or call to action.

Digital stories have come a long way since their inception in the early 1970s. Today, thanks to the cinematic crafting of stories for video games, they are not just a form of entertainment but a medium for storytelling. Video games have the unique ability to immerse players in a world that is crafted by the developers, and with new technology popping up all the time, we are able to imagine inhabiting these worlds. Because the story is an integral part of the video game experience, we have created transmedia properties and multiverses that require careful planning and execution to cross genres and demographics. The video game industry has seen some of the most iconic and memorable stories in the last few decades, and I'm sure you have your own opinions about how we will use these amazing stories to build the future – I certainly have mine.

REFERENCES

12 Years a Slave (2013) Directed by Steve McQueen [Film]. USA: Regency Enterprises.

A Bucket of Blood (1959) Directed by Roger Corman [Film]. USA: American International Pictures.

Aristophanes (c.411 BCE) *Lysistrata*. Various Editions Available.

Bal, M. (2017) *Narratology: Introduction to the Theory of Narrative*. 4th edn. Toronto: University of Toronto Press.

BBC Newsround (2024) 'Skibidi Toilet Explained: Why This Strange Meme Is Taking Over Your Screen', *BBC Newsround*, 8 February. Available at: https://www.bbc.co.uk/newsround/articles /c0r5550415ro (Accessed: 9 July 2025).

Bioshock (2007) XBox 360 [Game]. USA: 2K Games.

Bioshock (2007) PC [Game]. USA: 2K Games.

Boyfriend Dungeon (2021) Switch [Game]. Canada: Kitfox Games.

Brecht, B. (1964) *Brecht on Theatre: The Development of an Aesthetic* (Translated and edited by J. Willett). London: Methuen.

Campbell, J. (2004) *The Hero with a Thousand Faces*. NOvato, CA: New World Library.

Candy Crush (2012) Mobile [Game]. Sweden: King

Clancy, T. (2002) *Red Storm Rising*. London: HarperCollins.

Crisis Core: Final Fantasy VII Reunion (2022) Square Enix [Video Game]. Japan: Square Enix.

Death Stranding (2019) Playstation 4 [Game]. USA: Sony Interactive Entertainment.

Deliverance (1972) Directed by John Boorman [Film]. USA: Warner Bros.

Devil May Cry (2001) Playstation 2 [Game]. Japan: Capcom.

Dreams of Valor (2023) PC [Game]. Roblox.

Elden Ring (2022) PC [Game]. Japan: Bandai Namco.

Elden Ring (2022) PlayStation 5 [Game]. Japan: FromSoftware.

EVE Online (2003) PC [Game]. Iceland: CCP Games.

Fable (2004) XBox [Game]. UK: Microsoft Game Studios.

Fallout 3 (2008) XBox 360 [Game]. USA, ML: Bethesda Game Studios.

Fernández-Vara, C. (2015) *Introduction to Game Analysis*. New York, NY: Routledge.

Final Fantasy XIV (2010) PC [Game]. Japan: Square Enix.

Found In Translation (2022) *Interview with Hironobu Sakaguchi and Naoki Yoshida: On the Future of FFXIV and the Metaverse* [Online]. Available at: https://foundintranslation.games/interview-sakaguchi-yoshida-metaverse (Accessed: 10 July 2025).

Found In Translation (2023) *[FFXIV] YoshiP and Sakaguchi on the Metaverse (Eng Subs)*, 16 April 2023 [Online Video]. Available at: https://www.youtube.com/watch?v=Kn1ncqIJOm4 (Accessed: 20 April 2023).

Freaks (1932) Directed by Tod Browning [Film]. USA: Metro-Goldwyn-Mayer.

Grand Theft Auto V (2013) XBox 360 [Game]. UK: Rockstar Games.

Guild Wars 2 (2012) PC [Game]. USA: ArenaNet.

Hades (2020) Supergiant Games [Video Game]. USA, CA: San Francisco.

Halo: Combat Evolved Anniversary (Original Soundtrack) (2016) 343 Industries [Soundtrack]. USA: Xbox Game Studios.

Heavy Rain (2010) Playstation 3 [Game]. USA: Sony Computer Entertainment.

Heiner Müller (1995) *Theatremachine*. London: Faber & Faber.

Hitchcock, A. (1958) *Vertigo* [Film]. USA: Paramount Pictures.

Hitchcock, A. (1960) *Psycho* [Film]. USA: Paramount Pictures.

Hollow Knight (2017) PC [Game]. Australia: Team Cherry.

Horizon Zero Dawn (2017) XBox One [Game]. USA: Sony Interactive Entertainment.

Inside (2016) PC [Game]. Denmark: Playdead.

Isbister, K. (2006) *Better Game Characters by Design: A Psychological Approach*. San Francisco, CA: Morgan Kaufmann.

Journey (2012) PlayStation 3 [Game]. USA: thatgamecompany.

Journey (2012) Playstation 3 [Game]. USA: Sony Computer Entertainment.

Journey to the West: Conquering the Demons (2013) Directed by Stephen Chow [Film]. China: Bingo Movie Development.

League of Legends (2009) PC [Game]. USA: Riot Games.

Leonard, B. and Yorton, T. (2015) *Yes, And: How Improvisation Reverses "No, But" Thinking and Improves Creativity and Collaboration*. New York, NY: HarperBusiness.

Life Is Strange (2015) Playstation 4 [Game]. Japan: Square Enix.

Life is Strange (2015) PC [Game]. France: Dontnod Entertainment.

Little Big Planet (2008) Playstation 3 [Game]. United Kingdom: Sony Computer Entertainment.

Mass Effect. (2007–2012). Xbox 360 [Game]. Canada: BioWare.

Max Payne (2001) XBox [Game]. USA: Take-Two Interactive.

Metal Gear Solid (1998) Playstation [Game]. Japan: Konami.

McKee, R. (1997) *Story: Substance, Structure, Style and the Principles of Screenwriting*. New York, NY: ReganBooks.

Middle-Earth: Shadow of Mordor (2014) PlayStation 4 [Game]. USA: Monolith Productions.

Milgram, P. and Kishino, F. (1994) 'A Taxonomy of Mixed Reality Visual Displays', *IEICE Transactions on Information and Systems*, E77-D(12), pp. 1321–1329.

Minecraft (2009) PC. [Platform]. USA: Microsoft.

Moore, A. (1988) *Batman: The Killing Joke* [Graphic Novel]. New York, NY: DC Comics.

Phoenix Wright: Ace Attorney (2001) Game Boy Advance [Game]. Japan: Capcom.

Portal (2007) PC [Game]. USA: Valve.

Rainbow Six Siege (2015) XBox One [Game]. Ubisoft. *YoshiP*

Roblox (2006) PC [Platform]. USA: Roblox Corporation.

Rogers, S. (2014) *Level Up! The Guide to Great Video Game Design*. 2nd edn. Chichester: Wiley.

RuneScape (2001) PC [Game] Jagex

Schreier, J. (2017) *Blood, Sweat, and Pixels: The Triumphant, Turbulent Stories Behind How Video Games Are Made*. New York, NY: Harper Paperbacks.

Shenmue (1999) Dreamcast [Game]. Japan: Sega.

Spatial (2020) Metaverse Platform. USA: Spatial Systems Inc.

Speilberg, S. (1978) 'Science Fiction in Steven Spielberg's Suburbia By Chris Hodenfield', *Rolling Stone Archive 2018*. Available at: https://www.rollingstone.com/tv-movies/tv-movie-features/science-fiction-in-steven-spielbergs-suburbia-44190/ (Accessed: 9 July 2025).

Springs Rock High School (2023) PC [Game]. Roblox.

Tabula Rasa (2007) PC [Game]. USA: Destination Games.

Tekken (1997) Arcade [Game]. Japan: Bandai Namco Entertainment.

The Elder Scrolls III: Morrowind (2002) Bethesda Softworks [Video Game]. USA, ML: Bethesda Game Studios.

The Elder Scrolls V: Skyrim (2011). PC [Game]. USA: Bethesda Game Studios.

The Elder Scrolls IV: Oblivion (2006) Bethesda Softworks [Video Game]. USA, ML: Bethesda Game Studios.

The Elder Scrolls V: Skyrim (2011) XBox 360 [Video Game]. USA, ML: Bethesda Game Studios.

The Last of Us (2013) Playstation 3 [Game]. USA: Sony Computer Entertainment.

The Legend of Zelda: Breath of the Wild (2017). Nintendo Switch [Game]. Japan: Nintendo.

The Legend of Zelda: Breath of the Wild (2017) Switch [Game]. Japan: Nintendo.

The Mimic (2021) PC [Game]. Roblox.

The Sims 4. (2014). PC [Game]. USA: Electronic Arts.

Timmeh! (2021) PC [Game]. Roblox.

Truffaut, F. (1985) *Hitchcock/Truffaut*. Rev. edn. New York, NY: Simon & Schuster.

Tom Clancy's The Division (2016) XBox One [Game]. Ubisoft.

True Romance (1993) Directed by Tony Scott [Film]. USA: Warner Bros.

VRChat (2014) PC [Game]. USA: VRChat Inc.

World of Warcraft (2004) PC [Game]. USA: Blizzard Entertainment.

Wyatt, J. (1994) *High Concept: Movies and Marketing in Hollywood*. Austin, TX: University of Texas Press.

CHAPTER 9

A Life in the Metaverse

GENERATION BETA

I know, I know, the metaverse is still a relatively new and evolving concept, and as such, there is no clear demographic for metaverse users. However, it can be assumed that the users of the metaverse will be diverse, with varying ages, genders and backgrounds. That's a good thing (Yee, 2020; Hodent, 2018) (Table 9.1).

> 💡 **Business Takeaway:**
> Generation Beta is a term sometimes used to describe children born after 2025 (McCrindle, 2020). Here, we use it more figuratively to describe the next wave of metaverse natives, who will grow up with spatial computing, persistent digital identity and generative AI.

When *Minecraft* launched in 2011, it had been in beta for a while and had already undergone demographic shifts. Most people think *Minecraft* is a children's title. It isn't. It never was, until Microsoft bought it in 2014 and launched *Minecraft Education Edition* (Microsoft, 2016). But children absolutely played the hell out of it before then, especially those between four and ten. Ask your friends what their kids are playing and *Minecraft* will likely top the list. With over 126 million active players and 91 million monthly actives (Statista, 2023), the average *Minecraft* player today is male and 24 years old (Yee, 2020). *Minecraft* is, for the most part, story-less, and that's important.

Why am I telling you this? Because many metaverse platforms are primarily used by early adopters, tech enthusiasts and gamers. These users tend to be younger and more tech-savvy. But as technology becomes more accessible, we can expect a broader user base, just as we saw with *Second Life* (2003), where users skewed older and the content matured to match (Boellstorff, 2008).

Later platforms like *Avakin Life* (2004) show even more demographic diversity, particularly across age and geography (Lockwood Publishing, 2022). I'm obsessed with demographics when it comes to the metaverse because I believe it offers us bespoke experiences.

DOI: 10.1201/9781003615248-9

TABLE 9.1   Who's Who in the Metaverse?

Generation	Approx. Birth Years	Current Age Range (2025)	Tech Attitudes	Metaverse Entry Points
Gen Alpha	2010–2025	0–15	Digital native toddlers	*Roblox, Minecraft,* YouTube, *Fortnite Creative*
Gen Z	1997–2009	16–28	Gamified socialisation	TikTok, *VRChat, Roblox,* UEFN, Sandbox
Millennials	1981–1996	29–44	Tech-adaptive, nostalgic	*Second Life, Spatial, Rec Room*
Gen X	1965–1980	45–60	Tech-cautious but capable	*PlayStation Home, Meta Horizons*
Boomers	1946–1964	61–79	Occasional adopters	*Wii Fit, Brain Age, Zoom* Metaverses

These are places where we can find and be ourselves. They should be persistent, optionally social and fully accessible regardless of wealth, birthright or education level.

The ability to create and participate in unique, interactive experiences in a shared virtual space has the potential to appeal far beyond traditional gaming (Kim, 2018). So why, then, are some current metaverses locked behind NFT ownership, invite-only walls or age-specific branding with no educational rationale? This fragmentation, with metaverses just for dancers, construction workers or women, and worlds only open six months per year, makes no sense in a medium that should be global and inclusive. It's disappointing, but not surprising.

I remember visiting *Second Life, Kaneva* (2004–2016), and *SmallWorlds* (2008–2018). I lived through *Poptropica, Habbo Hotel* (2000) and *Club Penguin* in the late 2000s and early 2010s. Of those, *Habbo* and *SmallWorlds* were the most accessible. But even they lacked something essential. Perhaps it was narrative cohesion, or a reason to return beyond decorating avatars.

Working on AAA games with explorable worlds, I often imagined how easily those spaces could be layered over something like GeoCities. It's a theoretical design, not a practical one, but it stays with me (Table 9.2).

Be aware: These aren't just hobbies. They are low-friction prototypes of our future metaverse roles: hybrid, creative, self-directed.

In my day job, I advise Web3 studios and metaverse developers. In my evenings, when I'm not writing for books, like this one, I'm tending to my temple in Amazing Cultivation

TABLE 9.2   The Metaverse Jobs We Already Do: *Mini Metaverses, Real Workflows*

Game	Role	Skills Engaged
Amazing Cultivation Simulator	Spiritual leader	Systems design, mentoring, community management
Avakin Life	Hairdresser	Fashion styling, client interaction, aesthetic branding

Simulator, styling avatars in Avakin Life or managing my fashion boutique in Spatial. This fractured multitasking, this aesthetic and functional context-switching, is likely a blueprint for future work. But it's not seamless yet. If Sony hadn't shut down PlayStation Home in 2015, I might already be living in the metaverse of my dreams.

THERE'S NO PLACE LIKE PLAYSTATION HOME

PlayStation Home was a virtual world platform created by Sony Computer Entertainment for the PlayStation 3. It launched in December 2008 as a free-to-play service that allowed players to create avatars and interact in a 3D social hub (Sony, 2008).

The goal was to create a persistent social space for players to meet, play mini-games, customise apartments, watch videos and attend live events. Despite early interest, *PlayStation Home* struggled to maintain its user base and was plagued by glitches, load times and a frustrating update schedule. Critics also pointed to a lack of meaningful content and innovation in its later years (Eurogamer, 2015).

Sony officially shut down the platform on 31 March 2015, citing declining users and shifting priorities. The rise of mobile-first social networks like Facebook and Twitter further undercut *PlayStation Home*'s appeal, as did the growing dominance of free-to-play games on other platforms (IGN, 2015).

But that's not the whole story.

Sony first announced the concept of *PlayStation Home* in 2005, envisioning a 3D social experience inspired by *Second Life*, *The Sims* and the rapidly evolving world of social media (Nutt, 2007). The platform would offer customisable avatars, shared social spaces and premium in-world purchases. The business model relied on microtransactions and sponsorships, anticipating what we now call virtual economies.

As you can probably tell, I loved it. All of it. But I understand why it didn't succeed. And frankly, I'm not sure this kind of pipeline would survive in today's 2025 economy of cross-platform services and decentralised user preferences.

Then, in 2021, *PlayStation Home* came back from the dead. Sort of.

Not through Sony, but through the community-led revival project, *Destination Home*. It's rough around the edges, as fan-led restorations often are, but its contributors are players and developers, not shareholders. This distinction matters. The community is not chasing KPIs or investor decks. It's building the world it wanted all along.

> **Business Takeaway:** Why *PlayStation Home* Failed as a "Metaverse"
>
> - Walled garden: PS3-only, no cross-platform capability
>
> - Glacial updates: limited live ops and content refresh cycles
>
> - Passive users: little incentive for UGC or narrative worldbuilding
>
> - No persistent economic model beyond micro-purchases

Today, we see Home's legacy in more open, persistent and user-led platforms. But that original blueprint still haunts me. I saw potential. PlayStation Home could have evolved

TABLE 9.3   Social Worlds before and after *PlayStation Home*

Platform	Launch Year	Ownership	Strengths	Weaknesses
PlayStation Home	2008	Sony	Polished graphics, PS3 integration	Glitchy, walled garden, slow updates
Habbo Hotel	2000	Sulake	Accessible, pixel charm	Moderation issues, Flash reliance
IMVU	2004	IMVU Inc.	Customisation, roleplay culture	Niche appeal, inconsistent UX
Avakin Life	2013	Lockwood	Mobile-first, fashion-led	Lacks strong narrative
Horizon Worlds	2021	Meta	VR integration	User friction, inconsistent UX
Destination Home	2021 (revival)	Community-led	Nostalgia, archival purpose	Not cross-platform, fan-dependent

into something as ubiquitous and genre-fluid as *Fortnite Creative* or *Minecraft Realms* if it had just crossed the console border (Table 9.3).

My experience of *PlayStation Home* remains rose-tinted. As a developer, I want to believe it was the prototype for every metaverse that followed. Projects like *Habbo*, *IMVU*, *Avakin Life* and *Horizon Worlds* all followed. But Sony wasn't ready. It wasn't prepared for what players or, what *metizens,* truly needed.

Could it work now? Maybe. Perhaps *Destination Home* will prove it, if it ever fully launches. I like to believe the original Home would have outgrown its service platform and become cross-platform, maybe even interoperable. A bit like how *Fortnite* lets you bounce between mobile, console and cloud seamlessly.

But maybe that idea is for the birds.

THE SWANSONG

How do we talk about death in video games? Is it even appropriate? In a medium filled with combat, kill counters and endless respawns, death has often been reduced to a gameplay loop rather than a moment of consequence. From the over-the-top theatrics of *Zero Wing* to the frenetic kill streaks of *Call of Duty*, we have become somewhat desensitised to our most sacred and inevitable act: the ability to expire (Galloway, 2006).

Yet some games do dare to tread into deeper emotional and philosophical terrain, making death not a mechanic, but a meditation. In my own 2016 short story collection on post-human futures, I explored the concept of digital death as both a narrative device and a lived experience (Vero, 2016). Characters found themselves outlived by their avatars, data shadows and AI descendants. Death wasn't just biological; it was technological.

In the business of games and metaverses, understanding how death is represented tells us a lot about how these experiences prepare us for meaning, memory and loss. It's not only about grief. It's about closure, ritual and what it means to carry on (Salen and Zimmerman, 2004). Here are some games that handle death meaningfully:

Shadow of the Colossus (2005): A young man named Wander defeats sixteen towering beasts to resurrect a girl named Mono. The game's muted palette, slow pacing and vast empty world all underscore themes of sacrifice and moral ambiguity. It asks: *What would you give to reverse death?* (Consalvo, 2009).

What Remains of Edith Finch (2017): A first-person narrative game where you uncover the stories of deceased family members. Each death is stylised differently, turning loss into layered, experiential storytelling. The game is essentially a eulogy (Bissell, 2018).

Life Is Strange (2015): Max Caulfield discovers she can rewind time. This mechanic forces the player to confront the emotional consequences of death repeatedly. It questions whether preventing death always leads to a better outcome (Chess, 2017).

Final Fantasy VII: Crisis Core (2007) and *Final Fantasy VII: Advent Children* (2005): These titles in the *Final Fantasy* universe stir genuine emotional grief. The loss of Aerith and Zack is handled carefully but dynamically. Cinematics, character arcs and music work in harmony to create tear-worthy moments. These are not just cutscenes; they are catharses (Allison, 2006).
thatgamecompany, known for its deeply emotional and minimalist design, has built a catalogue of games that explore life, death, connection and transcendence (Chen, 2012).

Journey (2012): The player, a robed figure, moves toward a glowing mountaintop. With no dialogue and no instructions, the game becomes a metaphor for the human journey through hardship, discovery and rebirth. Other players appear anonymously, sharing the path. When they disappear, it can feel like a death. The final ascent is mythic and spiritual (Leaver and Willson, 2016).

Flower (2009): The player controls the wind to guide petals through environments. Initially a celebration of nature, the game subtly shifts into commentary on environmental decay and industrialisation. Its ending, interpreted by many as symbolic rebirth, feels like a eulogy wrapped in serenity (Flanagan, 2009).

flOw (2006): A meditative evolution simulator. It focuses on survival and transformation rather than death explicitly, but the visual feedback loop invites contemplation of biological cycles (Bogost, 2007).

Sky: Children of the Light (2019): A social adventure in the clouds, where players help lost spirits ascend. Death here is release. It's purpose. It's ritual (Kultima, 2020).

Business Takeaway: Why Game Death Matters for the Metaverse

- Emotional design increases retention. Players stay in worlds where their emotional labour is valued.

- Games exploring death provide a blueprint for memorialisation tools and digital legacies in persistent worlds (Bell, 2019).

- As older demographics enter the metaverse, concepts like ritual, grief and afterlife gain cultural relevance.

Lost Odyssey: The Gold Standard of Digital Grief

Lost Odyssey (2007) is a lesser-known but emotionally profound Japanese role-playing game (JRPG) created by *Final Fantasy* creator Hironobu Sakaguchi's creative studio Mistwalker. It tells the story of Kaim Argonar, a member of a tribe of immortals who has lived for over a thousand years and who, at the game's beginning, has lost all memory of his past.

Kaim has two children, Mack and Cooke, who have inherited his immortality. His wife, Sarah Sisulart, is mortal and dies early in the game. Her death is not a plot point delivered in cutscene alone, it becomes a rupture in Kaim's emotional world, a mirror through which the player experiences the cost of immortality (Harper, 2011). Unable to accept Sarah's death, Kaim embarks on a journey not just of battle and political intrigue, but of healing. He visits the land of the dead, where he is able to communicate with Sarah's spirit. She tells him she has found peace. This moment, understated but powerful, initiates his reconciliation with grief. It also models how persistent digital spaces might one day create opportunities for users to engage in symbolic acts of closure (Leaver and Willson, 2016).

Later in the story, Kaim meets Lirum, a young girl dying from an incurable illness. She is the daughter of Tolten, a political figure. As Lirum deteriorates, Kaim promises her father that he will help her pass peacefully into the afterlife. In this act, he becomes something more than immortal, he becomes a guide between life and death. Lirum's death is not avoided. Instead, it is marked by compassion, ritual and presence.

Through these scenes, *Lost Odyssey* invites players to witness and participate in a philosophy of care. Kaim's transformation is one of acceptance, not power. His children also begin to understand their place in a world that ages and dies around them. The game constructs a contemplative loop between player, character and world, a rare feat in game design (Nieborg and Poell, 2018).

> **Metaverse Insight:**
> *Lost Odyssey* presents a potential model for digital mourning, avatar retirement or memory-preserving rituals in persistent online spaces. As our digital lives become more enmeshed with our emotional ones, we will need metaphors and systems that help us process loss. We'll learn more about this later in the chapter.

The implications for metaverse design are clear. In worlds where avatars persist beyond their players, where social hubs act as both celebratory and commemorative spaces, we must look to narrative models that treat death with nuance. *Lost Odyssey* shows that death in digital worlds does not have to be about erasure. It can be about meaning.

Games have long flirted with the edge of death. But the most mature titles walk us over it, let us stand on the brink, and help us look back with something close to grace.

In metaverse design, this ability to embed *meaningful endings* may be just as powerful as offering infinite lives.

EARNING A LIVING

I won't deny that I'm a good, no great dancer, but I'm also pretty cool at *Dance Dance Revolution* (1998). This game is not about anything other than choosing a mode and dancing to music in time with the corresponding steps. Dance games, also known as exergames, have been shown to improve balance, coordination and cardiovascular health, which can reduce the risk of falls and other age-related conditions (Oh and Yang, 2010).

Video games that require problem-solving, decision-making and quick reaction times have been shown to improve cognitive function, including memory, attention and processing speed. This is particularly important as we age, since cognitive abilities tend to decline (Granic, Lobel and Engels, 2014). If, like me, you are an avid player of match-three or puzzle games, this could be good news for your ageing brain (Table 9.4).

> **Insight**: Serious games were never just about health – they were market expansion tools that positioned play as productivity.

Socialisation is also critical. Engaging with others can mitigate the risk of developing diseases such as Alzheimer's in later life. Some video games and metaverse platforms can provide a space for social interaction, which is particularly beneficial for older adults who may be isolated or lonely. Multiplayer games can foster a sense of community and connection (De Schutter and Brown, 2016).

Need to burn cortisol? Chronic stress is harmful and can contribute to hypertension and weight gain. Because video games (and to some extent spending time in the metaverse) can offer stress relief and mental escape, they provide a useful counter to these risks (Peng, Lin and Crouse, 2011).

The narrative, gameplay and entertainment value of games can also provide a source of joy and personal fulfilment. Especially for completionists like me, this is more than just fun. It's purpose. It got me thinking about the Nintendo DS. When I worked there in the early 2000s, I noticed a major trend in Japan where cooking games, brain trainers and even lifestyle titles like *Jamie Oliver's What's Cooking?* were being played not just by children, but by adults and retirees. This was a turning point.

TABLE 9.4 The Brain Game Boom – Who Played and Why?

Era	Region	Audience	Platform	Purpose
Early 2000s	Japan	Adults, seniors	Nintendo DS	Cognitive stimulation
Mid-2000s	Global	Casual gamers	Wii Fit	Physical activity
2010–2020	US and Europe	Health-conscious	Mobile apps	Brain training and mindfulness
2020s	Global	Cross-generational	Switch, mobile	Habit building, longevity

Dr Ryuta Kawashima, a Japanese neuroscientist, became central to this movement. His research focuses on cognitive function in ageing populations. He has conducted extensive studies on how cognitive training, particularly through interactive methods like games, can support mental acuity in older adults (Kawashima, 2003).

Kawashima was the key figure behind *Brain Age: Train Your Brain in Minutes a Day!* for the Nintendo DS. The game became a commercial sensation, selling more than 19 million copies globally and helping to legitimise the "serious games" genre (Nintendo, 2018). *Brain Age* included puzzles based on Kawashima's research, aiming to exercise memory, maths and logic through daily play.

He is also the author of several books, including *Train Your Brain: 60 Days to a Better Brain* and *Train Your Brain More: 60 Days to an Even Better Brain* (Kawashima, 2005; Kawashima, 2007). At Tohoku University, he leads the Department of Functional Brain Imaging and has received numerous awards for his work on neuroplasticity and interactive learning in later life.

Nintendo's strategic pivot with *Brain Age* was simple. They wanted to reach an audience beyond traditional gamers, including older adults, educators and curious non-gamers. It worked. It also helped establish Nintendo as a leader in wellness-oriented play.

> Business Takeaway: What Made Brain Age Work?

- Based on real neuroscience
- Daily short bursts of play
- Clear feedback loops ("Brain Age" scoring)
- Affordable hardware (Nintendo DS)
- Relatable UI for older users
- Marketed as a lifestyle product – not a game

Nintendo made brain training a cultural ritual, not just a digital product.

Since then, Nintendo has expanded its portfolio with the *Wii Fit* series and *Ring Fit Adventure*, which blend physical movement with game design. These products show that the gamification of health is not a gimmick – it is a long-term strategy (Nieborg and Poell, 2018) (Table 9.5).

TABLE 9.5   Serious Games vs Brain Training Apps

Feature	Serious Games	Brain Training Apps
Core format	Playful, immersive	Functional, test-based
Narrative	Often story-driven	Minimal or absent
Examples	*Ring Fit, Brain Age*	*Lumosity, Elevate*
Target Demographic	All ages, families	Adults, ageing populations
Monetisation	Console purchase, retail	Subscriptions, freemium

Business Takeaway: The most effective serious games don't feel like lessons. They feel like play with purpose.

Other platforms followed suit. Here are a few examples of serious games designed for cognitive health and brain training:

- *Lumosity* (2007): Web-based platform from Lumos Labs featuring daily cognitive exercises.

- *Elevate* (2014): Mobile app by Elevate Labs, focusing on communication, memory and processing.

- *Fit Brains Trainer* (2013): Created by Rosetta Stone, offering personalisation and progress tracking.

- *Peak* (2014): Developed by Peaklabs, featuring brain games backed by neuroscientific input.

While the clinical effectiveness of these platforms remains debated, they offer a low-barrier, engaging way to support mental health and stimulation into old age (Simons et al., 2016).

EVERYTHING MUST GO

I had no idea when I started working in game development that I would need to have a plan. We have all seen the tropes in entertainment, especially movies, where one person, usually a man, reaches out to another and begs him to burn all the evidence of his porn stash or insert your most embarrassing item here in case of an emergency. Yet this joke is on all of us, because very few of us, myself included, have made any kind of plan for our digital death. Why would we? We've spent years turning our lives into a narrative of zeros and ones. What's the point of deleting it now?

When I hosted one of the first metaverse events back in 2020, I wanted to explore where we had come from in the great digital shift of the last 20 or 30 years and where we were heading next. After all, I will be one of hundreds of thousands of people worldwide who will experience a fully digital end of life. I will expire physically and, eventually, as a digital footprint. The physical part is easy to grasp. But if I don't act now, my digital self could outlive me and become a liability.

In my 30 years of working in digital media and tech, I've accumulated more digital waste than I care to admit. Old rants on Blogger, a Doris Wishman retrospective on Fugu, dead Hotmail accounts full of heartbreak, and a Myspace profile drenched in nu metal and George A. Romero references; it's all still out there. My digital trail also includes NFTs, digital wallets, MP3 collections and CSVs of login credentials. The metaverse age demands that I start cleaning up, not just for me, but for those I leave behind (Leaver and Willson, 2016).

A positive legacy is a tidy one. I often tell audiences in my talks about working in a game studio: imagine you're hit by a bus. Have you documented your changes? Committed them? Are you wearing clean underwear? It's a joke, but also not a joke. This "bus insurance" is what makes continuity possible. In games and in metaverses, if your work isn't documented, it disappears with you.

> **Business Takeaway:** Digital Death Checklist
>
> Before the bus hits you, here's what to consider:
>
> - Have you documented your accounts and passwords?
> - Do your beneficiaries know how to access your digital wallet(s)?
> - Have you appointed a digital executor in your will?
> - Is your cloud storage labelled, sorted and named clearly?
> - Are your creative works archived or backed up somewhere accessible?
> - Have you left instructions for deleting or memorialising your social media?
>
> **Pro tip**: Use a password manager with legacy access, and update your digital will every two years.

My digital assets, from social media to email to online banking, have tangible value. Planning my digital legacy ensures these assets are distributed properly (Bell, 2019). It also protects sensitive data: private memories, photos, videos, notes or creative projects I may not want shared. Services like Google already warn us when our cloud limits are approaching. But what about the long tail of forgotten files? Who deletes those?

Even small digital wallets can become confusing legacies. I have enough Litecoin to maybe buy a weak coffee. But who inherits that? These are practical questions in a time when crypto, NFTs and virtual goods are real commodities.

Will the metaverse take care of me in return for the years I've given it? Possibly. And what about games? I've devoted my life to them. As I approach the other end of my career and my time, I wonder if games will help provide me with a good death (Table 9.6).

Leaving behind a digital legacy unintentionally, for example, on Facebook, highlights how deeply technology is integrated into our lives. Many people's profiles remain live long

TABLE 9.6   Grief, Games and Digital Ghosts

Digital Realm	Posthumous Presence	Cultural Impact
Facebook	Memorialised profiles	Public grieving, legacy timeline
Steam/Xbox/PSN	Inactive gamer tags	Lost achievements, idle digital identities
MMOs (*e.g. Final Fantasy XIV*)	In-game funerals	Collective rituals and avatar memorials
Cloud storage (Google, iCloud)	Auto-deletion or orphaned data	Family confusion, lost assets

after they're gone, raising issues about digital privacy, consent and ownership (Stokes, 2019).

Culturally, it also changes how we grieve. In the past, mourning was private. Now we light digital candles on Facebook and post Instagram tributes to those we've lost. It opens up new ways of sharing, but also complicates how we process loss. The online wake is becoming as significant as the physical one.

> **Design Insight**: As metaverses grow, platforms must build systems for digital death, not just onboarding.

Set those digital candles for 2053. Because everything, even our grief, is now online.

THE VAULTVERSE

Perhaps after I die, the metaverse will be my columbarium, a place to store my digital ashes, memories, assets and hidden treasures, encoded in ways only the curious or cryptographic could uncover.

As a virtual space where users can interact with people, AI and digital objects, the metaverse has the potential to meet real human needs in later life.

Social connection is one such area. As people age, they may experience greater isolation, particularly when mobility is reduced or social circles narrow. The metaverse can offer a persistent platform for companionship, shared experiences and community – from game nights and concerts to virtual tourism, all accessible without ever leaving the home (Marston and Shore, 2022).

> **Business Takeaway:**
> The most overlooked demographic in metaverse strategy is the ageing user. Designing for longevity, digital literacy and emotional care isn't niche, it's future-proofing.

The healthcare applications are equally promising. Virtual consultations with doctors or therapists could become part of a regular metaverse itinerary, especially for those living in remote areas or with limited mobility (Gorini and Riva, 2008). Meanwhile, smart assistants embedded in the metaverse could facilitate grocery orders, medication refills or even booking a digital car to get you from your metahome to your metaspace clinic.

Beyond utility, enrichment and entertainment remain a core offering: virtual museums, live performances, art galleries, historical reenactments and interactive storytelling. These experiences don't just fill time; they expand it, offering cultural and emotional engagement that might otherwise be inaccessible (Dionisio, Burns and Gilbert, 2013).

This got me thinking about the role of AI, chatbots and natural language processing in combating digital loneliness. Like Marella, the lonely millennial in *Prince of Tokyo* (Vero, 2016), or Will Smith's Granny in *I, Robot*, AI systems as assistants may one day keep us company, not out of dystopian necessity, but compassionate design.

Chatbots can already supplement care. AI companions such as ChatGPT can provide reminders, suggest activities, help navigate chronic health needs and prompt outreach to loved ones. For someone ageing alone, they are less about replacing humans and more about bridging the gap between solitude and sociality (Ta, Esper and Lerner, 2021).

AI assistants can also help seniors maintain a sense of purpose. They might suggest ways to engage in community life, reconnect with hobbies or even contribute to citizen science or digital art. When loneliness becomes chronic, digital companionship can be a lifeline (Neves, Franz and Judges, 2019).

Yet this landscape is not without risks. For Generation X and beyond, digital end-of-life poses new questions:

- Who owns our avatars after we die?

- Who can access or shut down our data?

- What happens to our AI companions, or the digital representations of ourselves?

The speed of technological change can be alienating. Not everyone is digitally literate, and not everyone wants to be. But the potential for creating meaningful, intentional and compassionate experiences at the end of life is enormous.

Design Takeaway: Digital Legacy is a Feature, Not a Flaw

Users will ask: *"What happens to my avatar/data after I die?"*
   Platforms should answer: *"We've built something meaningful for that."*

- Tools for digital will-making

- Memorialisation options

- Ethical data governance

- Legacy transfer mechanisms (assets, NFTs, accounts)

The metaverse may become more than a retirement home. It might become a memory garden, a living will or a refuge for the soul, provided we design it that way. It's up to us to determine whether we use it to preserve presence or erase it. Ultimately, how we navigate this new terrain will depend on personal values, comfort with technology and cultural openness to hybrid ways of living and dying.

I think we're going to be okay.

REFERENCES

Allison, A. (2006) *Millennial Monsters: Japanese Toys and the Global Imagination.* Berkeley, CA: University of California Press.

Bell, M. (2019) 'Digital Memorialisation in Gaming Worlds', *Journal of Virtual Worlds Research,* 12(2), pp. 1–17.

Bissell, T. (2018) *Extra Lives: Why Video Games Matter.* New York, NY: Vintage.

Boellstorff, T. (2008) *Coming of Age in Second Life: An Anthropologist Explores the Virtually Human*. Princeton, NJ: Princeton University Press.

Bogost, I. (2007) *Persuasive Games: The Expressive Power of Videogames*. Cambridge, MA: MIT Press.

Chen, J. (2012) 'Designing Journey', *Game Developers Conference*. Available at: https://gdcvault.com

Chess, S. (2017) *Ready Player Two: Women Gamers and Designed Identity*. Minneapolis, MN: University of Minnesota Press.

Consalvo, M. (2009) *Cheating: Gaining Advantage in Videogames*. Cambridge, MA: MIT Press.

De Schutter, B. and Brown, J.A. (2016) 'Digital Games as a Source of Enjoyment in Later Life', *Games and Culture*, 11(1–2), pp. 28–52.

Dionisio, J.D.N., Burns, W.G. and Gilbert, R. (2013) '3D Virtual Worlds and the Metaverse: Current Status and Future Possibilities', *ACM Computing Surveys*, 45(3), pp. 1–38.

Eurogamer (2015) *Why PlayStation Home Failed*. Available at: https://www.eurogamer.net

Flanagan, M. (2009) *Critical Play: Radical Game Design*. Cambridge, MA: MIT Press.

Galloway, A.R. (2006) *Gaming: Essays on Algorithmic Culture*. Minneapolis, MN: University of Minnesota Press.

Gorini, A. and Riva, G. (2008) 'Virtual Reality in Anxiety Disorders: The Past and the Future', *Expert Review of Neurotherapeutics*, 8(2), pp. 215–233.

Granic, I., Lobel, A. and Engels, R.C.M.E. (2014) 'The Benefits of Playing Video Games', *American Psychologist*, 69(1), pp. 66–78.

Habbo Hotel. (2000). PC [Game]. Finland: Sulake Corporation.

Harper, T. (2011) 'Immortal Loss: Representations of Grief in Lost Odyssey', *Game Studies*, 11(2).

Hodent, C. (2018) *The Gamer's Brain: How Neuroscience and UX Can Impact Video Game Design*. Boca Raton, FL: CRC Press.

IGN (2015) *Sony Shuts Down PlayStation Home*. Available at: https://www.ign.com

Kawashima, R. (2003) 'Reading Aloud and Arithmetic Calculation Improve Frontal Function of People with Dementia', *Geriatrics & Gerontology International*, 3(1), pp. 29–31.

Kawashima, R. (2005) *Train Your Brain: 60 Days to a Better Brain*. Tokyo: Kumon Publishing.

Kawashima, R. (2007) *Train Your Brain More: 60 Days to an Even Better Brain*. Tokyo: Kumon Publishing.

Kim, A.J. (2018). *Game Thinking: Innovate Smarter & Drive Deep Engagement with Design Techniques from Hit Games*. Palo Alto, CA: Game Thinking Press.

Kultima, A. (2020) 'Ritual and Social Play in Sky: Children of the Light', *DiGRA Nordic 2020 Conference Proceedings*.

Leaver, T. and Willson, M. (2016) 'Social Media and the Digital Afterlife', *New Media & Society*, 18(3), pp. 267–282.

Lockwood Publishing (2022) *Avakin Life Community Data Report*. Nottingham: Lockwood.

Marston, H.R. and Shore, L. (2022) 'How Digital Interventions Can Support Older Adults', *Digital Health*, 8, pp. 1–11.

McCrindle, M. (2020). *Generation Alpha: Understanding the Next Generation*. Sydney: McCrindle Research.

Microsoft. (2016). *Minecraft: Education Edition Launch Details*. Available at: https://education.minecraft.net

Neves, B.B., Franz, R.L. and Judges, R. (2019) 'Can Digital Companions Combat Loneliness?', *The Gerontologist*, 59(1), pp. 85–95.

Nieborg, D.B. and Poell, T. (2018) 'The Platformization of Cultural Production', *Social Media + Society*, 4(3), pp. 1–12.

Nintendo (2018) 'Nintendo DS Software Sales Data'. Available at: https://www.nintendo.co.jp/ir/en/sales/software.html

Nutt, C. (2007) *PlayStation Home: GDC Announcement Coverage*. Gamasutra. Available at: https://www.gamasutra.com

Oh, Y. and Yang, S. (2010) 'Defining Exergames and Exergaming', *Proceedings of Meaningful Play*, East Lansing, MI.

Peng, W., Lin, J.-H. and Crouse, J. (2011) 'Is Playing Exergames Really Exercising? A Meta-Analysis of Energy Expenditure in Active Video Games', *Cyberpsychology, Behavior, and Social Networking*, 14(11), pp. 681–688.

Salen, K. and Zimmerman, E. (2004) *Rules of Play: Game Design Fundamentals*. Cambridge, MA: MIT Press.

Second Life. (2003). PC [Game]. USA: Linden Lab.

Simons, D.J., et al. (2016) 'Do "Brain-Training" Programs Work?', *Psychological Science in the Public Interest*, 17(3), pp. 103–186.

Sony (2008) *Official PlayStation Blog: Welcome to Home*. Available at: https://blog.playstation.com

Statista (2023) *Number of Minecraft Players Worldwide as of 2023*. Available at: https://www.statista.com

Stokes, P. (2019) 'Ghosts in the Machine: Do the Dead Live On in Facebook?', *Philosophy & Technology*, 32(1), pp. 1–15.

Ta, V., Esper, S. and Lerner, M. (2021) 'Chatbots and Older Adults: A Review of Design Recommendations', *Proceedings of the 2021 CHI Conference on Human Factors in Computing Systems*, pp. 1–13.

Vero, K. (2016) *Prince of Tokyo*. Independently Published. Available at: https://www.amazon.com/Prince-Tokyo-Kelly-Vero/dp/1981035796

Yee, N. (2020). *Player Segments Based on Gaming Motivations: An Analysis of 400,000 Gamers*. Game Developers Conference, August.

CHAPTER 10

Introduction to User Experience

THE TERRIBLE DOGFISH: WHY MILO DROWNED IN A SEA OF WALLED GARDENS

Project Milo (2009) was a highly anticipated interactive video game project developed by Lionhead Studios and its founder, Peter Molyneux, for the Microsoft Kinect platform. The project was unveiled at E3 2009 and generated significant buzz due to its innovative use of the Kinect's motion sensing technology and its focus on emotional engagement and interactivity (Eurogamer, 2009). I remember exactly where I was when this was announced. I was glued to E3's live stream and I shook my head in disbelief, what a time this was to be alive, I thought. In this age of AI and NLP in 2023, I can't quite believe that *Project Milo* never saw the light of day.

Milo was a vision too early, and too locked in. It asked us to feel across hardware boundaries that didn't exist, and that's the point. What Milo lacked was interoperability: the ability to exist and evolve across different systems, platforms and devices – the missing limb of emotional AI. In today's metaverse conversations, interoperability isn't a buzzword, it's the connective tissue that binds persistent identity, emotional engagement and meaningful interaction (Interoperability Working Group, 2022).

The premise of the game was to create a virtual AI child named Milo, who players could interact with using the Kinect's voice and gesture recognition capabilities. The game would have used advanced AI and machine learning technologies to allow Milo to learn and adapt to the player's behaviours and preferences, making the interactions more personalised and meaningful (Edge, 2010). The guiding principles behind *Project Milo* were to create a new type of emotional connection between players and virtual characters, push the boundaries of what was possible with motion sensing technology and create an experience that would blur the lines between reality and virtual reality.

Project Milo offered a vision of an imminent future: one where adaptive technologies like gesture recognition let us connect (or should that be *Kinect*?) with virtual beings. The

DOI: 10.1201/9781003615248-10

avatars, AI and emotional interactivity we now crave were so prescient, the world simply wasn't ready.

It's difficult to say for certain whether *Project Milo* would survive in 2023, as the project was cancelled over a decade ago and the video game industry has evolved significantly since then. However, the concept of creating a virtual AI companion with emotional engagement and interactivity could still have relevance today, especially with the advances in artificial intelligence and machine learning technologies (Vincent, 2021). In recent years, we have seen the emergence of new AI-powered virtual assistants, such as Siri, Alexa and Google Assistant, which are designed to understand and respond to natural language commands and queries. Milo couldn't exist across systems, but in the metaverse, he'd have to, and technology would be waiting to support him (Ball, 2022).

Furthermore, the popularity of virtual and augmented reality technologies has also grown significantly in recent years, providing new ways to create immersive and engaging interactive experiences (Gartner, 2023). If the technology and AI capabilities needed to fully realise the vision of *Project Milo* have advanced enough, it is possible that a similar project could be successfully developed and released in 2023 or beyond.

Project Milo was over the moment the word "games" was used. Though envisioned as a unique video game experience where players could interact with a virtual AI child named Milo, the flaw was in its limitations. Milo was part of the game, and this game wasn't that good. The goal of the game was to create an emotional connection between the player and Milo, and to allow players to engage with the AI character in a more natural and immersive way than was previously possible (IGN, 2012).

Players would have been able to have conversations with Milo, teach him new things, play games with him, and watch him grow and develop over time. The problem was, by the time the development had come to an apex, maybe by the time the development had come to an apex, around Proof of Concept (POC) or MVP/Vertical Slice (early playable demo); Milo wasn't that much fun, or at least not in my recollection.

Though this game would also have featured a branching narrative system, where the player's choices and interactions with Milo would impact the story and the character's development, it was more like Haley Joel Osment's character in Artificial Intelligence (AI), staccato and overthought. Though interacting with Milo would have created a sense of agency and responsibility for the player, they would have felt accountable for Milo's well-being and emotional growth (Carstens and Beck, 2017).

Business Takeaway: No Interoperability = Metaverse Failure *Project Milo* failed not just because it wasn't fun: but because it couldn't scale.

Lessons for Interoperability:

- Locked platforms limit emotional design.
- AI companions demand persistent identity.
- Cross-device experience is critical for engagement.

In the end, the ideal Milo might actually have been closer to Cortana, another AI (but fictional and backstoried). In the *Halo* video game series, Cortana is a central character and serves as the AI companion to the protagonist, Master Chief. In the story, Cortana was created by Dr Catherine Halsey as part of the Spartan-II programme, which produced elite soldiers with enhanced physical and mental abilities (Bungie, 2001, p. 343 Industries, 2012).

In the game, this wonderful (yet objectified) Cortana assists Master Chief by providing tactical information, analysing enemy behaviour and hacking into systems. She also serves as a voice in Master Chief's ear, offering guidance and emotional support. Over time, Cortana develops a complex relationship with Master Chief and grapples with her own identity and existence as an AI (Lynch, 2021). At her core, she is not only combat support but also the brain of the game.

What the developers possibly wanted from Milo was for him to be the heart of gameplay. But that wasn't going to happen. Milo was designed to be emotionally engaging, learning and adapting to players over time via machine learning algorithms. Yet he never reached the usability or system compatibility required to scale.

From Master Chief to Microsoft's much lauded assistant, Cortana has also failed to meet the changing needs of operating systems in an AI dawn. From 2014 to 2023, Cortana, primarily a Microsoft voice assistant, provided assistance through connected smart/Microsoft devices. While she could process natural language, she could not provide the deep, emotional conversation that Milo envisioned. Replaced by Copilot, the less catchy, less relatable version of Cortana who carried enough fictional weight from her gaming origins. Let us not forget Clippy (1996), whose real name was Clippit, whose real-real name was Office Assistant and what he did with his Windows 97 shenanigans onwards. Cortana brought the cool. RIP (Table 10.1).

While *Project Milo* was not specifically designed with the metaverse in mind, its core concept, an emotionally intelligent AI companion, remains relevant. Some critics argued Milo was a solution looking for a problem. Others saw it as ahead of its time: a sandbox for emotionally engaging digital presence (Totilo, 2010).

If the metaverse becomes a shared persistent space for interaction, we'll need Milos, not locked in, but free to move with us. These companions could enhance emotional continuity, act as social bridges or even become co-creators of meaning.

Project Milo wasn't just a failed game. It was emotional design, trapped in a closed system. Today, our interactions with AI companions, from Siri to NPCs, demand not just intelligence, but portability. If the metaverse is to succeed, it must overcome what Milo

TABLE 10.1 *Project Milo* vs the Future

Feature	*Project Milo* (2009)	Metaverse Needs (2023+)
Platform	Xbox 360 only	Multi-platform, cloud-native
Interaction	Kinect (gesture + voice)	Natural language + emotional sensing
Persistence	Limited, local	Cloud-based, persistent ID
Emotional Design	Experimental, siloed	Central to UX across contexts
Interoperability	None	Critical

couldn't: emotional engagement that moves with us. Interoperability isn't optional: it's the architecture of meaningful presence.

REFERENCES

Ball, M. (2022) *The Metaverse: And How It Will Revolutionize Everything*. New York, NY: Liveright Publishing Corporation.

Carstens, D. and Beck, L. (2017) 'Emotional AI and Player Agency in Narrative Games', *Journal of Game Narrative*, 5(2), pp. 23–34.

Cortana (2014) Windows Operating System [Software]. USA: Microsoft.

Edge (2010) 'The Story Behind Project Milo', *Edge Online*, 4 June. Available at: https://www.edge-online.com/news/story-behind-project-milo/

Eurogamer (2009) 'Molyneux Unveils Milo and Kate', *Eurogamer*, 1 June. Available at: https://www.eurogamer.net/molyneux-unveils-milo-and-kate

Gartner (2023) 'Emerging Tech Impact Radar for 2023', *Gartner Insights*. Available at: https://www.gartner.com

Halo: Combat Evolved (2001) Bungie [Game]. USA: Microsoft Game Studios.

Halo 4 (2012) 343 Industries [Game]. USA: Microsoft Studios.

IGN (2012) 'Project Milo and the Decline of Kinect', *IGN*, 10 October. Available at: https://www.ign.com/articles/2012/10/10/project-milo-and-the-decline-of-kinect

Interoperability Working Group (2022) *Metaverse Standards Forum: Interoperability Overview*. Available at: https://www.metaverse-standards.org/

Lynch, D. (2021) 'From Cortana to Clippy: A History of Microsoft's Virtual Assistants', *The Verge*, 18 August. Available at: https://www.theverge.com

Project Milo (2009) XBox 360 [Game]. USA: Microsoft Studios.

Totilo, S. (2010) 'Project Milo Cancelled?', *Kotaku*, 27 May. Available at: https://www.kotaku.com.au

Vincent, J. (2021) 'The State of AI Companions', *The Verge*, 21 December. Available at: https://www.theverge.com

CHAPTER 11

Interoperability

THE DRIVE THRU

The metaverse is small when you think about it. It's the size of its user base and that doesn't even come close to how many people play *Call of Duty Mobile*, *Minecraft*, or who have a Disney+ account (Newzoo, 2023). So why are we trying so hard to build interoperability in everything that we do? Convenience mostly, for we live in inconvenient times. We are still human. We have to get up in the morning and go to work (even if we work from home), we have to walk the dog or feed the bunnies. We have to take our children to school, and we need to put food on the table. Interoperability should be making these tasks ever easier. But what is interoperability except for being a really big word in this really small technology town.

Interoperability refers to the ability of different systems and technologies to communicate and work with each other seamlessly (IEEE, 2022). In modern life, interoperability has become increasingly important due to the widespread use of technology and the need for different systems and devices to work together efficiently.

A few years ago, the Internet of Things (IoT) was the big buzzword du jour. IoT is a network of physical devices, vehicles, appliances and other items that are embedded with sensors, software and connectivity, which enable them to connect and exchange data over the internet (Ashton, 2009; Atzori, Iera and Morabito, 2010). These devices can be anything from smart home appliances, wearables, industrial equipment to smart cars and more.

The practice behind IoT is to create a seamless connection between the physical world and the digital world. The devices in an IoT network collect data from their environment and use it to perform various functions, such as adjusting their behaviour, sending alerts or triggering other devices or systems. This data can also be sent to the cloud for further analysis, processing and storage (Gubbi et al., 2013).

IoT devices communicate using wireless technologies like Wi-Fi, Bluetooth or mobile networks. This creates a mesh of interconnected devices that can be monitored remotely from anywhere. In theory, this sounds very James Bond. In practice, it's mostly clunky and it's mostly crap. It is not as joined up as you might think and it's eminently hackable

DOI: 10.1201/9781003615248-11

(Borgia, 2014). The manufacturers of IoT devices don't put as much effort into their applications to control the device or product as they do for the product itself, resulting in clunky user experiences and systems cobbled together from mismatched updates and half-built companion apps, making them less reliable than the devices themselves. Also, a lot of these applications and controllers are nice to have rather than need to have: manufacturers seldom see the difference between these two things. I can think of countless mobile phone apps which are native to the handset you've just bought but that are completely useless and take up more space in the phone than is necessary.

IoT has the potential to revolutionise the way we live and work, making our lives easier, safer and more efficient. Here comes the blue sky dreaming versus the reality of IoT (Gartner, 2023) (Table 11.1).

Are these examples really interoperable? Not very often. Even some of the big tech corporations have got this one wrong and need us to add three apps to our phone when one "hub" would suffice (Interoperability Working Group, 2022, Metaverse Standards Forum, 2023). Interoperability: it's important that we get this right; if we can, we will be able to enhance productivity through:

- *Improved efficiency*: Allowing different systems to communicate and work together, this can result in improved efficiency and productivity. In healthcare, interoperability between electronic health record systems could enable doctors and other healthcare providers to easily access patient data from different sources, which can lead to more accurate diagnoses and better treatment outcomes (HealthIT.gov, 2022).

- *Reduced costs*: Interoperability could perhaps help reduce costs by eliminating the need for custom integrations between different systems. Instead, standard interfaces and protocols can be used to ensure that different systems can communicate and exchange data seamlessly (IEEE, 2022).

- *Enhanced user experience*: Could interoperability improve user experience by making it easier for people to use different systems and devices? Of course! The interoperability between different smart home devices might allow users to control all their devices using a single app, rather than having to use multiple apps for each device (Borgia, 2014).

- *Innovation:* Fostering innovation using interoperability means allowing different systems and technologies to work together and share data. This can enable the development of new products and services that were not possible before (Ball, 2022).

TABLE 11.1   How IoT Should Work

Use Case	IoT Promise	Interoperability Reality
Smart homes	Single app control of all devices.	Most require separate apps.
Smart cities	Unified traffic and energy data.	Silos across city systems.
Wearables	Physical items that track activity and turn it into data.	Data protection becomes an issue across dashboards.
Industrial IoT	Monitor and control devices across manufacturing, logistics and agriculture.	Training across language and culture is difficult to sustain.

When I make products such as video games, I try to think about the bigger picture. In the previous section I explained the concept of Game Thinking and how designing for the player is much better than designing for a faceless corporate paymaster. The same goes for the metaverse. When I work with brands I try to get them to stop thinking about the data, and the image or the optic, but to get them thinking about discoverability (which is a form of optics) and to get them thinking about the metizen, before anything else. True interoperability will shape how the metaverse grows, not just how it functions. The moment users leave our product, we have to assume they aren't coming back.

Business Takeaway: Interoperability Drives Business Value

- Interoperability = retention: it keeps users within your ecosystem
- Interoperability = scalability: one asset, many touchpoints.
- Interoperability = protection: users don't feel locked in.
- Without it? You're selling blue party hats that disappear in customs.

THE BLUE FAIRY

Back in October 2021, I did a dumb thing. After writing a paper about a common framework for luxury and art (Vero, 2021), I then went on to secure it as a world trading standard for Non-Fungible Tokens (NFTs). Wow, that really put the cat among the pigeons. How could I try and standardise something in a decentralised space? I did it because I was mad, hopping mad about the millions of dollars people had spent on nothing more than jpegs even though I know art is worth what people are prepared to pay (Kastrenakes, 2021). Suddenly, things that had no tangible value outside of their own ego created a bubble effect that enabled a whole world of grifters and hustlers to develop a vapourware system of creating and selling NFTs, and that just was not ok for me.

NFTs are a type of digital asset that are stored on a blockchain and can represent ownership of a unique digital item, such as artwork, music or virtual real estate (Nadini et al., 2021). NFTs can be bought, sold and traded just like physical assets, and the ownership of the digital item can be transferred across different platforms and worlds (Dowling, 2022). That last section must have got your attention. Did it? I'll type it again: *transferred across different platforms and worlds*. But the phrasing here is "can be" because it's really hard to find anything that is truly interoperable in most NFTs.

NFTs need to be, like Collodi's *Pinocchio* (1881), real. Like Geppetto, we, the consumer, have to believe that what we have bought has some value. When I developed my model for this, I had one question: What makes value? And it was a balance of commonsense (Figure 11.1).

In the world of art and luxury, where provenance, authorship and exclusivity have always underpinned value, we can't afford to treat metadata as an afterthought anymore. It's the spine of everything. When we talk about digital objects, especially NFTs, the conversation can't just be about scarcity or blockchain vanity. We need to talk about the stuff

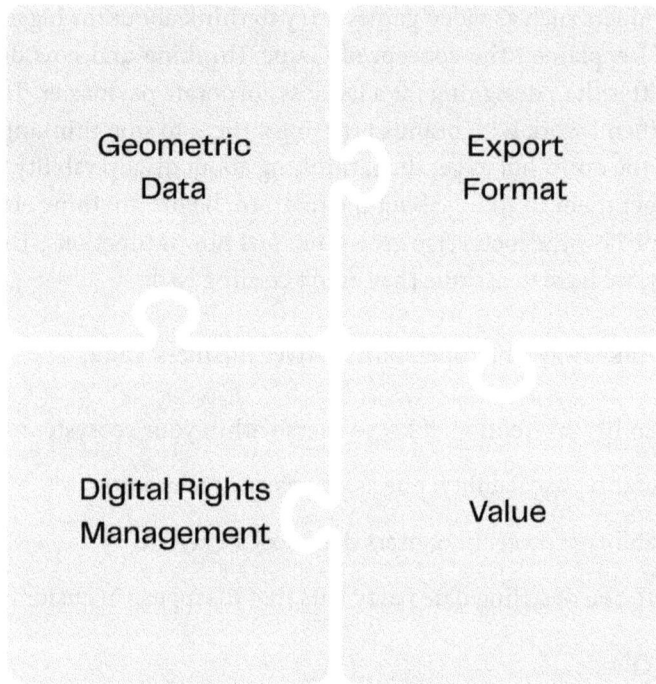

FIGURE 11.1   My paper "Luxury and Art: A Common Framework for Metadata in Practice" 2021.

under the hood: Geometric Data (what the object is), Export Data (where it's been and how it's travelled or will travel if we're creating it) and Digital Rights Management (who owns it, who touches it and who has permission to transform it). This is the critical foundation of value in the digital space. Without it, your NFT is just a JPEG with ambition.

If we don't bake that metadata into the object from the start, and more importantly, make it interoperable and readable across systems, we're selling vapour. True value in the metaverse or Web3 world isn't about hype; it's about persistence, trust and utility. If we want art and luxury to thrive in a digital-first economy, we need a common metadata framework that doesn't just support the object; it tells its story, its journey and its rules of engagement. That's not just good practice: it's the bare minimum.

As virtual worlds and metaverses have risen from practically nowhere in the last few years, virtual real estate has become a valuable digital asset. Players and investors have been able to purchase virtual land and buildings within these worlds, which can then be used for various purposes such as hosting events, selling virtual goods or even as a source of income (Dionisio, Burns and Gilbert, 2013). Hosting events seems to be the number one reason for buying a parcel or two of land in these virtual worlds. Some, most or all virtual worlds and games have their own currency systems, which can be used to purchase digital goods and services within the game. This virtual currency can sometimes be exchanged for real-world currency, allowing players to earn real money from their in-game activities through wallets and storage facilities (Lehdonvirta and Castronova, 2014). But it's confusing and about as useful as yelling "Bitcoin is gonna hit $150,000 in a decade" back in 2015. These universes that call themselves metaverses are many and not a single world has been interoperable. Developers have to keep the lights on, regardless. They have to believe that the next transaction will be the one. And for the land hosts, event planners and metizens? They get private and unfettered access without a single Blue Fairy to wish upon. No interoperability needed! In a world of decentralisation, who really has the keys (or should I say combination number) to the vault? AI Agents? That's a whole other book.

When we're trying to create products that we want everyone to access and utilise as they move through video games and metaverses, should we use regulations in an unregulated space to ensure ubiquity but also scarcity, or longevity but also viral, meme-approved transience?

MORE THAN MONEY

Interoperability also gives us strong use cases inside public policies and civic organisation of people and official capacity. When I attend global events, I always make a beeline for the NGOs using technology to streamline bureaucracy; it's just exciting to see how the metaverse or decentralisation might bring us even closer to the answers we seek. As you can tell, I'm an optimist.

A few technology tweaks between electronic health record (EHR) systems can help doctors and other health care providers access patient data from different sources, which can improve diagnoses and treatment outcomes (Adler-Milstein et al., 2017). Interoperability can also help public health officials track disease outbreaks and monitor population health (WHO, 2021). Now, that does feel a bit Big Brother, but in due course, technology might just bring us all together. During the global pandemic of the coronavirus, we relied upon the World Health Organisation to bring us towards solutions and help us find answers. Imagine if we could manage this process at an even more granular level? Emergency management systems can help emergency responders and officials communicate and coordinate their response efforts during a crisis or disaster. This can help to ensure that resources are deployed efficiently and that the public is kept informed and safe.

Help would find us quicker, and lives would be saved. *I remain the optimist.*

As our planet becomes hotter and the movement of people from the equator and tropics to the southern, and increasingly, the northern hemispheres, could interoperability help us find and support one another across systems and borders? I believe it can. Interoperability can play a crucial role in identifying and assisting refugees by improving communication and coordination between different organisations and government agencies involved in refugee resettlement (UNHCR, 2020). We can actually use technology, *game technology*, to help us build and learn.

Bury Me, Ly Love (2017) is a game you can play on your phone or tablet that tells the story of Nour, a young woman who is leaving her home in Syria to find safety in Europe. Her husband Karam is waiting for her in Germany and will use a messaging app to help her along the way. The game is inspired by messaging apps like WhatsApp and lets you talk to Nour in real time. You'll get notifications when she's available to talk, and you'll need to help her make choices and overcome obstacles. There are 20 different endings, depending on the choices you make. The game is based on real events and tries to recreate the experience of a migrant fleeing to Europe (Games for Change, 2022). It's also about the difficulty of not being able to help the people you love.

This was one of the first games to explore the process of migration or asylum from the perspective of non-fiction. There are many training games and simulators that do similar work, but this game, in particular, struck a chord with gamers because of the desperation of Nour's situation and how it depends on the player's choice. Additionally, it's a great grounding for assessing the needs of migrants as they cross borders or enter unknown or unwanted territories.

Game Takeaway: Design with Empathy

Bury Me, My Love (Case Study, 2022) offers a model for ethical storytelling: one that informs, empowers and respects its audience. Game mechanics here are not just tools; they are vehicles for emotional truth. Games can:

- Build policy understanding

- Simulate migration pressures

- Train responders and civil servants

- Teach players when systems fail

A wonderful use case of interoperability must therefore be identity. Interoperability can help to improve the accuracy and efficiency of refugee identification and registration processes. For example, if different organisations and agencies involved in refugee resettlement and assistance had interoperable databases, it would be easier to verify refugees' identities, track their movements and ensure that they receive the appropriate assistance from healthcare to employment or even education. There are no rules about who should own data or who should seek it or record it, so why can't it be our data? Why can't this information utilise blockchain technology rather than be something country-centric? (Zwitter and Boisse-Despiaux, 2020).

The metaverse has a golden opportunity to uplift not only decentralised technology but also IoT. Transport is a strong vertical for a use case. Imagine a world without borders (but that really is imagination currently); instead, imagine a world with decentralised or open mobility through digital wallets or wearable technologies. If you can pay with your Apple or Samsung watch, why can't you seamlessly zip around public transportation networks? Interoperability between transportation systems, such as traffic management systems and vehicle-to-vehicle communication systems, can help to improve safety, reduce congestion and increase efficiency (Gkoumas et al., 2019; UITP, 2022). It might also help us to get somewhere on time regardless of whether we are in Stockport or Shanghai. Wouldn't it be amazing to have the interoperability of travel? We could simply jump on public transport in any city without fumbling around at ticket machines or picking up a fine for travelling in the wrong zone. *I am obviously describing myself.*

What I'm not doing is making a rallying call for centralisation of information. The information belongs to us, *all of us*, but centralising data under personal control sounds empowering, but if that data is unusable across systems, it's just another silo. Blockchain can provide a transparent and immutable record of government and civic organisation activities, ensuring that information is easily accessible to everyone who needs it (Tapscott and Tapscott, 2016). This can help to promote accountability and prevent corruption too, so why hasn't it been adopted?

AMERICAN GODS

The original Technical Boy, but presumably without the arrogance of youth, must surely be Tim Berners-Lee. He created the World Wide Web to solve the problem of information management at CERN, the European Organization for Nuclear Research, where he worked in the late 1980s. At the time, CERN had a large and diverse research community that needed an efficient way to share information and collaborate on projects. However, the existing tools for information sharing, such as email and file transfer protocols, were limited in their capabilities (Berners-Lee, 1999).

Berners-Lee envisioned a system that would allow researchers to access and share information easily, regardless of their location or the device they were using. He developed the concept of the World Wide Web as a way to link documents or pages together using hyperlinks and to make them accessible to anyone with an internet connection.

The World Wide Web was built on a foundation of open standards, protocols and formats, such as HTTP and HTML, which allowed for the creation of a decentralised network of interconnected documents. Wait a minute. When did we move away from the openness of the internet? We might assume it was when young people started using it.

The rise of walled gardens in social media platforms and streaming services has created limitations in the flow of information and user data between their platforms and the rest of the internet (Zuboff, 2019). These closed systems make it more difficult for users to access and share information across different platforms and services. Add to that government surveillance, where the increase in surveillance and monitoring of internet activity in recent years has led to a decrease in online privacy and an increase in censorship and content restrictions in some countries (Snowden, 2019).

The internet has become increasingly dominated by a few large corporations too, such as Google, Facebook (now Meta Inc.) and Amazon. These companies have significant influence over the flow of information on the internet and can shape user behaviour through their algorithms and recommendations (Srnicek, 2016).

The early internet was epitomised by a sense of experimentation and exploration, as users and developers worked to create new tools and services and to improve the user experience. And in 2023 we find ourselves right back at that spot. If back then free-form architecture made it possible for anyone to publish and access information online, can't we utilise this decentralised system for interoperability towards a place of true openness and transparency? Communication, collaboration and knowledge sharing are more powerful than we ever imagined, but the guardrails are now on for all of us, not just children. This affects how we connect with everything around us.

There are documented notes and studies on the user experience of the early internet. In the early days of the internet, the user experience was very different from what we are used to today. The World Wide Web was mostly used by academics, researchers and computer enthusiasts.

One of the first studies on the user experience of the internet was conducted by researchers at Xerox PARC in the early 1990s (Johnson et al., 1993). You know Xerox PARC, right? The Palo Alto Research Center. Still not sure? What if I told you that Xerox PARC developed the Graphical User Interface (GUI)? Yeah, the photocopier folks.

The GUI lets users interact with their computers using visual elements such as icons, windows and menus, making it easier for non-experts to use computers (Moggridge, 2006). It's the staple of all good operating systems today and some might argue the benchmark for solid UX. Anyway, Xerox PARC found that users had difficulty navigating the internet due to the lack of standardisation and consistency in the design of websites. Users also found it challenging to locate relevant information, as search engines were not yet widely available.

Other studies from the early days of the internet also highlighted issues such as slow connection speeds, limited bandwidth and technical difficulties in accessing and using online services. No problem for Xerox PARC, like any good innovator should, they simply innovated out of the problem and gave us these bad boys:

- *Ethernet*: Yes, that Ethernet. The foundational networking technology that allowed computers to communicate with each other over a shared network (Metcalfe, 1973).

- *WYSIWYG editors*: What You See Is What You Get. Xerox PARC gave us editors that showed how our documents would look when printed or displayed, without needing to understand typography or layout (Smith and Irby, 1987).

- *Hypertext*: Thank Xerox PARC for this too. They developed the concept of hypertext, later adapted into the World Wide Web, which made navigating and linking information intuitive and powerful (Nelson, 1981).

Despite these early challenges, WWW users were often enthusiastic about the potential of the technology. Many saw the internet as a way to access and share information in ways that were not previously possible, and as a tool for collaboration and communication on a global scale.

Today we are looking at something bigger. We don't need to be educated on how to use browsers or when to burn cookies; but the user experience in Web3 technologies is *spartan*. There are areas in what we have created so far that have not prioritised users, yet claim to be open and for the people. I would disagree.

In Don Norman's book *The Design of Everyday Things*, some might argue the greatest book ever written; he shows us that good design is not just about aesthetics, but about making products and systems that are intuitive, functional and easy to use (Norman, 2013). By focusing on the needs and abilities of the user, designers can create products and systems that improve the user experience and ultimately lead to more successful outcomes. "Two of the most important characteristics of good design are discoverability and understanding" (Norman, 2013, p. 4).

TABLE 11.2   Web Types and Functions

Era	Web1 (1990s–Early 2000s)	Web2 (Mid-2000s–Present)	Web3 (Emerging)
Core idea	*Read*: static information publishing	*Read/write*: user-generated content	*Read/write/own*: dDecentralised ownership
Architecture	Decentralised (HTML, HTTP, open standards)	Centralised (platforms, cloud computing)	Decentralised (blockchain, peer-to-peer)
Identity	Anonymous or username-based	Central login (Google, Facebook, etc.)	Wallet-based, pseudonymous
UX	Clunky but open	Slick, intuitive, platform-locked	Complex, technical, uneven
Control	Individual website owners	Big Tech platforms	Users, DAOs, smart contracts
Monetisation	None or simple ads	Targeted ads, data harvesting	Tokens, NFTs, protocol economies
Examples	GeoCities, early blogs, forums	Facebook, YouTube, Amazon	Ethereum, OpenSea, Decentraland
Vibe	DIY, optimistic, information wants to be free	Share, connect, scale fast	Trustless, own your data, experimental

If I understand Web3 correctly, it is the container for a variety of Decentralised Applications (dApps) that operate on a decentralised network of computers and servers, rather than relying on a central server or cloud-based infrastructure (Zamfir, 2020). These dApps can be used for a wide range of purposes, including financial transactions, social networking, online marketplaces and more (Table 11.2).

If one of the key features of Web3 is the use of smart contracts, which are self-executing contracts with the terms of the agreement between buyer and seller being directly written into lines of code, we had better start figuring out how we're going to make Web3 even smarter.

Smart contracts should allow for secure, transparent and automated transactions, without the need for intermediaries. Right now, though? Web3 looks like a dumpster fire of burning egos. Every blockchain start-up is offering Smart Contracts-as-a-Service. But offering isn't the same as building trust.

Can we fix it? How?

Web3 aims to address some of the challenges and limitations of the current web, such as issues with privacy, security and control. It seeks to create a more open and transparent internet where users have greater control over their data and digital identities (Buterin, 2014). So let's start there.

Let's simplify the user interface. Why not? If Web3 technology is as complex and difficult to understand for many users, it needs to be simplified. Making the user interface more comprehensible and intuitive can help to improve the user experience. This can be done by reducing the number of steps required to complete a task, using clear and concise language and providing helpful on-screen guidance.

Web3 is for everybody! So if it is, an important consideration for any user experience is accessibility and inclusivity. Web3 technology should be designed with accessibility in mind, making it easy for users of all abilities to access and use the technology. This can be achieved by incorporating features such as screen readers, keyboard navigation and high contrast modes. Why is everything in Dark Mode? As someone with early macular degeneration, I struggle to read most things in dApps and browsers. Must we all have 20/20 vision to participate?

Some of my best friends are cybersecurity developers and they are afraid of Web3, not just because of the technology but because of us, the common meatsack. Web3 technology often involves sensitive financial and personal information, so security and privacy are critical. Users should be able to trust that their information is secure and that their privacy is protected. This can be achieved by using robust, sturdy and agile encryption, implementing multi-factor authentication and providing clear and transparent privacy policies that move with us, not against us (Reijsbergen et al., 2019).

Safety and privacy have been diluted or overlooked in favour of the one-size-fits-all Application Programming Interface (API) approach. How many times do we outsource our security to an ad-tracking API to enter a website or some online gateway? Users must take responsibility for their own security and rely on decentralised security mechanisms such as cryptography and consensus protocols.

Additionally, secure wallets and keys. Users control their own wallets and private keys in Web3, which are used to secure their digital assets. It is critical that users properly secure their wallets and keys, as any compromise of these could result in the loss of their assets. This happens more times than I've had hot dinners.

The confusion between what is public and private is a never-ending struggle for the end user. We made it too difficult for them and now they can't go a day without an axiomatic hack, and that's a nice way to describe it. Insecure smart contracts are by their very nature an oxymoron. Vulnerabilities in smart contracts can be exploited to steal digital assets or to cause other types of damage (Luu et al., 2016). Hot wallets? Cold storage? Please! Can someone help us!

Speaking of flaws, how's the network security in Web3? Well, it has the potential to be mostly poor. It relies on a decentralised network of nodes, and all those nodes must be secured to prevent attacks such as Denial-of-Service attacks and other types of network-based attacks.

As a designer, my biggest wish for Web3 is that we create more seamless experiences such as user-centric designs that focus on user needs and preferences, and by leveraging emerging technologies such as artificial intelligence and machine learning. That way we can bring user feedback upfront and incorporate it into the development process. This can help to identify pain points and areas for improvement.

The emphasis should be on the importance of designing for human cognition and behaviour (Norman, 2013), rather than forcing people to conform to the design of the product or system, especially for Web3. This sounds philosophical and it should because design 101 is about the philosophy of function rather than retrofitting for likes.

The need for designers to anticipate and prevent errors, rather than relying on users to correct mistakes on the tech side, will also make Web3 the most robust, the most water-tight and the most secure place for us to build a future. Technical Boy might not see it the same way, but Berners-Lee definitely had the future firmly in his mind when he brought us all together to collaborate, and surely that is worth protecting.

PRODUCT MARKET FIT

Video games are growing up, big time. We're in a beautiful place where games want to leave home and as video game developers we have to let them. Their home has always been in the PCB at the arcade, the console on your TV, or in your PC or laptop. In the last 10–15 years we're now fully mobile through handhelds like the Nintendo suite and even Steam is getting in on the act with the Steamdeck. Developers have a love and hate affair with publishers; and brands are eating up the metaverse because game publishers are mostly jealous gods. It's disappointing that video games that are owned and operated by huge publishing corporations haven't welcomed more brands with open arms; but this is about money more than it is about the game. So thankfully over the last few years the idea of Web3 gaming has appeared in our newsfeeds and today it's a credible vertical of the industry.

All good games boil down to three things: autonomy, mastery and purpose (Pink, 2009; Kim, 2018). It doesn't matter how this is done; we've seen games take on as many guises and forms as you can imagine, but successful games all have just these three things in common (Table 11.3).

Together, autonomy, mastery and purpose can help to create a gameplay environment that is engaging, rewarding and fulfilling for players. By providing players with the freedom to figure things out, develop their skills and find a sense of purpose in what they do sometimes day in and day out, that's the benchmark for success in games. Does it sound too simple? Maybe, but that's all there is. Teach your players this and you win.

A lot of brands, creators and developers lose their user base quickly because they don't seem to be able to apply it in a gamified environment. They don't understand it, so they can't make it work. Applying this simple methodology to Web3 games and the metaverse too is going to change the entire landscape in any creator's favour. Let's dig deeper:

In the context of gameplay and user experience, autonomy is about giving your player as much onboarding to the point that things feel natural to them without making it seem like we think they are stupid. It's the hardest thing for game designers and metaverse creators to get right because for them this is a point of ego. Sophisticated means that some designers (not this one) feel that comprehensive = uncomplicated. Not true. There is a great deal of sophistication in simplicity. Autonomy ultimately is freedom, but in games, freedom is not something that happens easily for players, unlocking their freedom and that organic

TABLE 11.3 Loops of Engagement and Loyalty

Principle	Definition	In Games/Metaverse
Autonomy	Freedom to choose and self-direct	Sandbox play, UGC, DAO governance
Mastery	Skill growth and challenge	Rank progression, crafting, earning badges
Purpose	Meaning beyond the moment	Community roles, contribution, legacy

nature of playing without forced or micromanaged direction can help the player to master their progression with ease.

Mastery is just that! Mastering the game is a bit like middle age: you know all those mistakes you made earlier in life, and you know what you did wrong earlier in the game. It is here in the middle age of gameplay and hindsight that mastery needs expertise to sustain. It needs the player to attend to its needs. In game development, this is a dangerous place to develop for because instead of expertise, often the player errs on the side of complacency. Good habits in the game should probably happen here rather than rehashing the old habits from the autonomy part of the game.

Purpose is that transcendence, a bit like in Maslow's Hierarchy of Needs (1943), where we realise self-actualisation and we want to be the best that we can be with absolutely no catches. Gamers who do purpose well are the ones that boost younger or less-experienced players in the game. Purpose players are the ones that get to play new expansions or levels before everyone else. They're also hugely involved in the community of the game. If the game is like going through school, these guys aren't the teachers, they're the seniors, the ones who have been through the system and have come out the other side to this self-actualisation. Game developers also have one helluva time trying to satisfy purpose players. This is where I feel it is the hardest for game developers. What are they supposed to do with a player who knows everything? Do they celebrate them? The truth is, they don't know how to. It also plays into my hands a little because I often get a call asking me to come and have a look at the core loop or the inner mechanics of the game.

Business Takeaway: Use AMP for Retention, Not Just Play

- **Autonomy = return visits**: Let users shape their path or content.

- **Mastery = stickiness**: Offer challenges with visible growth.

- **Purpose = advocacy**: Give players a reason to bring others in.

Brands that ignore AMP? They lose attention, trust and community.

What most game developers don't understand (except for RPG developers) is that games are tribal. Listen, I love *Devil May Cry* (2001) as much as the next person, but I couldn't care less about *Bayonetta* (2009) or *Dark Souls* (2011), but I *should*. Again, it's about good habit forming and it's got a lot to do with developing a very strong (stronger than Superman's jockstrap) forever loop. Whether developing for femtech or a simple mobile app which tells the time in AR, there has to be a reason for the user to return again and again. Remember my golden rule? No one leaves the keyboard, the game, the console. We can't leave a player behind ever (Table 11.4).

When we create Web3 tools or even use Web3 tools, we have to maintain the same intentions towards our users. Why would the metaverse be different from *Devil May Cry*? The game itself is not persistent, but the metaverse is, so use all that persistence brings to your brand, IP or experience. The combination of blockchain and NFTs can help to create a decentralised metaverse that provides users with the autonomy, mastery and purpose they

TABLE 11.4   User Experience Gold Standards

Game	AMP Example	User Experience Application
Minecraft (2009)	Autonomy playground	User-generated content (UGC) design
League of Legends (2009)	Mastery loops	User interface (UI) and deep game progression design through repetition not story
Final Fantasy XIV (2010)	Purpose through community roles	Player-centred progression boosting, matching, forums, cosplay (outside of the game)

need to fully engage and participate in virtual worlds. By creating a new ecosystem that incentivises creativity, innovation and collaboration, the metaverse has the potential to become a powerful new platform for social interaction, entertainment and commerce. In the metaverse, autonomy can be achieved by giving users the freedom to create and interact with virtual worlds in their own unique ways, such as through user-generated content. Blockchain and NFTs can be used to create decentralised platforms that allow users to own and control their digital assets, giving them the autonomy to create and trade within the metaverse as they see fit (Tapscott and Tapscott, 2016).

Mastery in the metaverse can be achieved by providing users with the tools and resources they need to develop their skills and abilities within virtual worlds. Blockchain and NFTs can be used to create incentivised learning systems that reward users for acquiring new skills and expertise within the metaverse.

Purpose can be achieved by creating virtual worlds and experiences that have a meaningful impact on users: set up the flow inside your brand activation or experience to make this happen (Kim, 2018). Try to avoid creating a ready-made activation that just turns the metizen off. Blockchain and NFTs might be used to create new economic models that reward users for contributing to the development of the metaverse, and for creating experiences that are valuable and meaningful to other users.

These types of offers exist in luxury brands but as yet seem hugely distanced in terms of making sense to everyone else. It's made me think that up until recently all I could do with an NFT is look at it or put it on the wall of my digital apartment or office in *Spatial* (2016) or *Avakin Life* (2004). Very sad. Can I use it to enter secret spaces or actually use it as a Proof of Attendance Protocol (POAP) rather than a PFP (Picture, or Photo for Profile)?

MY SECOND SECOND LIFE

I'm a hairdresser in *Avakin Life* (2004). People come to my salon and I cut their hair for 20 crowns or whatever the going rate is currently. I choose my work in the metaverse. In games, choices are pre-determined (so technically it isn't choice at all) by design. It's part of the narrative, not the experience. I have no control over having a job: if I'm a farrier in *Fable* (2004) or a table dancer in *Final Fantasy VII: Reunion* (2022) it's because it's a task, it's how I earn gold, gil and experience points (XP); or how I will eventually defeat my level boss. XP should be the thing that takes us between all those player states of Autonomy, Mastery and Purpose (Pink, 2009; Kim, 2018).

Progression is important to us, not just as players but as people. We move forward in our lives because the cost of living rises, because we want a pet rabbit or because we're tired of being single. Games are no different. To get this, you need to do that. The reward? Currency and XP. Every time. That hit of completion, that dopamine loop: we crave it. And here's the bigger idea: XP might be our future credential.

What if proof of work in the metaverse or across interoperable digital spaces wasn't just a gamified task, but a badge of competence? What if your XP became a portable, verifiable record of skills and learning? This mirrors the logic behind Mozilla's Open Badges initiative: a framework for recognising and validating learning across formal and informal environments (Mozilla Foundation, 2013). It's credentialing built on contribution. This is more than a job, it's a signal.

> **Business Takeaway:** *XP vs Real Work*
> In games, XP is a currency of growth. In work, it's… well, sometimes it's just exhaustion. But what if metaversal platforms allowed us to redefine progression, not just as titles or salaries, but as mastery loops, proof-of-impact or contribution badges?

If we work in the metaverse, are we completing a task or are we really doing a job? That kind of depends on the virtual platform, really. The work you do in *Avakin Life* (2004) is possibly gamified to keep you interested in playing in their gamified experience. Getting a job in NVIDIA Omniverse (2022) might be a different set-up because that metaverse is focused on the world of work anyway. It is a 3D collaboration platform which makes use of Universal Scene Descriptions (USD) for the development of digital twin technologies. Siemens and Microsoft are just two of many platform partners at NVIDIA Omniverse.

Other "real" jobs in the metaverse might include Virtual Tour Guide: Virtual tourism could become a significant industry in the metaverse. Virtual tour guides could lead visitors through virtual destinations, providing information and insights about the place. In *Second Life* (2003), folks with physical jobs in physical embassies around the actual physical world were also working digitally as their avatars assisting metizens and citizens with questions they may have had about anything to do with their particular country (Chowdhury, 2007). So you see, the metaverse and the future of work are not as cut and dried as we might imagine. Though there is a definite will to go completely digital, we are not Jobe in *Lawnmower Man* (1992). We are not able to pass through fibres and wiring to be inside a machine handling queries or assisting metizens with random connections.

The future of work is likely to be shaped by a range of factors, including technological advancements, economic and social changes, and evolving attitudes towards work and employment. The COVID-19 pandemic has accelerated the adoption of remote work and flexible schedules, and this trend is likely to continue in the future. As Cathy Hackl and John Buzzell argue, the future of work within the metaverse isn't just about novelty, it's about reconfiguring economic systems entirely (Hackl and Buzzell, 2021). More people are likely to work from home or other remote locations, with flexible schedules that allow them to balance work and personal life.

Then, perhaps advances in automation and AI are likely to continue to change the nature of work, with machines and algorithms taking on more routine and repetitive tasks. This will require workers to develop new skills and adapt to new forms of work. This leads to different education pathways with the more traditional areas of work being left behind. If I had a dollar for every time I heard someone say that they wanted to work on *Grand Theft Auto IV* back in 2008 I would be at least $100 better off but seriously, if you switch out GTA for a ChatGPT Prompt Engineer, you get the general idea of where the future of work is taking us. As technology continues to evolve and new skills become more valuable, lifelong learning and upskilling will become essential for workers to remain competitive and adapt to changing work environments.

If you are anything like me, you will have noticed that the gig economy and freelancing are likely to continue to grow, with more people working as independent contractors or freelancers rather than traditional employees. That's bad for me, but it's great for people who feel more comfortable in freelanced capacities. Incidentally, the word freelance comes from a knight who was not affiliated to any particular flag and worked for himself. So one might argue that we might not have moved as far into the future as we think we have!

More workers are likely to seek out purpose-driven work and social impact, looking for opportunities to make a positive difference in the world through their work. But at the heart of everything we do, should we still look for opportunities that offer collaboration and co-creation too? These are likely to become increasingly important in the future of work, as organisations seek to harness the power of diverse teams to solve complex problems and drive innovation. Epic launched its Unreal Editor for Fortnite (UEFN), allowing players to develop inside the engine, and they really do. It proves that there is an appetite for players to continue their engagement with any brand IP inside the *Fortnite* universe. Since it supports creator economies too, the player actually becomes the developer, which is even better for turning XP into currency.

It is highly likely that people will work in the metaverse as it continues to evolve and become more widely adopted. However, the specifics of how people will be paid within the metaverse are still uncertain and will likely depend on various factors, including the specific metaverse platform being used, the type of work being performed and the preferences of both employers and employees.

Let's assume that people will be paid in cryptocurrency or other digital assets that are native to the metaverse platform (or native to the metaverse, period – that's the goal). This could involve earning tokens or other forms of virtual currency for completing tasks or providing services within the metaverse, which could then be exchanged for real-world currencies or goods and services. I don't see that the traditional payment systems like payroll apply here. Here's why: open banking or universal banking methodologies must have a say in how we operate everything in this space. The interoperability of finance or DeFi gives rise to changing every process thereafter including taxation and administration. New and innovative payment models that are unique to the metaverse will win us over. My folks couldn't grasp PayPal when it launched: why should the next generation cling to legacy systems? Additionally, people could be paid based on the value they bring to a virtual community or for the intellectual property they create within the metaverse.

I suppose that until we have a good rationale for currency as a whole we can't really make decisions on how future generations will pay and be paid for work. For now, I'm going to dream of video game currency and monetisation models as leading the way (don't you just love spending Simoleons and Septims on stuff?)

REFERENCES

Adler-Milstein, J., Everson, J. and Lee, S.-Y.D. (2017) 'EHR Adoption and Hospital Performance: Time-Related Effects', *Health Services Research*, 52(3), pp. 1364–1383.

Ashton, K. (2009) 'That "Internet of Things" Thing', *RFID Journal*, 22(7), pp. 97–114.

Atzori, L., Iera, A. and Morabito, G. (2010) 'The Internet of Things: A Survey', *Computer Networks*, 54(15), pp. 2787–2805.

Avakin Life (2004) Lockwood Publishing Ltd [Mobile Game]. Available at: https://avakin.com

Ball, M. (2022) *The Metaverse: And How It Will Revolutionize Everything*. New York, NY: Liveright Publishing Corporation.

Bayonetta (2009) PlatinumGames [Video Game]. Japan: Sega.

Berners-Lee, T. (1999) *Weaving the Web: The Original Design and Ultimate Destiny of the World Wide Web by Its Inventor*. New York, NY: HarperOne.

Borgia, E. (2014) 'The Internet of Things Vision: Key Features, Applications and Open Issues', *Computer Communications*, 54, pp. 1–31.

Bury Me, My Love (2017) Mobile [Game]. The Pixel Hunt. FR: Arte.tv.

Buterin, V. (2014) 'A Next-Generation Smart Contract and Decentralized Application Platform', *Ethereum White Paper*.

Buzzell, J. and Hackl, C. (2021) *The Augmented Workforce: How AI, AR, and 5G Will Impact Every Dollar You Make*. New York, NY: Wiley.

Chowdhury, N.R. (2007) 'Maldives Opens Virtual Embassy', *Hindustan Times*, 23 May. Available at: https://www.hindustantimes.com/world/maldives-opens-virtual-embassy/story-ywf NCEGWBvQNYrEpI72DiP.html (Accessed: 14 July 2025).

Dark Souls (2011) FromSoftware Inc [Video Game]. Japan: Bandai Namco Entertainment.

Devil May Cry (2001) Capcom [Video Game]. Japan: Capcom.

Dionisio, J.D.N., Burns, W.G. and Gilbert, R. (2013) '3D Virtual Worlds and the Metaverse: Current Status and Future Possibilities', *ACM Computing Surveys*, 45(3), pp. 1–38.

Dowling, M. (2022) 'Is Non-Fungible Token Pricing Driven by Cryptocurrencies?', *Finance Research Letters*, 44, p. 102109.

Final Fantasy XIV: A Realm Reborn (2010) Square Enix [Video Game]. Japan: Square Enix.

Games for Change (2022) 'Bury Me, My Love – Case Study'. Available at: https://www.gamesfor-change.org (Accessed: 18 July 2025).

Gartner (2023) 'Emerging Tech Impact Radar for 2023', *Gartner Insights*. Available at: https://www.gartner.com

Gkoumas, K., et al. (2019) 'Smart Mobility and Transport Interoperability: Evaluation Frameworks', *European Commission Science Hub*. Available at: https://publications.jrc.ec.europa.eu

Gubbi, J., Buyya, R., Marusic, S. and Palaniswami, M. (2013) 'Internet of Things (IoT): A Vision, Architectural Elements, and Future Directions', *Future Generation Computer Systems*, 29(7), pp. 1645–1660.

HealthIT.gov (2022) *Interoperability and Health IT*. Available at: https://www.healthit.gov

IEEE (2022) *Interoperability in Emerging Tech Ecosystems*. New York, NY: IEEE Press.

Interoperability Working Group (2022) *Metaverse Standards Forum: Interoperability Overview*. Available at: https://www.metaverse-standards.org/

Johnson, J., Roberts, T., Verplank, W., Smith, D.C. and Irby, C. (1993) 'The Xerox Star: A Retrospective', *IEEE Computer*, 22(9), pp. 11–26.

Kastrenakes, J. (2021) *Beeple Sold an NFT for $69 Million, The Verge.* The Verge. Available at: https://www.theverge.com/2021/3/11/22325054/beeple-christies-nft-sale-cost-everydays-69-million (Accessed: 18 July 2025).

Kim, A.J. (2018) *Game Thinking: Innovate Smarter & Drive Deep Engagement with Design Techniques from Hit Games.* Burlingame: gamethinking.io.

Lawnmower Man (1992) [DVD]. Directed by Brett Leonard. USA: New Line Cinema.

League of Legends (2009) Riot Games [Video Game]. USA: Riot Games.

Lehdonvirta, V. and Castronova, E. (2014) *Virtual Economies: Design and Analysis.* Cambridge, MA: MIT Press.

Luu, L., Chu, D.H., Olickel, H., Saxena, P. and Hobor, A. (2016) 'Making Smart Contracts Smarter', *Proceedings of the ACM SIGSAC Conference on Computer and Communications Security (CCS)*, Vienna, Austria.

Maslow, A.H. (1943) 'A Theory of Human Motivation', *Psychological Review*, 50(4), pp. 370–396.

Metaverse Standards Forum (2023) *Interoperability Principles for the Open Metaverse.* Available at: https://www.metaverse-standards.org

Metcalfe, R.M. and Boggs, D.R. (1973) 'Ethernet: Distributed Packet Switching for Local Computer Networks', *Communications of the ACM*, 19(7), pp. 395–404.

Minecraft (2009) Mojang Studios [Video Game]. USA: Microsoft Studios.

Moggridge, B. (2006) *Designing Interactions.* Cambridge, MA: MIT Press.

Mozilla Foundation (2013) *Open Badges for Lifelong Learning.* Available at: https://openbadges.org/ (Accessed: 15 July 2025).

Nadini, M., et al. (2021) 'Mapping the NFT Revolution: Market Trends, Trade Networks, and Visual Features', *Scientific Reports*, 11(1), pp. 1–11.

Nelson, T.H. (1981) *Literary Machines.* Sausalito, CA: Mindful Press.

Newzoo (2023) *Global Games Market Report.* Available at: https://www.newzoo.com

Norman, D.A. (2013) *The Design of Everyday Things: Revised and Expanded Edition.* New York, NY: Basic Books.

NVIDIA Omniverse (2022) NVIDIA. Available at: https://www.nvidia.com/en-us/omniverse/ (Accessed: 15 July 2025).

Pink, D.H. (2009) *Drive: The Surprising Truth About What Motivates Us.* New York, NY: Riverhead Books.

Reijsbergen, D., Gramoli, V., Gervais, A. and Esteves-Veríssimo, P. (2019) 'Security Issues in Blockchain Technology', *Computer*, 52(6), pp. 20–28.

Second Life. (2003). PC [Game]. USA: Linden Lab.

Smith, D.C. and Irby, C. (1987) 'The Star User Interface: An Overview', *Byte Magazine*, 12(9), pp. 237–247.

Snowden, E. (2019) *Permanent Record.* London: Macmillan.

Spatial (2016) Spatial Systems Inc [Virtual Platform]. Available at: https://spatial.io

Srnicek, N. (2016) *Platform Capitalism.* Cambridge: Polity Press.

Tapscott, D. and Tapscott, A. (2016) *Blockchain Revolution: How the Technology Behind Bitcoin Is Changing Money, Business, and the World.* London: Portfolio Penguin.

UITP – International Association of Public Transport (2022) *Interoperability in Public Transport Systems.* Available at: https://www.uitp.org (Accessed: 18 July 2025).

UNHCR (2020) *UNHCR Innovation – Blockchain and Refugee Identity.* Available at: https://www.unhcr.org/innovation (Accessed: 18 July 2025).

Vero, K. (2021) Luxury and Art: A Common Framework for Metadata in Practice, LinkedIn (July 1, 2021), Available at: https://www.linkedin.com/pulse/luxury-art-common-framework-metadata-practice-kelly-vero/ (Accessed: 18 July 2025).

WHO (2021) *Digital Health Interventions for Emergency Response*. Geneva: World Health Organization.

Zamfir, V. (2020) 'The Ethereum Governance Crisis', *Crypto-Economics Explorer* [Online]. Available at: https://vitalik.ca (Accessed: 14 July 2025).

Zuboff, S. (2019) *The Age of Surveillance Capitalism*. London: Profile Books.

Zwitter, A. and Boisse-Despiaux, M. (2020) 'Blockchain for Humanitarian Action and Development Aid', *Journal of International Humanitarian Action*, 5(1), pp. 1–7.

CHAPTER 12

User Acquisition

USE IT OR LOSE IT

Roblox is a Massively Multiplayer Online (MMO) game with a user-generated content platform that was first released in 2006. It was created by David Baszucki and Erik Cassel under the company name "Roblox Corporation." The platform was designed to allow users to create their own games and play games created by others in a 3D virtual world.

When Baszucki and Cassel created a physics simulation software in 2004, they called it "DynaBlocks" (TechCrunch, 2018). The software was later renamed to *Roblox* and officially launched in 2006. Initially, the platform was available only on Windows and Mac, but it later expanded to other platforms, including mobile devices and game consoles.

In its early days, *Roblox* had a small but passionate user base. However, it quickly grew in popularity due to its user-generated content and the ability for players to create their own games. In 2011, *Roblox* hit a major milestone of having 5.4 million monthly active users.

Since then, *Roblox* has continued to grow in popularity and has become one of the most popular gaming platforms in the world. As of 2021, *Roblox* has over 200 million active users and has been valued at over $38 billion. The platform has also expanded beyond gaming and has been used for educational purposes, virtual concerts and other events.

Roblox has come a long way since its early days as a physics simulation software. It has grown into a massively popular game creation platform and virtual world with a passionate user base and a wide range of uses beyond gaming.

While researching and writing this book, the Key Performance Indicators (KPIs) for its success are the same as what I'd find in most of the platforms I'm researching. They are built from a place of passion. I'm a very passionate gamer. If you know me, you will know that I have a frieze of *Final Fantasy VII* characters and environments from that particular universe tattooed on my arm. I was not an easy user to acquire. I had never played a *Final Fantasy* game before FFVII, but I was passionate about story in games even back in 1997 when I was early in my video games career. My genre passions may have distilled down to titles now, but I'm still an avid gamer. Therefore, I think it is important to play all game genres in order to understand how games work. There is never a one size fits all to the

DOI: 10.1201/9781003615248-12

design and neither to the user. *Roblox* knows this even if it does skew closer to the younger age range.

According to Roblox Corporation (2021), 55% of daily active users are over age 13, and 33% of total users are between ages 17 and 24, which is the fastest growing age group on the platform. Note that 45% of their user base is under 13. Like *Minecraft*, they have obviously needed to find a strategy where the platform grows with the player. But user generation isn't the only benchmark of their success as they try to connect with players of different demographics.

- *Accessibility*: *Roblox* is available on multiple platforms, including mobile devices and game consoles, making it easily accessible to a wide range of users. It also has a low barrier to entry, with many of the games being free to play.

- *Community*: *Roblox* has a strong and active community of players and developers, who collaborate, share ideas and support each other. The platform also has a robust social feature set, including chat and groups, which allow players to connect and interact with each other. Additionally, because some of their users are young, content must also be moderated, and *Roblox* provides this.

- *Monetisation*: *Roblox* offers multiple ways for developers to monetise their games, including in-game purchases, ads and a virtual currency called Robux. This incentivises developers to create high-quality games and content, while also providing a source of revenue for the platform. However, unlike SAND or MANA, this currency is not yet tradeable. I'm sure that will happen.

- *Innovation*: *Roblox* is constantly evolving and introducing new features, tools and technologies to the platform. This keeps the platform fresh and exciting, while also allowing developers to create more advanced and immersive games and experiences.

I have already explained the traditional and new models for building apps and experiences, but how should we measure them? What are we looking for and why should we try? A lot of games and metaverse developers are so convinced by what it is they have built that they don't seem to know how to bring users on board and retain them.

If we apply some of the early hypotheses into our metrics, planning the middle bit is the game/metaverse/experience. So in a sense, we're wrapping up our experience into an actual product. We crunch data as we go through the processes of watching you, the user, consume the product. We want to measure the things that are measurable:

- *User behaviour*: What time and when do players play? How does that fit our hypotheses and our bold appraisal of the end user?

- *Time vs Money*: We've already explored how long players play or how long users visit platforms, but how much are they spending? And how does the time vs money analysis fit your best guesses when designing, or, more simply, how will you balance the experience?

- *Player experience*: Sometimes players have problems because they can't do something or get somewhere, they give up. Don't let them. Instead, analyse their First-Time User Experience (FTUE) and measure it against your measurables.

- *Bottlenecks and pain points*: Sometimes these are tech related, but mostly they are user-centric. Players or metizens just will not move a muscle if they cannot make something happen that best suits them.

- *Sales*: Like the time vs money, it's sometimes very surprising what and how much users spend on your product. Take some time to find out why and then you'll know how you can improve the metric using simple methodologies.

In casual apps and games versus serious games, we see different responses from the same or similar parts of the brain in different users; however, these tend to boil down to the same segments of data. For example, in casual apps we might look for certain traits or behaviours in our users. In serious games these things are pattern-orientated. Number-related activities which heighten things like dopamine in our brains (such as kill streaks in entertainment games like *Halo: Combat Evolved* (2001)) relate to the feelings of completion in more serious or task-focused experiences. In preferred storylines, fictions or contexts, these things are the same. If we're looking at the spend of users in our app, game or experience, we might be looking for reason or motivation in a serious game. Spending time or money invokes the same brain responses to being or feeding motivation.

Asking questions of the end user is all well and good, but we also have to turn that line of questioning on ourselves as creators. When I worked for a huge mobile game developer in Scandinavia, one of the big questions for them was always what does success look like? They didn't have a pedigree of hit games, and they were not traditional game developers, but they were on the outside and I suspect that's a strong motivator for them becoming as successful as they were. Their structure for what success looks like was to work up to the question by asking other questions first:

- What do you want the user to do/feel/experience/play?

- What measurements prove your game/app/experience?

- How do you reward and how is that measured or balanced?

- Which targets do you set for your end user? How high or low are they?

The performance of any activation, regardless of its destination, should be focused on metrics and demographics working together to guide everything from design to content.

CHEAP ≠ BAD

Unless it's on a luxury handbag, I don't like paying for anything. Who does? I can hear you all shouting into this book. But I'm going to stick my neck out and say that the cost of User Acquisition (UA) in games did this to me.

What is user acquisition, and does it have key performance indicators relevant to your studio or business?

User Acquisition, in video games anyway, is the process of attracting and converting new users to a game or platform. It involves identifying potential users, creating awareness about the game or platform and convincing them to download or sign up for the game or platform. In reality and away from the niceties of press releases and interviews in some kind of flex-related publication, user acquisition boils down to getting bums on seats. These strategies can take many forms, such as targeted advertising campaigns, influencer marketing, social media outreach and search engine optimisation.

The goal is to drive traffic to the game or platform, and to convert that traffic into active users, and UA is therefore a critical metric for game developers and metaverse platforms, as it directly impacts the growth and success of the product. A high rate of user acquisition is generally seen as a positive sign, as it indicates that the game or platform is resonating with users and has the potential for continued growth (Table 12.1).

Here's the thing though, once you start UA, it's pretty difficult to stop. It really is the first step in the user lifecycle. The stuff I talked about previously still stands. You have to follow that process of feedback loops as well as core loops. Retention management is tough, but if the product is right, it's much easier. The product needs to have some strong elements to connect with users. Think about some of the cool games you've played and if you don't play games, think about great app experiences you've had which make the dream work for you. In all experiences, the user interface should be intuitive and easy to navigate, allowing users to quickly find what they are looking for. It should also be visually appealing and consistent with the theme of the game.

The gameplay or activity should be engaging and challenging, but not too difficult. Users should feel like they've done something, anything that fires their synapses when completing tasks and achieving goals. The experience should provide ample opportunities for social interaction among users too. This can include chat features, group activities and events that bring people together.

The metaverse should perform well and load quickly, allowing users to enjoy the experience without any frustrating lag or glitches. The developers should be committed to continuous improvement, regularly releasing updates and new features to enhance the user experience and keep users engaged.

TABLE 12.1   User Acquisition Lifecycle Overview

Phase	Key Action	Metrics Tracked
Awareness	Marketing, outreach	Impressions, Click-Thru rate (CTR), Traffic
Acquisition	Signup/install	Cost per install (CPI), cost per acquisition (CPA)
Activation (FTUE)	First five minutes of use	Drop-off rate, user experience (UX) friction
Retention	Return visits, repeat sessions	Daily active users (DAU), monthly average users (MAU), stickiness ratio
Monetisation	Spend, upgrades, unlockables	Average revenue per user (ARPU), conversion rate
Referral/community	Sharing, word of mouth	Net promoter score (NPS), viral coefficient

The priority for most metaverse experiences is customisation and users should be able to customise their avatars and their virtual environments, allowing them to express their personality and create a unique experience; add to that the community and bingo! You've got an awesome KPI list to explore the possibilities of your product and build a metric plan to measure your product against.

I said at the top of the chapter that I don't like spending money; there is a perceived value that just because something costs X amount, you should pay it. There's also a great deal of tribute to pay to those designers and developers who work hard at the coal seam, bringing users through communities. But at the end of the day, UA is something we should all do and that we can learn from. I don't profess to go far enough down the rabbit hole to be an expert in this field, but any form of digital development is not cheap, so adding UA onto the budget is going to be a knife to the heart if you're a small indie. You need it, but UA also needs you. So a good rule of thumb is to apportion 80% of the development budget into marketing and UA. Hopefully, you have a strong publisher or investment who will swallow that up for you without question. If you don't, I feel bad for you. This might hurt a little bit.

Business Takeaway: UA Doesn't Have a Flat Fee
UA costs can vary widely depending on a number of factors, including the platform, the type of game or app, the target audience and the marketing strategy used.

In general, costs can range from a few cents to several dollars per user, with some highly competitive markets and genres commanding much higher costs. For example, mobile games in highly competitive genres like puzzle and strategy games can have user acquisition costs ranging from $1 to $5 per install, while some top-performing games may have user acquisition costs of $10 or more per install. If you apply those estimates to your platform or world, even if it is in the *Sandbox* (2012)or *Decentraland* (2020), you are looking down the barrel of a sniper rifle rather than a sidearm.

UA is typically measured using a metric called Cost Per Install (CPI), which is calculated by dividing the total cost of a user acquisition campaign by the number of installs generated (AppsFlyer, 2023). It's worth noting that user acquisition costs are only part of the equation when it comes to measuring the Return On Investment (ROI) of a game or app. In addition to user acquisition costs, factors such as retention rates, in-app purchases and ad revenue also play a role in determining the overall profitability and success of a product.

Business Takeaway: What Is CPI?
Cost Per Install, is a key metric to understand the cost-efficiency of user acquisition.

UA is an important consideration for game developers and metaverse platforms, as it directly impacts the financial viability and growth potential of whatever it is you are making or have made. In video games, we take this on the chin because in most cases we have the support of the publisher, but metaverses tend to have similar relationships or none at all. If one publishes to *Roblox* or *Decentraland*, this is a safe investment in terms of user acquisition: provided the demographic and the user experience are in line with the destination, the user acquisition has a good chance of bringing ROI for you. Building your own platform and then failing to secure users because of how UA has been implemented is a really big faux pas, regardless of how much tech, design or even games experience you have. I've seen mighty developers get taken down by their own games, a bit like being hoisted by your own petard because that confidence of endless publisher budget carried through into the indie or sole developer. The publisher can't support you and even worse, if you're going into the metaverse, even if you do partner up with *Roblox*, *Decentraland*, the *Sandbox* or whoever: they aren't obliged to find users for you.

Like playing games, UA is a grind if it's done organically, and the pressure is eased if done with a solid support mechanism or tool. It's the difference between grinding yourself or farming your way to success. Farming, in case you aren't aware, is the act of getting a bot to do all the work for you while you sit back and relax or focus on something else. It's fairly frowned upon in game circles, with the onus of earning gold to trade being more of a motivation than the activity itself.

KICKING SOMEONE'S DOG

You should know by now how passionate I am about my games and even more about my metaverses. My opinionated diatribe is not just for the pages of this book; it spills like a barrel of bile (sorry if you are eating) into almost every talk I do and every article I write.

I am a heavy player of games, but I also stan luxury handbags, I collect sneakers and I love Japanese food but only when it is made in Japan. I don't like coriander, Oasis (the band) and I can't stand getting my feet wet. These facts make me a bit of a pain in the pro-verbial when it comes to telling you why I think something is good and something is bad. I have no filter for the things I love (strong word) and hate (even stronger word). It's ok though, we're all guilty of it.

Someone recently told me: *she who holds the mic has the power.* It's not a quote from *The Wedding Singer* (1998), but much like when Robbie says, "I have a microphone and you don't, so you will listen to every damn word I have to say!" – it captures the power of plat-form. Rather than list out a million reasons why I think something is good or bad, I want to help you understand why you should care.

Working in the games industry has taught me to understand other opinions but as a weird chimaera of creative and technical, I should never have to agree with them, and you shouldn't either. Moreover, I want to tell you the stories of how I came to these often con-troversial and polarised opinions and let you make your own minds up.

The metaverse is full of opinion, and I think it's because the internet is rife with opinion and video games are too. These things are important to us in creating something for our users that only they can judge. As developers or creators, we're too close to the problem or the solution often. We can't see how or why something doesn't work, or why someone doesn't want to rate or review us.

The first-ever video game review is widely considered to be a review of the game *Spacewar!* which was published in the May 1972 issue of Rolling Stone magazine. The review was writ-ten by Stewart Brand, who was a writer, editor and cultural commentator at the time. In the review, Brand described *Spacewar!* as a "mind-twisting display of pyrotechnics, pinball machine effects, and stellar simulation" and praised the game's design, stating that it was "fun, addictive, and stimulating" (Brand, 1972).

Second Life (2003) and *Habbo Hotel* (2020) were both popular virtual worlds that gained a significant following when they were first launched. Though we view this era through rose-tinted spectacles, it was definitely not without criticism. *Second Life* was praised for its immersive environment and for offering users a high degree of creative freedom; that was 20 years ago. However, *Second Life* was also criticised for its steep learning curve and for being too complex for many users to navigate. Steep learning curves, if you have been paying attention, are actually good for players to engage over a long period of time. This might not have been the best element of the critique, but from a playing perspective this is a good sign of longevity. Additionally, the game's adult-oriented content and mature themes sparked controversy, and some critics accused the game of promoting unhealthy behaviours. Despite these criticisms, *Second Life* remained popular throughout the 2000s and continued to attract a dedicated fanbase.

Habbo Hotel launched in 2000 and quickly became one of the most popular virtual worlds for teenagers and young adults. The game was praised for its vibrant, cartoonish graphics and for its focus on social interaction. It was also criticised for the presence of sexual content and inappropriate behaviour among some of its users. In 2007, the game was temporarily shut down in several countries following allegations of sexual misconduct involving minors. *Habbo Hotel* is still in the hearts and minds of people who look back at early metaverses fondly. It remained popular for many years and has continued to attract a large audience of young users.

Why in an age of openness and transparency would we still pin our trust on review and score aggregation? Metacritic is a score aggregation website which gathers reviews from various sources, including professional critics and user reviews, and calculates a composite score based on these reviews. This aggregation provides a snapshot of critical consensus and user sentiment about a particular movie, game or other forms of media. It allows people to quickly gauge the overall quality and reception of a product. We know the impact it makes on consumers of our products; any review or score is fairly intrinsic to our overall approach, or it should be. If it isn't, we should call the whole thing off.

Scoring/review systems help consumers make informed decisions and as metaverses, like games, we have to put ourselves out there. I would go (even) further to say that every digital product should now position itself to be easily reviewed by its consumer. By providing a numerical or qualitative assessment of a product's quality, this assists potential buyers in determining whether a particular video game or other digital or creative media product is worth their time and money. They serve as a helpful tool in evaluating the potential enjoyment or value of a product.

What impact will this have on an industry that is just getting started? Review aggregators such as Metacritic (Fielder, 2020) significantly influence consumer and critical reception. Since the popularity of video games has grown (maybe from the Super Famicom onwards), game developers' financial performance and critical acclaim are often linked to Metacritic scores. Higher scores can lead to increased sales and improved reputation, while lower scores may have the opposite effect. This creates an incentive for developers to strive for high-quality products.

Feedback and comparison is not just about the appetite for purchase against the end user's buyer or player behaviour. It creates a paper trail of trend analysis. The establishment of historical context allows consumers and critics to evaluate how a particular product stacks up against others. This fosters discussions, debates and analysis within the media industry; these are exactly the reasons for creating a survival plan. I love stats as much as the next person, and God knows there are plenty of books about the metaverse mostly focused on stats, but I care much more about the qualitative nature of feedback throughout the entire creative process. It helps the launch manifesto, and it makes QA really happy if they know they have minimal testing to do, or at least a plan of how this pile of faecal matter is going to make it to a console/app store/other.

FLOWERS IN THE ATTIC

QA, an abbreviation for quality assurance, but should really stand for *Questioning* and then *Answering* the bloody-mindedness of game development. QA is not something that should ever be left to the back of the production when making any form of digital product. It plays a crucial role, if not the most crucial alongside design in video game development. QA teams are responsible for ensuring that the game meets high standards of quality, functionality and player experience before it is released to the market. But wow how QA is treated.

I have been fortunate enough in my career to deliver workshops and then sit on everything from funding to career panels about the games industry and every time I take a look at a rookie indie team's "plan" or "go to market" QA is listed as happening in the last few weeks of development. The bit before soft launch and, er, launch. While one might argue that we should take the raincoat or the umbrella from the inside of the door or coat rack before we leave the house, QA doesn't work that way. It's not something one can just pick up or take off. If QA is even a raincoat, it's a sou'wester *and* a raincoat that you put on *before* you go out into the rain of game development. It's not the protective coating or seal on a roof, it's the roof. QA isn't a band-aid placed over a crack in a bulging wall, QA is the wall. It holds up a business like nothing else on Earth and yet, it is the last thought, the forgotten child, the flowers in the attic.

While you're having a knees up in a bar with your engineers because you've gone alpha, QA is meticulously searching for bugs, glitches and technical issues within your game. They conduct thorough playtesting to identify and document any defects, such as graphical anomalies, broken mechanics, crashes or audio issues. This helps developers understand the problems and fix them before the game's release; or in the case of most games I've ever worked on, shortens the time in the pub by about an hour.

Some of my best friends are really famous. They became famous by working up the ranks from QA to creative directors, executive producers, visionaries and living legends. QA people have been the brains behind *Grand Theft Auto* (1997) and *Gears of War* (2006). The responsibility of testing the game's functionality across various platforms, hardware configurations and operating systems is immense and, to be honest, too much. The success of a game often depends on whether these wonderful QA people have done their checks and balances. They verify that all features, mechanics, controls and interfaces work as intended. This isn't a 5 week stand. If compatibility testing has also to be conducted to ensure the game functions correctly, these folks spend time creating test environments for different devices and configurations. QAs can code, they're good too! So it amazes me that in an era of metaverses and virtual worlds, we're happy to put any old crap out there without a single idea of how it will be received. We spend time, and we spend investor money on building the perfect world, which breaks the moment we try to make it interoperable, for example.

It wasn't so long ago that someone showed me their MVP, a metaverse world for mobile with an NFT platform for monetisable content. I was excited. I had just sat through their talk, seen their roadmap, relished their white paper (though I'm still unsure as to why they don't just call white papers design docs when that's what they are). The talk was a success, and now it was time to dive in and be immersed. Her fingernails were manicured with small rainbow ceramic beads as though her talons were the branches of a Christmas tree and it was there that I noticed her hands shaking. She knew before I did that she had maybe a 20% chance of the MVP working the first time, 40% the second time and maybe a 50% chance of the world loading from the local network the third time. But the opposite was true. The scale of probability slid down a little like Nagashi somen; but this wasn't summer and we were not in Kyoto.

Listen, you only get one chance to make a first impression. This is why you need QA. From evaluating game performance by measuring stability, frame rates, loading times and resource usage, this testing helps optimise the game's performance to deliver a smooth and enjoyable experience for players.

If we can learn anything from what we want to do in the metaverse, it's that everything we develop as an infrastructure in our business has to reflect what we've learned in video games. During the pandemic I would carp about why digital fashion creators should get a game developer in their business from day one because most folks that don't have games experience and are using game technology to make their breakthroughs are trying to squeeze the size of a melon (a massive game engine and all its moving parts, worlds and items) into the size of a lemon (that's the mobile phone). It doesn't have to be this way.

QA is not about localisation testing. It's a small facet: in the case of games intended for international markets, QA teams verify the accuracy and appropriateness of translated text, audio and cultural references, as ensuring that the game's content is correctly adapted for different languages, cultures and regions is key to finding an audience, which is also a design trait, and it's something that definitely belongs in my earlier chapter on Design and Game Thinking (Chapter 7).

So are you coming around to the idea that QA is a vital part of the entire creative process? You should be. If you can't find a QA team in time for your project's kick-off, go back a few pages because the skills needed are centred on objectivising the users' requirements rather than that of the studio making the game, if you see what I mean? Getting QA to evaluate the user experience by analysing gameplay flow, difficulty balancing, menu navigation, tutorials and overall player satisfaction is big, a playtest or a user focus test can't do this. Users do not have the academic capacity or work experience to get into the weeds. QA folks do! Feedback from User Experience (UX) testing helps improve the design and accessibility from every angle, so cover all those bases.

For the metaverse, regression testing is a huge element to how the mindset should change to accommodate the users. As developers make changes or add new features to the experience, QA should focus on performing regression testing to ensure that existing functionalities have not been negatively impacted. I spoke to legendary producer, QA professional and friend Nelle Stahl, previously of IO Interactive, CCP Games and more recently Riot Games. She told me that the developer creates the change but rarely do they consider how this change will affect the game on ALL platforms. This, a lot of the time, is a problem with design, especially for live games. Since we want products to have cross-platform support, usually it is QA that actually is the one holding the torch there. Design and engineering team(s) might come up with great rough solutions for how it could work for each type of platform, but the crucial point is when the feature actually gets to QA and is being scrutinised on all platforms (or at least a large subset of them). "If people leave QA to the last minute they are then most certainly planning to fail because there is no way the precious feature will perform or even work on half the platforms" (Stahl, 2023). By retesting previously tested areas, QA helps maintain the overall quality of the game.

I get tension headaches when I think about the times I have been in trouble in my industry. As a writer working on young adult games for well-known toy companies, it is forbidden to say the word "kill," for example, or "murder." "Destroy" is fine, as is "exterminate." As a producer working on shooters, it was important to avoid the gaze of age rating bodies and government organisations at a time when geopolitics affects everything including video games. I'm working on children's games; however, there are relatively no problems.

Children's experiences need compliance throughout the design and implementation process; therefore, if there was ever an opportunity to use QA from day 1, it would be for children's metaverses and games. Compliance testing ensures that whatever is being made (from toys to metaverses and apps) adheres to industry standards, guidelines and legal requirements. This includes verifying age ratings, content restrictions, accessibility features and data privacy regulations. I worked on a children's game with Nelle Stahl, who again has a strong opinion on this and ranked the three main problems she ran into in the order of number of occurrences:

> Protecting kids from kids (i.e bullying, restricted language and content added by the kids themselves), protecting the product from the kids (even 10 year-olds will hack the shit out of your product and do whatever it takes to get free stuff or cause things to break just because it is fun). Finally, sleazy old people trying to pick up kids by faking accounts.

Oh dear.

I like to be Children's Online Privacy Protection Act (COPPA) compliant as a developer, and adherence to this element of Federal Trade Commission law is vital because vulnerable adults need to be protected too. COPPA is a powerful force in protecting children's privacy and online safety due to its comprehensive regulations and enforcement mechanisms; it specifically targets the online collection of personal information from children under the age of 13 (FTC, 2024). It requires operators of websites and online services directed towards children or with knowledge of child users to obtain verifiable parental consent. This bit is really important. Consent is a really important part not just of data but also of participation. Participating in something we can understand is easier, especially for children under the age of 13 or vulnerable adults, if it is monitored by a responsible guardian or custodian of personal information before it is collected, used or disclosed. Children under the age of 13 and vulnerable adults cannot make those decisions, and why should they?

As well as parental consent policies, COPPA sets forth strict requirements for operators, including providing clear privacy policies, implementing security measures and maintaining the confidentiality of children's information. These requirements help ensure that operators handle children's data responsibly and protect their privacy.

COPPA is enforced by the Federal Trade Commission (FTC) in the United States. Famous for being name-checked in an Eminem song, the FTC has the authority to investigate and take legal action against operators who violate COPPA's provisions, including imposing significant penalties for non-compliance. This enforcement power makes COPPA an effective tool in holding operators accountable for protecting children's privacy, and accountability as we build a better metaverse is vital to our understanding of how the metaverse will ebb and flow in the future. I mentioned previously that design has nothing to do with us but also something and everything to do with us? Accountability is no different when we're passing the metaverse on to other generations to maintain.

> **Legal Note:** COPPA protects users under 13 from data exploitation.
> Consent is legally required. This is not an opt-in/opt-out choice for creators, designers and publishers.

Right now COPPA empowers parents to have control over the collection of their children's personal information online. It requires operators to obtain verifiable parental consent before collecting such data, enabling parents to make informed decisions about their children's online activities and safeguard their privacy. What will it do in the future? How will it operate in a truly decentralised world? What input will Gen Z have on, say, Gen Alpha when it comes to making something truly and transcendentally accessible?

NO ONE'S CUP OF TEA

Already well established as shade-thrower extraordinaire, I am adept at spilling the tea on metaverses and their ridiculous pitches for a better world. Come on, *any fool knows* that most of these platforms and NFTs are a ploy to get rich quick. The thing is, this methodology is slowing down as the metaverse begins to grow up. Gone! The grifters that are selling empty dreams (and land packets). Gone! The hot air merchants who talk a good metaverse but have never made one or even played a game.

Back when games were golden – in the 1980s, when we had some nostalgic joy for all things pixel – there were some really terrible games that we look back on with a vintage glow, but really games such as *Custer's Revenge* (1982) for the Atari 2600 or *Dr Jekyll and Mr Hyde* (1988) for the Nintendo Entertainment System should never see the light of day again. Look them up if you must, but it feels as though consigning these ideas to the bin comes from a result of knowing, back then, that video games were so important to the consumer that we could do anything for money. The indulgence of getting product to market was appealing but occasionally "haphazard" (to say the least!).

With that assumption in mind, we must also accept that your daily active user numbers might not be the big thing that you thought they would be. I talked a little about the DAU and MAU and why these numbers are important to game developers; however, metaverse creators should also take note that creating a metaverse that everyone wants to be in is simply not your responsibility, unless you are really sure that the metaverse is being created in your vision and your tool sets; which it isn't.

The metaverse is about choice as much as it is about belonging. Users will use your metaverse however they see fit, and you simply have no control over this. I talk to game developers about this subject regularly, they are convinced their games will be used for what they are originally designed for. When some of my friends worked on *MotoGP 10/11* (2011) for Capcom back in the late 2000s, one of the things that made them laugh and cry in equal amounts was how the player would try and ride Casey Stoner (famous motorcycle rider) into a brick wall over and over again for fun. Not because they were malevolent, quite the opposite, this was the players' way of showing their appreciation for good avatar ragdoll physics. *VRChat* (2017) is used for chat in virtual reality, of course it is, but did you know that it's also used for drinking games? The ways that users adopt technology will not always be the way one might expect. That's what makes good design in my opinion: when the user experiences design (simply and silently), or they find a good use case for design, the results are really amazing.

Some key turn-offs for metizens are the kinds of things you think are very good as a developer or a creator, because you would have liked to have seen those things in your fave games or in the metaverse platform you are working on now. Whatever it is you are thinking of right now as a cool new feature that you would like to see in your metaverse, forget it. Complicated UI with overlay inventory? Nope. High-priced luxury fashion items – because you're doing a Metaverse Fashion Week with your weird metaverse pals? Nope. Metaverse pets? For some people yes, for most people, nope. I want to tell you why your metizens don't want to be on your server. They have other places to be. And that's it.

Tragic isn't it? To read that in a metaverse book. But we're not in a pandemic anymore. We don't need to chain ourselves to our desks with nothing to do but watch Travis Scott in *Fortnite* (BBC, 2020). We actually have physical friends (some of us) and some of us even want to go to meet people or buy things from an actual store. I think they're all crazy, but you might want to take note of this, because you are not there with them. And you should be. When I go to the store, my FitBit goes with me; it's on my wrist. When I sit on long train journeys or wait for a late arriving plane at the airport I am playing a game or reading a newsfeed, why aren't you there for the ride? Why isn't your news at the top of my newsfeed?

Why aren't you the device or game that I am holding or playing? Because you are still making experiences for a pandemic which is over.

REFERENCES

AppsFlyer (2023) *The State of Gaming App Marketing.* Available at: https://www.appsflyer.com/resources/reports/state-of-gaming-app-marketing/ (Accessed: 16 July 2025).

Brand, S. (1972) 'Spacewar: Fanatic Life and Symbolic Death Among the Computer Bums', *Rolling Stone*, 7 December. Available at: https://www.rollingstone.com/culture/culture-news/spacewar-19092/ (Accessed: 15 July 2025).

Custer's Revenge (1982) Atari 2600 [Game]. USA: Mystique.

Decentraland (2020) PC [Platform]. Unknown: Decentraland Foundation.

Dr. Jekyll and Mr. Hyde (1988) NES [Game]. Japan: Toho.

Federal Trade Commission (2024) 'Complying with COPPA: Frequently Asked Questions', *FTC .gov*. Available at: https://www.ftc.gov/legal-library/browse/rules/childrens-online-privacy-protection-rule-coppa (Accessed: 15 July 2025).

Fielder, A. (2020) *Scoring Games: The Rise of Review Aggregation.* London: Game Insight Press.

Final Fantasy VII (1997) PlayStation [Game]. Japan: Square.

Fortnite's Travis Scott Virtual Concert Watched by Millions (2020) *BBC News*. BBC. Available at: https://www.bbc.com/news/technology-52410647 (Accessed: 16 July 2025).

Gears of War (2006) Xbox 360 [Game]. USA: Microsoft Game Studios.

Grand Theft Auto (1997) PlayStation [Game]. Scotland: Rockstar North.

Habbo Hotel (2000) PC [Game]. Finland: Sulake Corporation.

Halo: Combat Evolved (2001) Xbox [Game]. USA: Microsoft Game Studios.

MotoGP 10/11 (2011) PlayStation 3/Xbox 360 [Game]. Japan: Capcom.

Roblox Corporation (2021) 'Q4 Earnings Report', Roblox Investor Relations. Available at: https://ir.roblox.com/ (Accessed: 15 July 2025).

Second Life (2003) PC [Game]. USA: Linden Lab.

Stahl, N. (2023) Industry Examples of Child Protection Online. Interview by Kelly Vero 17 June.

TechCrunch (2018) *The Untold Origin of Roblox.* Available at: https://techcrunch.com (Accessed: 16 July 2025).

The Sandbox (2012) PC/Mobile [Platform]. China: Animoca Brands.

The Wedding Singer (1998) [Film]. Directed by F. Coraci. Burbank, USA: New Line Cinema.

VRChat (2017) PC [Platform]. USA: VRChat Inc.

CHAPTER 13

Communities and Influencers

THE LUNATICS ARE TAKING OVER THE ASYLUM

Vocaloid is a singing voice synthesiser technology developed by the Yamaha Corporation. It allows users to create songs and produce vocal performances by inputting lyrics and melodies into the software. Vocaloid utilises a database of pre-recorded phonetic samples and vocal samples of different singers to generate realistic-sounding vocals. As a huge fan of Japanese singer Gackt, I am consciously aware of the impact Vocaloid has had on modern popular music, especially in Japan.

The core component of Vocaloid is the Vocaloid software engine, which processes the input data and generates the synthesised vocals based on the provided lyrics, melody and parameters. The software provides controls for adjusting pitch, tone, dynamics and other vocal characteristics to shape the output according to the user's preferences.

You might be mistaken for thinking that it's enough to mess around with the human voice, plugging it into various flanges and coming out sounding like Cher; but don't confuse Auto-Tune (1997) with Vocaloid, these are very different beasts. Vocaloid doesn't need the human voice to create some kind of human sound, but Auto-Tune does.

Each singer within the Vocaloid system is represented by a virtual character, sometimes a *moé* anthropomorphised character (where the character was never human in the first place but takes on human affectations) to create the "cosplayification" of our imagination.

Hatsune Miku's persona is depicted as a 16-year-old girl with long turquoise hair, and she is known for her signature outfit featuring a futuristic and stylish appearance.

What sets *Miku* apart and contributes to her fame is her ability to sing and perform on stage, despite being a virtual character. Using Vocaloid technology, *Miku*'s voice is synthesised by combining pre-recorded phonetic samples to generate vocals for songs. This allows users to create music using her voice and bring her performances to life.

"*Her(!)*" popularity surged in Japan and internationally due to her catchy songs, energetic performances and the enthusiastic support of her fan community. She has held numerous virtual concerts where fans can experience her performances through holographic

DOI: 10.1201/9781003615248-13

projections and elaborate stage setups. *Miku's* concerts have gathered thousands of fans and have even taken place in different countries.

What makes *Hatsune Miku* unique is her interactive nature. Crypton Future Media encourages users and fans to create their own music, artwork and animations featuring *Miku*, leading to a vast array of user-generated content and a strong fan culture around her.

Her success has had a significant impact on the perception and acceptance of virtual idols and virtual performers in the entertainment industry. She has inspired the creation and popularity of other virtual idols and has become an icon of the Vocaloid movement.

Other characters such as *Kagamine Rin and Len, Megurine Luka* and many more have distinct voice qualities and personas, where users can create songs and performances using their voices. Vocaloid technology has had a significant impact on the music industry, contributing to the rise of virtual idols and virtual singers; but we shouldn't care too much about that, it's a by-product of technology. Vocaloid has also inspired a dedicated fan community and has opened up opportunities for collaboration between producers, artists and virtual idols: this bit, as an architect of the metaverse, is something I really care about for it is here that we plot the course for the rise of the virtual influencer.

> **Community Takeaway**: Vocaloid showed us that audiences can create the culture if given the tools.
> From fans producing music for *Hatsune Miku*, to modders building with Kagamine Rin: this is scaffolding in action. The lesson for the metaverse? Empower the user, don't just entertain them.

Let's start our journey with the humble human being (just joking): Jake Paul, the PewDiePie, MrBeast; yes, people are still losing their minds over humans, but it's not the same as when I had a small cut-out from a magazine – Sting and Mark Hamill, side-by-side, laminated. Is it? So much has changed.

A digital influencer is an individual who leverages social media platforms to build a following and influence their audience's opinions, behaviours and purchasing decisions. They typically create and share content related to various topics such as fashion, beauty, fitness, travel or lifestyle. Digital influencers gain popularity by engaging with their followers, creating compelling content and collaborating with brands for sponsored posts or endorsements.

I'm a Gen X female, and so I have a bit of difficulty in surmounting the cut-through of content to the brain. I need some time to process what I'm seeing whether it is on film, in video or even video games. The thing about digital influencing is that it's part of fan culture and fan culture throughout history has been monetised. One only has to study the intricacies of George Gordon, Lord Byron's poetry release regimen to understand that he was very aware of how to monetise his legions of fans against how and when he released books and poems. And if Lord Byron is the ultimate OG of fandom, it's fair to call MrBeast as the new Byronic hero (Table 13.1).

But because we live in a digital world, our connection to Jake Paul is perhaps not as deep as our relationship with Commander Shepard, even if Commander Shepard is a predefined

TABLE 13.1 Digital vs Virtual Influencers

Influencer Type	Definition	Example	Control Level	Key Risk
Digital influencer	Human using digital platforms	MrBeast, PewDiePie	Medium	Burnout, scandals
Virtual influencer	CG persona managed by a team or AI	*Lil Miquela*	High	Lack of authenticity
Hybrid/avatar influencer	User-driven virtual avatar	VTubers	Variable	Identity confusion

character within the Mass Effect series and does not have an independent existence beyond the game. They do not have social media accounts or interact with users outside of the game's narrative framework. Virtual influencers *do*.

They are computer-generated characters or avatars that have been programmed to interact with users on social media platforms. These virtual influencers are created using advanced technologies like AI, computer graphics and motion capture. They have realistic appearances and unique personalities, and they engage with their audience through posts, comments and even live streams.

Virtual influencers represent an exciting development because they combine the growing influence of digital media with the capabilities of AI. They offer brands and marketers new opportunities for promotion and advertising, as they can be easily customised and controlled to align with specific brand values or campaigns.

Lil Miquela is one of the most well-known virtual influencers. She has a significant following on Instagram and is recognised for her fashion-forward style and engaging storytelling. She isn't the first or last attempt at virtual influencing (I'm a strong believer that Hatsune Miku might have been the first of their kind). I agree with Gemma A Williams that outside of video games and internet memes "most virtual influencers are focused on luxury or beauty" (Williams, 2023). This adoption from its original or natural space and state has been great for brands but terrible for the consumer. Instead of the perfection of Kate Moss or Karli Kloss, we should instead accept a substitution of the same but virtual? No thanks, I want *me* as a virtual influencer but with Cara Delevingne's skin (and eyebrows) please. If everything we've done so far is to find that version of ourselves in the metaverse, why would we outsource our psyche to a perfect datapoint?

Virtual influencers have the potential to provide more consistent and predictable content creation, as they are not subject to human limitations such as fatigue or schedule constraints. I can get with the latter part of this, but will we really accept predictable content as the normalisation of our access? I thought we wanted something democratised?

The rise of digital and virtual influencers is already having a significant impact on the way we consume and engage with content, and their influence is likely to continue shaping the future in various ways. Perhaps we're thinking about this all wrong, and that virtual influencers, if done correctly with some deep connection rather than a fleeting acquaintance, might enable us to push the boundaries of possibilities in the metaverse? After all, it worked for *Final Fantasy XIII*'s (2009) Lightning didn't it?

Virtual influencers can be tailored to specific brand values, target demographics and marketing campaigns. With advancements in AI and technology, virtual influencers have the potential to deliver highly personalised content and experiences to their followers. This level of customisation could deepen the connection between influencers and their audiences.

Virtual influencers could further blur the lines between reality and fiction, opening up new possibilities in entertainment and media. We may see virtual influencers starring in movies, TV shows or even virtual reality experiences. This could revolutionise storytelling and offer immersive entertainment experiences beyond traditional mediums.

Virtual influencers have the power to shape trends, opinions and behaviours. As their reach and influence continue to grow, they may play a significant role in driving social and cultural discussions, impacting topics such as fashion, beauty standards, sustainability, activism and hopefully inclusivity.

But the emergence of virtual influencers raises questions about authenticity, transparency and ethics (Dennehy, Conboy and Sammon, 2020). Is it really that crucial to distinguish between virtual and human influencers, and ensure transparency regarding AI-driven content creation and endorsement deals? As developers, we are not even equipped to care about our users in some cases; look at how many developers have infringed the privacy of children and vulnerable adults through data collection. The impact on the mental health and well-being of both digital influencers and their virtual influencer audiences also requires attention.

CATCHING HONEY WITH FLIES

External scaffolds in digital products and media, such as games and metaverses, help us to connect our belief in the product via other tools or outlets. So as an example, when *Love Island* (2018) was released on mobile by Fusebox Games, it was bolstered by the strong scripted reality on the TV, allowing us as players to fully immerse ourselves in the game. *Forza Horizon* (2012) is also a great example of how games can present solid passive marketing results too. I mean, who doesn't want to drive a Mercedes-AMG ONE just once in their lives? I do. My knees don't, but I would happily walk through broken glass and salt to drive a supercar.

Loyalty marketing strategies are another form of external scaffold that involve techniques aimed at cultivating and maintaining user loyalty and engagement. Loyalty programmes, VIP memberships and special promotions are examples of loyalty marketing initiatives. These strategies provide additional incentives, exclusive content or privileges to loyal users, encouraging them to remain engaged and fostering a sense of belonging and value. By recognising and rewarding user loyalty, loyalty marketing efforts reinforce positive user experiences and create a stronger connection between users and the product or brand.

Experiences where the motivation of exploring "long-term engagement with extrinsic rewards is a fool's errand" (Kim, 2018), it makes sense that game design needs to do the job of engagement and retention; rather than marketing. In more expansive fictional media, this external scaffolding of off-game marketing has to be done. NFTs supply this short-termism of campaign marketing, but external scaffolds are part and parcel of initial user acquisition that need to be done as part of the release structure. What I'm saying is that the metaverse will cave in if it isn't supported by a constant stream of UA tools and techniques like loyalty marketing, or other supporting documentation and activities like tutorials, onboarding and reward systems. These components play a crucial role in enhancing user experiences and facilitating engagement.

In the good old days of video games, we might use documentation to provide users with information, guidelines and instructions. In the context of games, documentation can include game manuals, online guides, FAQs and knowledge bases. It helps users understand game mechanics, controls and features, ensuring they have the necessary information to navigate and enjoy the game effectively. Well-written and easily accessible documentation contributes to a smoother and more engaging user experience. The problem is, we live in a fast brain food universe where we need more than something to read.

The VARK learning style questionnaire developed by Neil Fleming in 1987 gave me, the game designer, a better understanding of how players play (Fleming, 1987). VARK, or Visual, Auditory, Reading/writing and Kinaesthetic (or learning by doing), provides the general ground rules for designing anything: not everyone learns at the same speed or in the same way. Where previously we would use tutorials and onboarding processes to act as external scaffolds to guide users in learning how to interact with a game or digital product, we need to shift our thinking. Tutorials provide step-by-step instructions, explanations and demonstrations that help users become familiar with the gameplay mechanics and controls. More effective onboarding experiences are the ones that use VARK to introduce new users to the product's features and functionalities gradually (or at speed with the (X) action button on a controller), ensuring the player understands how to navigate and utilise key aspects. By providing clear guidance and support, tutorials and onboarding processes facilitate a positive user experience and reduce barriers to entry.

If we implement interactive in-game guides that provide contextual information and instructions to users when they navigate the metaverse, these guides can be triggered based on user actions or events, offering real-time assistance and explanations. Integrating the documentation directly into the metaverse by way of AI or voice-controlled tutorials means users can access information seamlessly without the need for external sources, so finally the metizen or player won't need to leave the experience.

We can introduce embedded tooltips and contextual help throughout the user interface; tooltips can provide brief explanations or instructions when users hover over specific elements or interact with certain features. Contextual help or reporting can be accessed through a dedicated help icon or menu, offering detailed information and guidance when needed.

If we can regularly review and update the documentation to reflect any changes or updates to the metaverse, we can promptly address user feedback and questions to improve existing documentation and address any gaps or areas of confusion for the end user. As new features or functionalities are introduced, we should ensure that the documentation, in whichever format, is kept up to date.

Reward systems are external scaffolds that operate outside of gamified experiences. They involve mechanisms that provide users with incentives and rewards for their actions and achievements. In games, rewards can take the form of virtual currency, experience

TABLE 13.2 Types of External Scaffolds in Games and Metaverses

Scaffold Type	Example	Purpose	Metaverse Equivalent
Tutorial	VARK-based onboarding	Onboard and train	Contextual onboarding bot
Loyalty systems	Starbucks Rewards	Retain and reward	NFT campaigns (caution!)
Community spaces	Love Island game forums	Drive engagement	Instanced hubs, Discord
Documentation	Game manuals, FAQs	Reduce churn	AI in-world help

points, items or unlocking new levels or content. These rewards reinforce positive behaviour, motivate users to engage further and provide a sense of accomplishment: offering tangible benefits for progress and achievements contributes to user satisfaction, engagement and long-term retention.

In a seamless world we need to rethink what this might be for a metaverse, and the external scaffolds that live in our realities have to step up considerably to reflect the needs of future generations against advancing technologies (Table 13.2).

AR, in particular, uses robust search functionalities within their interfaces, allowing users to quickly find relevant documentation based on their queries. Have you played *Pokémon Go* (2016)? It's one big query disguised as a game. If you're not that clandestine, consider creating a user-friendly navigation system that organises documentation into logical categories and sections, making it easy for users to browse and access the information they need.

THE NEXT FACTOR

There's no doubt that the metaverse or something like it will be the platform of tomorrow. Ideally, I would love it to be more of a base layer system. I also want to support the metizen, or the end user, whatever it is that they will be called, but it won't be player, or will it? The platforms of tomorrow need to be supported by users rather than ideation alone. We can dream all day long but unless we start making what non-*Roblox* or non-*Minecraft* players want (these two are the most popular metaverse platforms, but have been made for kids), we won't ever transition outside of short-lived experiences, or popularly called brand activations; expensive press releases!

Platforms should prioritise user experience and cater to the needs, preferences and abilities of users. It's so important to go through that Game Thinking model to figure out what those missing links are between traditional consumer access and Gen Z or Gen Alpha consumption models. Results need to be tweaked, so gathering user feedback and iterating on platform design based on user input is essential to develop a consistent product.

> **Business Takeaway:** Designing for Gen Z and Gen Alpha
> If your metaverse doesn't pass the 3-click or 3-second rule, it's already lost Gen Alpha. Think short loops, visual onboarding and built-in feedback. These users aren't waiting for your UX to improve in v2.

Fostering a sense of community within the metaverse platforms is crucial. Encouraging collaboration, social interaction and meaningful connections among users can create a vibrant and supportive environment. Implementing features like chat systems, forums and shared experiences can help facilitate community building. Don't assume that inserting some kind of AI is enough to satisfy moderation and a constant stream of activities for the metizen to immerse themselves in and feel a part of, because of that platforms must also put user safety first. Security, and well-being, while could be argued the responsibility of the player or end user, it's our responsibility as creators to ensure that our focus is on them returning. If we don't make our infrastructure and interactions safe, we can't expect our users to stay. That's just the way it is.

Implementing robust measures to combat harassment, hate speech and inappropriate content is essential. Providing reporting mechanisms, moderation tools and clear guidelines can contribute to a safe and inclusive metaverse environment. We must also make user privacy and data protection priority #1.

In a Web3 world, transparent data practices, clear privacy policies and user consent mechanisms are essential, but for Web2 experiences they're not the easiest to find. Platforms should strive to minimise data collection and ensure secure storage and handling of user information.

Fostering collaboration and open standards as well as embracing interoperability and open APIs can allow for seamless integration of different platforms and encourage innovation. Collaborating with developers, content creators and researchers can drive continuous improvement and expansion of the metaverse ecosystem. That's what we need. However, this really has to come from a place of understanding. In the metaverse currently (as I write this) there are simply not enough grown-ups in the room. Not nearly enough. What we will continually fail to provide, given current metaverse benchmarks, is some form of standardisation which I believe has to be 30/70 on the side of game developers. Why? If you've already read this book to this point you'll know why, and if you haven't, let me make this as simple as possible for you. The games industry has already made every single mistake so you don't have to.

The 30% of the 30/70 split is something the metaverse can own really comfortably, well, if you don't count the number of egos and elitists on the NFT side. The consideration and acknowledgement of ethical challenges is vital: this includes issues such as algorithmic bias, content moderation, fair compensation for creators and responsible use of user data. Platforms should proactively engage in ethical discussions, involve diverse perspectives and strive for fairness and accountability. There are some great metaverse platforms which do this already, and some who do this with really great results. Games still have a way to go, and remember that games in 2023 at least are still walled gardens of data and gameplay. Some notable developers in the Web3 space are trying to build games with these requirements in mind from day one. Look to studios that present not just an understanding of democratisation, but also the evidence or use cases of how they are applying it in this new era of game development. Platforms should have a forward-thinking approach, anticipating and adapting to evolving user needs, technological advancements and societal changes; these guys and girls definitely do. Embracing emerging technologies, such as AI and virtual reality, while considering their ethical implications, can drive the development of future-proof platforms.

By focusing on user needs, fostering community, ensuring safety and privacy, promoting collaboration, addressing ethical considerations and embracing innovation, the metizen will most definitely be supported, and the platforms of tomorrow can be nurtured to create engaging, inclusive and sustainable metaverse experiences (Figure 13.1).

I mentioned the uneasy bedfellows relationship of games and the metaverse: the more that we try to assume that there is a fork in the road of games and the metaverse, the more that we will find a confluence between the two states. The argument that Web3 gaming is the changeling here is premature to say because we are looking for an omniverse rather than a simple metaverse. Interoperable assets and financial technologies supported by distributed ledgers will bring together the traditional nature of gameplay with the sustainable future of automation, mechanisation and applied industrial techniques, but I never said how that might happen.

Did I tell you the one about how I went for a tattoo of *Final Fantasy VII*, *Advent Children* and *Crisis Core* on my left arm? I selected the composition mostly based on the beautiful ruins of Midgar with Vincent Valentine (in *Final Fantasy VII: Crisis Core*) in the foreground and Kadaj, Yazoo, Loz (from *Final Fantasy VII: Advent Children*) as sinister shadows of the fading blue light pollution of the post-apocalyptic city.

I didn't work on that game or on that part of the IP at all. I didn't have to know it inside and out. I'm an end user, a player and a viewer. A superfan. I'm a collector of FFVII books, stories, action figures and games of course.

Cloud is not the most important thing on my tattoo, Midgar is. Yet in the original PlayStation game, Midgar was just an environment. But it was an environment that I wanted to live in, even back then in 1997. So, as the game grew in popularity and spin-offs,

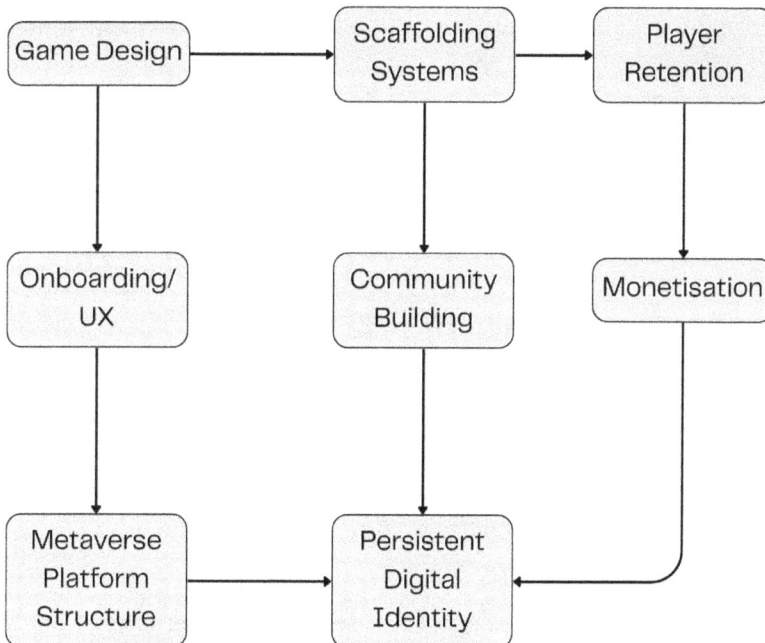

FIGURE 13.1 From games to metaverses: a flow of influencer basic instincts.

so did the immersive nature of the IP, and as an end user, that gave me the raison d'etre for that particular IP.

The thing about Square Enix is that for *Final Fantasy* at least, it is masterful at creating experiences that evolve. There were no Kadaj, Yazoo and Loz in the first game on the PlayStation; those dynamics simply could not work in the limited graphical interface of pre-evolved renders. And more importantly, what might we learn from actually living in Vincent Valentine's decaying Shinra Manor? A metaversal experience would give us the opportunity to buy an instanced manor that we might call home, or rent a room and work in the caves below. We might do our shopping at a grocery store in Nibelheim (Cloud Strife's hometown) or we might work the post-lifestream fields in the hinterlands. If you know, you know.

Now let's change Cloud in *Final Fantasy VII* and replace him with Martin Rauch in *Deutschland 83*. What is *his* Berlin like? Can we live in the barracks in West Germany during Operation Able Archer? Can we work (and party!) in 1980s West Berlin? The point is that we can live inside and do anything that has a strong enough connection to the user; what we can't do with the metaverse is create a base layer where the end user has to wonder what they're doing next: because that's game design. *Final Fantasy VII* and *Deutschland 83* (along with its sequels) represent things that are unattainable in real life, right now. What we already have in our metaverses are the boring bits: the mundanities of nipping to the store for a pint of *vilk* (that's virtual milk, you know). This is our physical life. Why phygitise it? The attraction to our metaversal experiences only becomes more appealing when we realise we're in a world that we have to create (because it doesn't exist) or a place that exists in our collected human history (that we can refer to). Don't you want to live in pre-eruption Pompeii? I do. How about living in Algol from Hitchhiker's Guide to the Galaxy? Yep! I'm labouring the point now; but we have the technology to make this happen, so what's stopping us?

Most user experiences are speculative and depend on the specific implementation and development of the metaverse. The actual user experiences may vary based on technological advancements, adoption rates and creative innovations by developers and users alike. If the metaverse is created as a base layer or universal operating system, it would fundamentally reshape the way we interact with computers and digital information.

- Users could have a persistent digital identity that carries across various platforms and applications within the metaverse. This would enable a seamless transition between different virtual environments, social networks, games and other online experiences.

- The metaverse could provide an immersive computing environment where users can interact with digital objects and information in three-dimensional space. This could involve gesture-based controls, voice commands and even haptic feedback to enhance the sense of presence.

- With the metaverse as a base layer, applications and experiences would be compatible across different devices and operating systems. Users could seamlessly switch between desktop computers, mobile devices, virtual reality headsets and other connected devices while retaining access to their digital content and experiences.

- The metaverse could offer virtual workspaces that facilitate collaboration among individuals and teams regardless of their physical location. Users could engage in real-time communication, share and edit documents, and interact with virtual tools to enhance productivity.

- Users would have the ability to customise their virtual spaces within the metaverse. They could design and decorate their own virtual homes, offices or gathering places, reflecting their personal tastes and preferences.

I often argue that this integrated omniverse is probably going to come as a 3D internet first. For me as a practitioner in this space and someone who builds experiences for users with this as a starting point, it certainly feels that the end user or users at large have more cognisance with the metaverse being something that they can touch and feel or hear and see to understand. No amount of multicoloured wires carrying millions of bytes in a split second will ever convince a metizen that this is the future. Or *their* future, even. Users are looking for:

- A 3D internet within the Metaverse would allow users to navigate websites and online content in a three-dimensional space. Instead of clicking through links, users could physically explore virtual environments to discover information and interact with digital objects.

- Shopping experiences would become more immersive, with virtual storefronts and marketplaces within the 3D internet. Users could browse virtual shelves, try on virtual clothing and make purchases within the Metaverse.

- The 3D internet could facilitate social interactions in virtual spaces, enabling users to meet and communicate with others in more engaging ways. Virtual gatherings, events and concerts could provide a sense of presence and shared experiences.

- The 3D internet could revolutionise education and training by creating interactive and immersive learning environments. Students could explore historical sites, conduct virtual experiments and engage in collaborative projects within the Metaverse.

- The 3D internet would offer a new dimension to entertainment and gaming experiences. Users could enter virtual worlds, participate in multiplayer games and engage in immersive storytelling that goes beyond traditional flat screens. Meta are trying to bring that hybrid of entertainment and gameplay to their Horizon Worlds/ Workrooms concepts to varying degrees of success.

By leveraging the existing infrastructure and experiences of video games, developers and platform providers can lay the foundation for a comprehensive metaverse that incorporates elements of a base layer or universal operating system and a 3D internet. However, it's important to note that the metaverse is a complex concept, and its realisation will require collaboration and integration across various industries, technologies and platforms beyond just video games. But yes, video games can play a significant role in bringing together the elements of a base layer or universal operating system and a 3D internet to create a relatable and comprehensive metaverse. Video games have already demonstrated their potential in providing immersive experiences, social interactions and virtual economies, which are key components of the metaverse concept.

Multiplayer video games have long been facilitating social interactions among players, and this is too important to ignore if we're building a metaverse that can sustain. In the context of the metaverse, video games can serve as hubs for social gatherings, enabling players to connect, communicate and collaborate with others. Features such as voice chat, real-time multiplayer interactions and shared gameplay experiences can enhance the social aspect of the metaverse.

Many video games provide tools and platforms for players to create and share their own content, such as custom levels, mods and virtual items. These user-generated creations can extend beyond the boundaries of a single game and be incorporated into the metaverse, allowing players to showcase their creativity and contribute to the overall richness of the virtual ecosystem. *Yahaha* (2020) and *Minecraft* (2009) are the new gods of this technology, but start-ups like *Anything World* (2018) show us that game engines are just foundational concepts, we can build anything on top of them with a bit of help from AI.

Finally, some video games have intricate virtual economies where players can trade in-game assets and currencies. This will change everything in our metaverse. Because these economies can be expanded into anything, creating a unified virtual marketplace where users can buy, sell and trade digital goods, services and experiences across multiple games and applications will almost certainly spill into phygital and physical realities.

REFERENCES

Anything World (2018) AI-Powered 3D World-Building Platform [Software]. London: Anything World Ltd.

Auto-Tune (1997) Audio Plugin [Software]. USA: Antares Audio Technologies.

Dennehy, D., Conboy, K. and Sammon, D. (2020) *Differentiating Digital Influencers: An Exploratory Study on the Antecedents of Influencer Credibility in Social Media Marketing*. Journal of Research in Interactive Marketing, 14(3), pp. 269–286.

Final Fantasy XIII (2009) PlayStation 3 [Game]. Japan: Square Enix.

Fleming, N.D. (1987) *VARK: A Guide to Learning Styles*. Available at: https://vark-learn.com

Forza Horizon (2012) Xbox 360 [Game]. USA: Microsoft Studios.

Hatsune Miku (2007) Vocaloid 2 [Software]. Japan: Crypton Future Media.

Kim, A.J. (2018) *Game Thinking: Innovate Smarter & Drive Deep Engagement with Design Techniques from Hit Games*. Burlingame: Game Thinking Press.

Lil Miquela (2016–) Instagram Virtual Influencer. USA: Brud.

Love Island: The Game (2018) Mobile [Game]. United Kingdom: Fusebox Games.

Minecraft (2009) Mojang Studios. PC [Game]. USA: Microsoft.

Pokémon Go (2016) Mobile [Game]. USA: Niantic, Inc.

Williams, G.A. (2023) *Should Brands Use Virtual Influencers in China?*, *The Business of Fashion*. Available at: https://www.businessoffashion.com/briefings/china/should-brands-use-virtual-influencers-in-china (Accessed: 20 July 2025).

Yahaha (2020) Cross-Platform 3D Creation Platform [Software]. Finland: Yahaha Studios.

Afterword

SOME KIND OF WONDERFUL

Thanks so much for reading. I've spent a lifetime inside video games. From the dusty arcade machine at the end of a Spanish street to the procedurally generated worlds of today, I've never really left that first cabinet.

This book has argued, again and again, that building a metaverse isn't magic, it's memory, logic, imagination and empathy. Most metaverses won't survive because they forget their reason for being. Unless they serve a clear purpose, or offer a community something they can't find elsewhere, they're nothing more than castles built on zeroware: destined to float out to sea.

Communities are not passengers in this journey, they're the pilots. They are fragile and fierce. If the metaverse doesn't feed them, they won't feed it.

I hope this book has offered a few strategies and a few provocations that help you build something lasting. Not just another experience, but a world worth remembering.

Index

For Product Safety Concerns and Information please contact our EU
representative GPSR@taylorandfrancis.com
Taylor & Francis Verlag GmbH, Kaufingerstraße 24, 80331 München, Germany

www.ingramcontent.com/pod-product-compliance
Lightning Source LLC
Chambersburg PA
CBHW081535220326
41598CB00036B/6449